# Acknowledgements

KU-703-561

I would like to thank Alain Anderton for his help at a crucial stage in planning, etc., and the editors of Macmillan Education, who have been especially supportive in seeing the project through to publication. My thanks go also to Judy Hobden for her typing, to the many other friends who helped with ideas, cups of coffee and 'offices' for work, and to my long-suffering family who had to put up with so much, and do without so much else, during the writing of the book. Any faults that remain are, of course, my responsibility alone.

A.L.

The author and publishers wish to thank the following who have kindly given permission for the use of copyright material:

Gillon Aitken for an extract 'Rags to riches to .... what?' from *Among the Believers – Islamic Journey* by V. S. Naipaul.

Associated Newspapers Group for extracts, 'Dear Boss, I've just got your job' (21.3.84), 'The Young Today' (26.1.83), 'Young People's Pay – too high a price?' (7.1.83), 'Millions from under the sea' (5.3.84), 'Forged £50 note turns up in a pension' (26.4.84), 'Making a pet project pay' (21.3.84), 'Bouquets to last for ever' (8.2.84), and data (26.4.84), from the *Daily Mail*.

Bank of England for data from the *Quarterly Bulletin*.

The Consumers Association for extract, 'Harry Hawkins on the dole', from *The Which Book of Money* (1982).

The Economist for extracts 'Drought in Africa' (10.9.83) and photograph, 'Mr Shilling's Motoring History' (12.11.83), 'Christmas Gobbledegook' (24.12.83), 'Spurred on to Market' (18.6.83), 'Brits out, Mexicans in' (14.1.84) and data obtained from the *The World in Figures* (1978) and the 12.2.83 and 19.2.83 editions of *The Economist*.

The Financial Times for data obtained from 'Where cows make way for machines' (18.6.84), and extract from 'Commodore Moves to Corby' (21.3.84).

Guinness Superlatives Ltd for extracts from the *Guinness Book of Records* 1985.

The Controller of Her Majesty's Stationery Office for data from *Annual Abstract of Statistics* (1984), *Annual Abstract and Monthly Digest* (1984), *Business Monitor* (1979), *Financial Statistics*, the Bank of England, *Regional Trends* (1984), *Social Trends, Financial Statement and Budget Report 1984–85* and *UK Balance of Payments* (1983).

Ann Hills for extract, 'The couple with a lot of bottle' from the *Guardian* (13.12.83).

The Joint Matriculation Board, the London Regional Examining Board, the University of London Schools Examinations Board, the University of Oxford Delegacy of Local Examinations, the Southern Regional Examinations Board, the Welsh Joint Education Committee and the West Midlands Regional Examination Board for questions from past examination papers.

London Express News and Features Service for 'Where are the jobs of tomorrow?' (3.5.84), 'Don't get caught in the Gold Rush' (17.2.78) and 'Take a bow' (4.5.84) from *The Sun*; and 'The dentists who drill for gold' (5.6.84), 'How Mark Watts escaped' (21.1.83), 'Floating Palace fit for a King' (24.5.85), 'The Case for Keeping Britain on the Rails' (21.1.83) plus photograph, 'The Stockbrokers' (21.9.83), 'Penny Pinchers' (12.3.84) and 'The Miners' Strike' (7.3.84) from the *Daily Express*.

Macdonald Educational Limited for diagram from *The Divided World*, by Lionel Grigson (1975).

Peter North for a redrawn illustration based on his original in 'Where cows make way for machines', *Financial Times* (18.6.84).

Christopher Pond for his letter to *The Times* (20.12.83).

Queens University, Belfast and Karen Trew and Rosemary Kilpatrick for an extract from 'The Daily Life of the Unemployed' (1983).

Reuters Limited for extract and information taken from Reuters Holdings PLC 'Offer for Sale by Tender.'

Routledge and Kegan Paul Ltd for extracts from *The Book of Heroic Failures* (1980).

Daily Telegraph for extract from 'Third rate state firms' (1.11.83) and 'English £195 worse off than Scots' (15.9.78).

The Times for extracts 'Economic time bomb warning' (9.12.83), 'House plant industry wilts' (8.5.84), 'Waiting for a mineral tidal wave' (12.1.83), 'Beef Sirloin Buyers must work extra 45 mins' (14.2.84), 'Breaking the Tobacco Habit' (27.2.84), 'Why Britain's coal industry may be booming by the year 2000' (20.3.84), 'Calm after tea price storm' (17.1.84), 'Bank of England supports sterling'

(4.4.78), 'Falling pound may bring tourists in' (11.1.84) and 'Trade Figures fire a warning shot' (25.11.83) from *The Times*; and 'Are Britain's Highest Paid Directors really worth the money?' (3.6.84), 'Software, Hard Cash' (4.3.84) and 'Who's where in the UK Grocery League' (2.3.80) from *The Sunday Times*.

US News and World Report Inc for extract from 'Banks view; Business not out of the woods yet' and 'Why no stampede?', *US News and World Report,* issue 1.11.82.

The author and publishers wish to acknowledge the following photograph sources:

Banking Education Service pp 110, 114, 120;   Jim Brown-bill pp 38, 74, 99;   Camera Press Ltd p 77;   J Allan Cash p 145;   Ron Chapman pp 73, 150;   Conservative Party p 132;   Consumer Association p 119;   Crown Copyright (Central Office of Information) p 20 top;   Daily Mail p 29;   Daily Mirror p 164;   Economist Newspapers p 148;   FAO p 33 top;   Ford Motor Co Ltd p 80;   Health Education Council p 22;   Mike Hicks (Brent Cross Shopping Centre) p 67;   Hoover PLC p 99;   Institute of Economic Affairs p 131;   Rodney Jennings pp 58, 91;   Labour Party p 132;   London Express News Service p 38;   Mansell Collection p 16;   Matthews Norfolk Farms p 81;   N McCloud, 'Free Trade' p 151; McDonald's Hamburgers Ltd p 52;   Photo Source pp 25, 125;   Popperfoto p 33 bottom;   Post Office p 20 bottom; National Westminster Bank PLC p 109;   David Richardson p 37;   John Topham Picture Library p 13; SDP p 132;   Shell Photographic Service p 59;   Sun Newspaper p 88;   Times Newspapers Ltd p 61.

Every effort has been made to trace all the copyright holders but if any have been inadvertently overlooked the publishers will be pleased to make the necessary arrangement at the first opportunity.

Illustrations by Gecko Ltd
Cartoon illustrations by Tony Ellis

CXO 0004041 XD

5. 95

# Action Economics
## A coursebook for GCSE
Andrew Leake

MACMILLAN
EDUCATION

© Andrew Leake 1986

All rights reserved. No reproduction, copy or transmission
of this publication may be made without written permission.

No paragraph of this publication may be reproduced, copied
or transmitted save with written permission or in accordance
with the provisions of the Copyright Act 1956 (as amended),
or under the terms of any licence permitting limited copying
issued by the Copyright Licensing Agency, 7 Ridgmount Street,
London WC1E 7AE.

Any person who does any unauthorised act in relation to
this publication may be liable to criminal prosecution and
civil claims for damages.

First published 1986
Reprinted 1986, 1987

Published by
MACMILLAN EDUCATION LTD
Houndmills, Basingstoke, Hampshire RG21 2XS
and London
Companies and representatives
throughout the world

Printed in Hong Kong

British Library Cataloguing in Publication Data
Leake, Andrew
Action Economics
1. Economics
I. Title
330     HB171.5
ISBN 0-333-37311-1

WESTERN EDUCATION
YOUTH
LIBRARY
SERVICES
LIBRARY BOARD

YH010675

# A note for teachers

● This is a course-book for students working towards GCSE examinations in economics.

The book is divided into 56 learning sections which relate to one another and fit together, but can be read individually over the period of perhaps two years of a GCSE course.

The sections are grouped into seven parts which build from personal concerns, such as work and shopping, towards more general issues like inflation and the EEC. Teachers may prefer to approach topics in a different order, and should find that the book suits this approach. But they may find that Part 1 serves best as a general introduction to the range and nature of the course as a whole, and that some of the later theoretical topics from micro and macro economics may suit the more advanced students.

● The parts are structured to develop from simple to more complex analysis. They generally start by introducing basic terms and ideas, with examples as appropriate, then consider the issues that use those ideas. For example, 'What are banks, how do they earn their living, and what is their importance in the economy?'

Each section contains a variety of material to interest all students. There are short case studies, chosen to relate wherever possible to the students' own experience and interests, and to raise important social and moral as well as economic issues. There is data, given where appropriate as factsheets, on important aspects of the UK economy. This information is made as clear and accessible as possible, to help students to develop their numerical skills. There are checklists to summarise the main points studied.

● The book includes many questions and points for thought or discussion. Each section has structured questions, worth a total of ten marks. These are of data response form, and are included with the factsheets and case study material. Suggestions on answers to these questions appear at the end of the book, but are intended for the teacher's use rather than the students' on their own. There is also a full section of past examination questions on the topics covered in the book. These questions are of the different forms and are chosen from some of the different Boards that students are expecting to meet at GCSE level. Teachers may wish to use these questions to mark the end of a half or whole-term's study.

● The book aims to help teachers to offer something of value to all students of economics. Most of the material will suit those taking the subject only up to GCSE, and will help them to understand important ideas and be interested in them. Teachers should find also that the book raises questions and shows a type of work that suggests the appeal of studying economics to higher levels.

# Contents

# Part 4 Buying and selling

# Part 5 Finance

# Part 6 Steering the economy

# Part 7 Trade

# How to use this book

This book aims to show you all you need to know about economics for the GSCE exams. But it tries to do a lot more also. It shows how economics fits in with other things, and how much a part it is of our everyday lives. You meet economics when you go to work, deal in business, or buy and sell. Economics is all around us in the money we use and the things on which we spend it at home and abroad.

This book will help you to see economics in action, to see how it fits in with the news, Spurs, smoking, the dole, Christmas turkeys, young people's pay, and much, much more.

What does this book ask of you? Mainly, you must question what you read, question what you see about you, and question your teacher. You must play an active part in order to make sense of economics and to check that you have learned its ideas well. There are questions in each section of the book to help you do this, and the book ends with a section which shows the kinds of questions you will meet in GCSE exams.

You will find things to enjoy, things to use, and things to interest you in the pages of this book. Economics is a lively and changing subject – no-one knows all the answers. Economics is often open-ended. That may be the best thing about it.

What is economics about? Mainly it is to do with choices. These are of many kinds, but in each case there is an opportunity cost.

1927 was a good year for Al Capone. He earned over $100 million, which is more than £300m in today's money. (See the Guinness Book of Records.) On his business card, Capone called himself a 'Second Hand Furniture Dealer'. But clearly he did not make his money, or his enemies, selling old chairs. What did he do?

He knew about economics. He knew that you must choose how to run your life and that many choices are economic ones. People must choose how to work, and in what line of business. They must buy and sell and use money to pay each other. They must pay taxes to the government, which makes choices for us about how to spend and how to steer the economy. People buy and sell with other countries through trade.

Economics is all about this. These are the questions that we cover in this book. Economics is about how people choose what to do. It is not just economics, but more a way of life.

## Choosing what to do

It was quite easy for Al Capone to choose what he would do. He was interested only in himself and would do whatever he wanted in order to make money. It was the time of prohibition in America, when making or selling alcoholic drink was against the law. Capone made and sold more drink than anyone in Chicago. He also ran gambling halls, dog tracks, dance halls and other 'rackets'.

He chose to work these ways to earn his living. He made his income from this work as people paid him for what he gave them – drink, drugs, protection from his own killers, and so on. He chose these lines of business because they made him most money at that time. His buying and selling was against the law, but people were still willing to pay him for what he provided.

This made it easy for the government to choose as well. In terms of his own private income, Capone was doing very well. To the government and the country as a whole, however, he was public enemy Number 1. Capone was arrested in the end, not for murder or theft, but for not paying his taxes.

You, of course, would choose quite differently from Capone. But you do face many of the same sorts of choices. What work should you aim to do, in what line of business? How do you buy and sell things? How do you borrow or lend money? What should you expect of the government? Should you buy from other countries or your own? You must choose one way or another, and face the cost in each case.

Opportunity cost – you cannot have your cake, and eat it.

2

# DROUGHT IN AFRICA

## Malthus's children

**The continent of Africa should be one of the greatest food-producing areas of the world. Instead, it cannot feed itself. Governments blame the weather. It is true that in many areas of Africa there is a desperate shortage of water. Farmers long for rain. But many of the continent's food problems are man-made.**

The English economist Thomas Malthus argued that populations tend to increase faster than their ability to feed themselves. He forecast that worldwide famine would result. In 1983 the rains failed across Africa, where two thirds of the world's poorest people scratch a living. Now, some 150 years after Malthus's death, they may be facing a continental Malthusian crisis.

In 18 black African countries, according to the United Nations Food and Agriculture Organisation, more than 20m people are facing starvation: around 600,000 tonnes of extra food was needed in 1983 to help them stay alive.

Since 1960 the amount of food produced in Africa has increased by less than 2% a year and the growth rate is now falling. During that time, the population has increased by well over 2% a year and the rate is now rising. Africa is the only part of the world which now grows less food for each of its people than it did 20 years ago. The World Bank estimates that nearly 200m people – more than 60% of Africa's total population – eat fewer calories each day than the UN thinks are required to provide a survival diet.

The population boom is most noticeable in the towns, many of which are doubling in size every 10 years. In 1960, one African in 10 lived in a town; by 1980, the proportion was one in five. If the trend continues, half the population of Africa will live in towns by the end of the century.

The new town-dwellers want food like bread or rice that can be prepared quickly. They are willing to pay for it. The staple crops of the local countryside, like cassava and millet, are cheaper than wheat and rice but take a good deal longer to cook. As a result, Africa's towns are fed mostly by imported food while the rural areas remain stuck in subsistence agriculture. Cereal imports into Africa nearly quadrupled in volume between 1960 and 1982.

Government policies discourage farmers. Nearly every African country has a state marketing board with powers to buy and sell food at fixed prices. Throughout the 1960s and 1970s, these prices were too low to encourage farmers to produce a surplus for sale to the boards. Low food prices, it was thought, mistakenly, would keep urban wages low, and help new industry to grow.

Late in the day, African governments have discovered the error of their ways. There has been a desperate rush to help farmers. But higher food prices have upset consumers. In almost every African country, governments are more sensitive to urban opinion than to that of the countryside. When governments increase food prices in urban markets, street riots often follow.

Higher food prices should encourage subsistence farmers to produce more and to start to sell their surplus output. But there are other problems:
● Roads. The cost of transporting food over Africa's vast distances is huge. Some towns are fed by imports because it is cheaper to ship grain from America or Asia than it is from inland.
● Farmers are often not paid regularly by marketing boards, nor are their crops always collected on time.
● Most loans are made to large farms, because the state-owned banks think lending to peasants is too risky.

The FAO reckons that Africa needs to double food production this decade to have enough to feed itself. It is a modest target. More than half the unused farmland in the world is in Africa. If it were all made to yield the best that can be obtained elsewhere, on the same kind of soil, Africa could grow at least 100 times more food than it grows now.

The Economist, 10.9.83

## Africa's dry lands

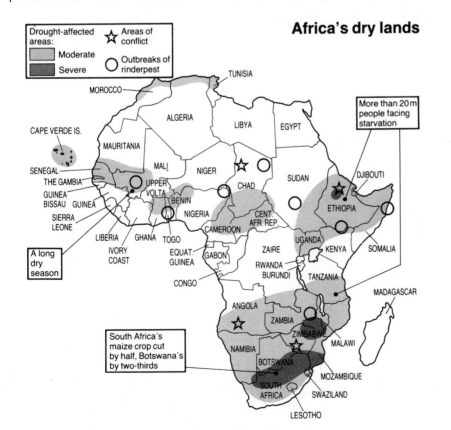

## Questions

1   Show how Africa's food problems have been made worse by peoples' choices about–
    (a)   where to work, and in what line of business,   (2)
    (b)   which types of food to buy and sell,   (1)
    (c)   how the government should change farming,   (2)
    (d)   whether to buy from home or abroad.   (1)
2   What is opportunity cost? Why is the opportunity cost of water greater in some parts of Africa than in others?   (2)

# The cost of choosing

You cannot choose to be both a gangster and a cop. You cannot choose to spend all you have on records, and all you have on films. Every choice you make is a choice between one thing and another. You choose one way instead of the other. You have one thing but go without another.

This is the cost of choosing. Whatever you choose costs you something else. In economics this is called an *opportunity cost*, because you lose the chance to have something else. *Opportunity cost* measures the cost of anything in terms of the next best alternative that you do without. Every true cost is an opportunity cost.

Suppose you choose to buy a hamburger with all the money you have on you. You could have used the money to buy many other things instead; for example a milk shake. As an economist, you see the cost of the hamburger as that milk shake that you now cannot drink.

Al Capone was a public enemy because his choices cost other people so much. He cost them not only their money, but perhaps their happiness, their freedom, or even their lives as well.

## Go catch a bus

Cost of fares on a bus

| | |
|---|---|
| single adult fare | 40p |
| single child fare | 20p |
| retired person fare | 0p |
| season travel card | £10 + 0p for each ride |

### Question

1  What is the opportunity cost of a bus ride, in terms of money, to
   (a)  a family of a mother, a retired person, and a child?  (1)
   (b)  someone with a season travel card?  (1)

# Is economics good for you?

You must choose one way or another in every part of economics. You study the subject to help you see how choices are made and why they matter. But it is still up to you to decide what you will do in your life. It is up to the government to decide what it will do to help to steer the economy. Some choices may help poor people, some may help the rich, but they are all economic choices.

# 1.2 Working and spending

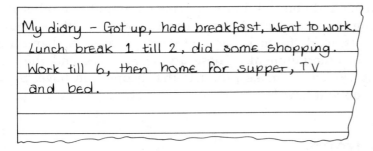

My diary – Got up, had breakfast, went to work.
Lunch break 1 till 2, did some shopping.
Work till 6, then home for supper, TV
and bed.

People spend their time either working or spending. They act as producers and then as consumers in the economic system. How does this all come together in the circular flow of income?

People pass a lot of time either working or spending money, but usually there are different times for each. You work for perhaps 8 hours a day, 5 days a week, most weeks of the year. But this still leaves around seven-eighths of your time free for spending, saving or sleeping.

# Beef sirloin buyers must work extra 4.5 minutes

WORKING TIME (Minutes)

|  | 1970 | 1983 |
|---|---|---|
|  | April of each year | |
| 1 lb beef sirloin | 47.5 | 52.2 |
| 1 lb fresh cod (fillets) | 23.0 | 23.9 |
| 800 g sliced loaf (wrapped) | 9.9 | 7.2 |
| 1 pint fresh milk | 5.0 | 4.0 |
| 1 lb back bacon (smoked) | 36.2 | 27.4 |

(for a married man with 2 children, on average earnings.)

The average family man in 1983 had to work longer to earn the price of Britain's favourite luxury meal, steak and chips, than he did in 1970, according to the Treasury. But the cost in working time of fish and chips was about the same while the traditional British breakfast cost a good deal less.

The Times, 14.2.84

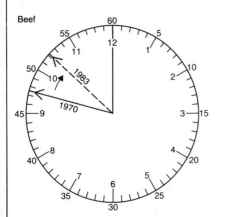

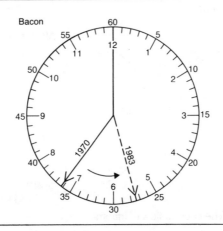

## Questions

1  What was the opportunity cost to the average family man in 1983 of 1 lb of cod:
   (a)  in terms of minutes of work,
   (b)  in terms of pints of milk that could be consumed?  (2)
2  Which of these products became relatively *cheaper* in exchange between 1970 and 1983?  (2)

What do we mean by 'work' in economics? You work when you help in *production*. Production uses your effort and other resources to make for example, cars, hamburgers, clothes and much, much more. Production gives us almost all we need to live. It supplies water that is taken from lakes and rivers, cleaned, and piped to your homes. It supplies pens that are made in factories far away, then are bought and sold by shops, and finally bought by you when you want them.

Most people who work in production are paid to do so. They are paid for the cost of working, for giving up their free time. They work in the water industry for example, or in a shop, for their eight hours a day. Other people may feel that they try as hard as this, but do not help in production at all. You may study as hard as you can and please your teacher and yourself, but you make no output that other people are willing to pay you for. You are not a producer in the economy.

Producers work to make an output such as cars, hamburgers, holidays or entertainments. These are all *products*, and the aim of economic work is to make products that people can have. So what products do you have?

# Consumers

Your spending on products such as jam and coffee is part of *consumption*. Consumption uses what the economy produces to make people feel better off in some way. You consume when you go shopping in your lunch break for clothes, presents or records. You consume when you pay for food and drink, or for plates or washing-up liquid. You consume even when you are asleep at home, with the fridge using electricity and the house itself costs rent or mortgage and rates.

Consumers spend to get the things they want. Some things you can make yourself. If you are good at do-it-yourself you may be able to make furniture rather than buy it. If you are good at sewing you may be able to make clothes rather than buy them. But most of what you buy is made by other people, perhaps even in other countries. How can you afford to consume these products?

You need an income. You can use the income you have as money to spend on what you want. This gives you income as you really want it – as clothes, food, travel and so on. But people earn their incomes by working, before they spend on what they want. Work leads to spending, and spending keeps people at work, in a *circular flow of income*.

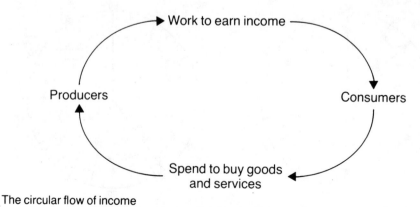

The circular flow of income

# The couple with a lot of bottle

Washing nappies in a freezing stream sharpened Cath McGoldrick's appetite for challenges, she says from the relative comfort of her 17th century Pennine farmstead. These days she's got running water, electricity via a generator, 100 hens for fresh eggs and geese. And her children are now four and five.

What Cath didn't realise in the stream-washing days was that the water from her small woodland spring was going to become business. Cath, 31, and her husband Tom, 42, are just launching Allendale Spring Water at 35p a bottle with distribution in Newcastle and beyond. It rises, says the label, from a source in the high Pennines at the centre of Britain.

They both come from the North-east – he from Sunderland, she from Newcastle. They had each tried their hand at many jobs. Tom had been a croupier and auctioneer, a window cleaner and a shop assistant. Cath had been a fashion student and a psychiatric nurse, a postwoman and a gardener for the parks department.

They bought their remote 16 acre smallholdings, at Low Turney Shield in Northumberland, eight years ago for £2,300, "which seemed a large sum as it was nearly derelict."

When visitors from Newcastle brought bottles to take home supplies of the water – "which hasn't already been through other people's kidneys" – they hit on the idea that it could be sold.

The equipment cost a few hundred pounds – the main items being an ultra violet purifier and a six-bottle filling tap (the water had already been pumped uphill, to flow into a barn at the back of the farmstead).

"Our maximum production will be 6,000 bottles a week. I won't mind doing it for hours: it's like weeding – the mind can wander." Thousands of plastic bottles at 10p each (glass would have cost more) and boxes are arriving. The other cost will be distribution. But the water is theirs for the taking, flowing at 45 gallons a minute.

The bottled water market is now worth some £30 millions a year, mostly in the hands of multi-nationals. Cath and Tom will be distributing to local wholefood shops and pubs. "It's a godsend," says Tom. "We think it will let us pay our way here and put some money back into the land. We've already planted a couple of thousand trees."

The Guardian, 13.12.83

## Questions

1   Find 2 products that the McGoldricks are making. What did they do in production before taking on the smallholding? (2)
2   Find 4 other products they must use in order to sell their water. (2)
3   What is consumption? Explain why the McGoldricks plan to sell their water. (2)

# Exchanging work and products

Suppose you fix your bike or make your own clothes; first you do the work but then you have what you want – a bike that goes or clothes to wear. You exchange your own work for a product you can have, and act as both producer and consumer.

Most exchange is between different people. People work at shops, offices or factories, making certain products. Then they go out, or go home, to consume products very different from the ones they have made. But everything they consume was produced somehow, and everything that is produced is owned by someone as a consumer. Producers exchange with consumers as a whole in an economic system.

Income flows around the economic system in a circle. People work as producers to make all the different products in the economy. Other people consume those products as their income. They are fed, clothed, housed and entertained. Then they go out to work once more. This completes the *circular flow of income* and the exchange of work for income.

People specialise to produce different kinds of goods and services. Why is this, and why are jobs changing so much?

## Questions

1  What service do shops offer?   (1)
2  Find 2 examples of shops selling
   (a) goods, (b) services.   (2)

## Checklist – what are the main areas of production?

- primary production extracts materials from the ground and sea – in farming, fishing, mining, etc
- secondary production manufactures goods such as cars, TVs and medicines
- tertiary production offers services such as banking, entertainment and administration

Tinker, tailor, soldier, sailor, or computer programmer! The jobs may have changed but we still seem to see people in terms of the work they do. Can you see yourself as a plumber, a nurse or a teacher? Each job is different and seems to make you into something of a different person.

People *specialise* in their work. Most people do just one job, and have training and experience to help them do it well. They work to make a product, but their product is different from those made by other people. This means that there is a whole range of different things that you can choose to consume. So what are the main types of products?

Let's say that you set off from home one morning. You take a bus ride and buy a magazine to read on the way. You have bought two products already, but they are quite different. You can read and keep your magazine and hold on to it for as long as you want. It is a product that stays just as you bought it, like a car, a TV or a pair of shoes. These are all called *'goods'* because you see a good reason for buying them.

What's so different about a bus ride? You bought that too and saw a good reason for doing so. It is produced just as goods are. But a bus ride is a *'service'* that helps you without giving you anything you can keep and hold on to. Hairdressers, cafés and banks also offer services to their customers, and so do shops, football teams and doctors. You have their products only while you pay for them. In the end there is nothing solid left to show.

## The main areas of production

People specialise in different jobs when they work for firms. Some are manual workers who use their hands, others are non-manual workers who perhaps use their minds a little more. But firms also specialise in different areas of business. Let's say that you could work for one of three firms. One is a farm, the second a plastics factory, and the third sells insurance.

Your work at the farm is to take products from the land. The farm sells its products as food and materials to other firms, who then turn them into finished goods and services for the general public. You may produce strawberries to go into jam, or grain to feed chickens. This is called *primary production*, because we need to extract raw materials from the land as a first stage in all production. Agriculture, forestry, fishing and mining are in this same area of production.

Factory work is different. This uses raw materials to make goods of one kind or another. Your plastics factory may make buckets, bottles and clothes pegs that are finished products ready for sale to the general public. It may also make parts for cars or for radios and hi-fis, that are components, or intermediate goods, for use by other factories. All manufacturing work in factories is part of a *secondary* stage in production.

Most of the products we use every day come from the manufacturing industry. We take toasters, TVs and toilets almost for granted and forget how difficult it is to make these goods. Light industry makes chairs, belts, clocks and other small consumer goods. Heavy industry makes steel, chemicals and other semi-manufactures that are used in production elsewhere.

Suppose you get a job selling insurance. Here you do not produce a solid end product, but you offer a service instead. This makes your customer feel more secure because your firm will help if he falls victim to theft, fire or accident. Services make up a third stage of production that is again different and is called *tertiary production*. It includes banking, health and education, travel and selling.

# Why do jobs change?

If you had been born 250 years ago it is very likely that you would have worked on the land. Some people worked as blacksmiths or potters, in manufacturing; some were soldiers, sailors, merchants or actors. But most worked on farms.

The industrial revolution changed all that. People were needed to work in factories, making all sorts of goods, using mass-production. If you had been born 100 years ago you would probably have worked in secondary production.

Now the picture is different again. The factsheet shows where the jobs are now. Around two in every three people working in the UK are in services of one kind or another. Why have jobs changed like this? The main reasons are to do with economic growth.

*Economic growth* is a rise in output from all three forms of production together. This happens partly because there are more machines and equipment for people to work with, and partly because of technical progress. Producers find out how to make new products and how to use new methods of production which require fewer workers. They can increase output or use fewer workers or both. Economic growth gives us more goods and services and raises our incomes. So we buy more products and different products.

The first industrial revolution came when we needed more workers in factories and fewer in farming. Now there are still fewer people who work in primary production. Farms and mines have more machines and better ways to do the work instead. A second industrial revolution seems to be upon us now, as we need fewer workers in manufacturing industry. As at the time of the first industrial revolution, there are machines and methods to replace the old sorts of jobs. We need more jobs in services to make up for those being lost.

# Is it good to specialise?

When jobs change, specialised people are put out of work. Specialised work brings other problems as well. You may find that you do the same

## Factsheet – where the jobs are now

Which areas of production do people work in?
For every 100 workers in 1982

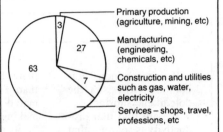

- Primary production (agriculture, mining, etc)
- Manufacturing (engineering, chemicals, etc)
- Construction and utilities such as gas, water, electricity
- Services – shops, travel, professions, etc

**What are the main changes?**

Lost – 1 in 3 jobs in metal manufacturing and textiles and 1 in 5 in manufacturing as a whole

Gained – 1 in 12 jobs in insurance, banking, professional, scientific and some other services

but only 1 in 30 in services as a whole

So more jobs lost than gained (all changes for 1976–1982)

**What are the main areas of production?**

| | | number of employees 1982 (m) |
|---|---|---|
| Primary – | agriculture, forestry, fishing, mining, etc | .354 .326 |
| Secondary – | food, drink, tobacco | .622 |
| | chemicals | .415 |
| | metal manufactures | .295 |
| | engineering, etc | 2.646 |
| | textiles, etc | .616 |
| | other | 1.158 |
| Tertiary – | construction | 1.049 |
| | gas, electricity, water | .340 |
| | Services – transport & communications | 1.383 |
| | distribution | 2.706 |
| | insurance, banking, etc | 1.321 |
| | professional & scientific | 3.768 |
| | public administration | 1.549 |
| | other | 2.554 |
| | TOTAL 1982 = | 21.102 |

(Source – Annual Abstract of Statistics, 1984)

# WHERE ARE THE JOBS OF TOMORROW?

It's the question everyone keeps asking:

If Britain's industry is booming, why isn't the dole queue shorter?

We are told that productivity is soaring, that New Tech is replacing old wrecks and that we are set for a bullseye on growth targets.

But none of this activity is generating jobs.

Frank Turner manufacturing director of Rolls-Royce, foresees huge factories run by one man and a dog.

He says, "The dog is there to stop the man touching anything. And the man is there to feed the dog."

It's a fantasy – for the time being, at least. But at R-R's Derby plant fact is catching up. The company has spent more than £4m on an automated production line making turbine blades for its aero engines.

Microprocessors, robotised handlers and advanced machine tools have transformed an operation which used to be slow, labour-intensive and unreliable.

Three men per shift are now producing what once required 30. Turner can see considerable scope for increasing output but no one expects it to produce new jobs.

So where will the new jobs come from?

The simple answer is – the service industries, which have grown over 20 years across Britain.

But the Government is very defensive about these Mickey Mouse jobs, as critics call them.

The information technology minister, says: "I know some will sneer. They claim that Britain will become a nation of hairdressers, waiters and video salesmen.

"I would reply by saying that people who do these jobs are no less worthy than those who make the scissors for the hairdressers, or grow the vegetables for the restaurant, or make the electronic circuits for the video machine."

The new jobs of tomorrow will be concentrated in management and administration, literary, artistic and sports occupations, the engineering, scientific and technical field, the professions – outside teaching – and the security business.

The Sun, 3.5.84

## Questions

1 From the article, find one example of primary production, one of secondary production and one of tertiary production. (2)
2 Explain why Rolls-Royce automated their production line. Why could they not do this 20 years ago? (3)
3 If this happened in the same way to all manufacturing industry, how many jobs would be lost? (Use the factsheet.) (2)

difficult jobs over and over again. This can become boring. Specialised workers may know that their firms cannot do without them, and so demand high wages. Yet most people train and work in just one sort of job. What is the advantage in specialising like this?

We can all gain from *division of labour*. Perhaps you can fix your own bike or sew your own clothes, but you may get the job done better if it is done by an expert. This leaves you free to do what you are better at. We can all divide work between us so that we each do a different job. We can produce more, and make it better, by dividing our labour.

People have different abilities – for example, not everyone has the patience to sew well. People gain experience by doing just one type of work and learning how to do it better. For example, you must repeat your revision several times to remember it well in the exams. It takes time for people to change jobs, to move from one machine or one place to another. A moving production line, for example, can serve a number of fixed workers doing different jobs. In all these ways, division of labour improves production. It gives us more goods and services to enjoy, and it gives us different jobs to do.

# 1.4 Yours and mine – income and wealth

Let's say that there are 100 people in your year at school, and that the richest person has an income of £10 a week. How much would everyone else have if their incomes were in line with the country as a whole? The richest ten people would have about £5 each, those in the middle would have around £1.30, and the poorest twenty-five would have less than 50p. This gives an idea of the differences in what people earn in the UK. There are clearly great differences in income.

What can you do with your money? You can buy goods and services as you choose. The richest person in your year, could buy more than twenty times as much as the poorest. You can spend your money on the things you want.

## Wants

We all want many different things. What would you like to have? A car of your own, a holiday in the sun or lunch at the Ritz? Once you start to make a list of everything you want you soon find out one of the most important ideas in economics. *Wants* are endless. You may have a lot already, but there is always something more you want. Even if you have enough, there is someone somewhere else who wants more.

You try to buy the things you want most, but there can never be enough money to buy all that you want. You have to choose which goods and services you want and face the opportunity cost of going without something else. If you choose well, you can satisfy as many of your wants as possible. Rich people have more to spend and can satisfy more of their wants. They may be able to buy caviar and champagne while poor people can only afford bread and water.

## Resources

How do you make your money? People are paid in many different ways, and some have pocket money, some pensions, and some supplementary or unemployment benefit. In economics we must be careful to ask if people work for their money or not. Gifts and other benefits are ways to *transfer payments* from one person to another but they are not earned by work.

Income is earned from work in one way or another. You work to help produce goods and services and your pay is a reward for doing so. You earn pay because you put your *resources* into production. You may earn more pay if you offer more resources and so gain a higher income. So people who earn a high income are usually putting more resources to work than poor people. But what are these resources?

Are you rich or poor? Some people have much more income and wealth than others. Why is this?

In the summer of 1924 a Scottish conman managed to sell, to American tourists, Big Ben for £1000, Nelson's Column for £6000, and Buckingham Palace for a deposit of £2000.

11

Resources are all that firms use to produce goods and services. You already own some resources in your ability to work with your hands and your mind. People offer these human resources when they go to work in offices and factories. You may also have savings in the bank, or property such as land or shares in owning a company. These are also forms of resources although they are clearly not human.

Human and non-human resources are generally used together to make up production. We will see how they are set to work in Part 2 of this book, and how firms use them in Part 3.

# Are Britain's highest-paid directors really worth the money?

Is a retired chairman who left his company owing £200m of debt to its bankers worth a £137,000 golden handshake? Dunlop shareholders thought not at last week's noisy annual meeting. It added insult to injury. From 1981 to 1983, as Dunlop's losses piled up, Sir Campbell's salary increased to £85,000, taking him comfortably into the top 100 of Britain's best paid directors.

Dunlop shareholders were silenced, but it will have reminded many a company director that their salaries and perks will not wash with their shareholders unless the company performs.

Dick Giordano, Britain's highest paid director, earned £522,000 last year. Surprisingly, he "only" managed a 9% rise in two years at BOC. But then BOC profits rose just 4%.

Some of the biggest rises have been in the retailing and service sectors, reflecting the consumer boom of the past 18 months. Michael Hollingbery enjoyed a 145% salary rise in two years before selling his stake in the Comet chain to Woolworth for a princely £55m in April. Yet his shareholders had few causes to complain at a £194,000 salary, for profits grew by 184%.

But then for many a chairman or highly paid director, his salary is simply the loose change in his pocket. Tiny Rowland earned over £4m in the final Lonrho dividend in 1983 from his £56m stake in the company, compared to a mere £265,000 salary in 1983.

*The Sunday Times, 3.6.84*

| Highest-paid director | Company | 1983 salary £000s | Position amongst highest-paid directors |
|---|---|---|---|
| Dick Giordano | BOC | 522 | 1st |
| Tiny Rowland | Lonrho | 265 | 3rd |
| Michael Hollingbery | Comet | 194 | 10th |
| Sir Campbell Fraser | Dunlop | 85 | 92nd |

## Questions

1 What 'resources' do top company directors offer in their work? (1)
2 Which two sources of income are mentioned here? (2)
3 Why do some company directors deserve to earn a higher income than others according to the company shareholders? (1)

# Wealth

Resources such as land and machinery are property that you can own. But you can also own other forms of property such as paintings or the house you live in. These are never likely to be used by firms to produce goods and services. All forms of property together make up the wealth of a country.

It is difficult to measure how wealthy you are. Perhaps you can tell how much your possessions cost when you first bought them, but what are your clothes, records, furniture, and so on worth now? You must guess the price you could sell them for. In the same sort of way we can try to see how much the wealth of the country would be if that were put on sale. Some of this is held as money, some as stocks and shares and some as other financial loans. How much is there altogether in the UK?

## Floating palace fit for a king

The wraps came off the world's most luxurious yacht yesterday.

The £30 million dream boat was custom built as a floating pleasure palace for King Fahd of Saudi Arabia.

It is a little gift from a Greek shipping billionaire.

But its breathtaking opulence is enough to make even the fabulously wealthy king pause from counting his oil wells.

The cabins are decorated with gold and silver and the finest woods – ebony, teak and mahogany.

The marble floors are covered with the richest carpets, and Old Masters hang from the walls.

The yacht also has the obligatory swimming pool, helicopter pad and fully-equipped hospital with an operating theatre for performing emergency operations at sea.

But the pleasure palace is also a floating fortress for the security-conscious king.

It has armour-plated windows and a missile detection system. Anti-aircraft missiles may be added later.

Daily Express, 24.5.84

### Questions

1 Why are King Fahd and other Arab Princes so wealthy? (1)
2 What special wants does this floating palace satisfy? (1)

The factsheet gives the official figures. It shows that possessions were worth almost £10 000 in 1981 for each person in the country. Do you have a fair share of all this? It is most unlikely, for the average measure shows only what everyone would have if the total were shared out equally. In fact shares are not at all equal.

Suppose again that wealth is shared out amongst your school year of, say, 100 people, in a way that matches the shares across the country as a whole. The richest person would have almost a quarter of all the wealth. The poorer half – fifty of your year – would have only about 6 per cent or £6 in every £100 of wealth to share between them.

The distribution of wealth shows that it is shared out unequally between people. The rich are much better off than the poor. How did this come about?

## Income and wealth

Wealth is made up of possessions such as savings, houses and paintings. You buy these things with your income but then keep them as long as you wish. So wealth is made up of products bought with income, that have been held and added to over the years. Much wealth is passed on from parents to children so that most rich people are born rich.

13

# Factsheet – income and wealth in the UK

## How is people's wealth made up?
Much is as buildings and investments.

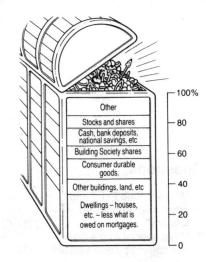

(Source – Social Trends, 1984)

## Questions

1  How much of people's incomes comes from (a) their work as human resources, (b) transfer payments?  (2)
2  Explain why you would prefer to be rich in terms of (a) income or (b) wealth.  (2)

## How much income each?
The top fifth of households has almost half of all income, but taxes and benefits reduce this considerably.

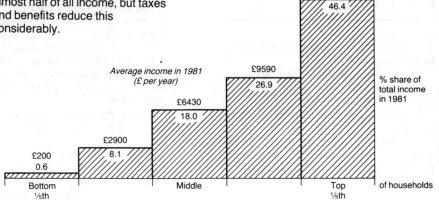

*Average income in 1981 (£ per year)*

£16540 — 46.4
£9590 — 26.9
£6430 — 18.0
£2900 — 8.1
£200 — 0.6

% share of total income in 1981

Bottom ⅕th | Middle | Top ⅕th | of households

## Where does this income come from?
Most is earned as wages and salaries –

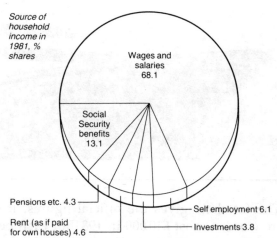

*Source of household income in 1981, % shares*

Wages and salaries 68.1
Social Security benefits 13.1
Pensions etc. 4.3
Rent (as if paid for own houses) 4.6
Self employment 6.1
Investments 3.8

## How much wealth each?
The most wealthy 1% of the adult population owned 23% of all marketable wealth in 1981
The most wealthy 10% owned 60% of all wealth
The most wealthy 50% owned 94% of all wealth.

Income and wealth are different. A rich widow keeps her husband's wealth without 'working' for it, although her investments may work and earn income for her. You may start work young and earn a high income but not have many possessions to show for it at first.

But once you have wealth you can use it to earn income. You can own resources and use them in production to earn more income in future. Rich people usually stay rich.

The taxman changes this somewhat. Income taxes take away a share of people's incomes and take a greater share from the rich. Wealth taxes take a share of people's wealth, for instance when they die. These taxes make the distribution of income and wealth a little more equal but great differences still remain.

# 1.5 At what price? A first look at supply and demand

What can you make from an hour's work? Clearly this depends on whether your rate of pay is high or low. But also you will want to spend your money on the things you want. What will it be – fruit, textbooks or extra games for a video machine?

How much of each can you get? This is set by the *prices* of goods and services. £1 buys one £1 textbook, two 50p boxes of strawberries or ten 10p games. Prices are different and you must pay more for some of the things you want than for others. The price of one good is high when seen next to the price of something else. We call this its *relative price* because it measures what you must pay for one thing compared with another.

The price of some textbooks is higher than the price of video games. These relative prices tell you how much of one you must go without to gain an extra amount of the other. This measures the opportunity cost of buying each good. The textbook costs you ten extra games, for example.

You could afford to buy more of all these goods if you could earn more pay. Your rate of pay is also a price – in this case the price paid for your work. A higher price means that you get more money. So you meet prices in all you do, as a seller of your own work and as a buyer of goods and services.

Prices are set by supply and demand. So what are the effects of changes in these market forces?

## Markets and prices

Why are prices different from each other? In economics we look at how price is set for each product when it is bought and sold in a market. A *market* brings buyers and sellers together to exchange a product.

Each product and service has its own buyers and sellers, and so has its own market. The market may take place in a certain building at a certain time, as in an auction of paintings, for example. An auction is where everyone wanting to buy can make offers, and the best offer wins. Other markets are spread across the world and go on at all times, as with sales of petrol, for example.

Markets can take in a number of products that are all about the same, such as a take-away chip shop, or just one product that is seen to be different from all others, such as Rolls Royce cars. In all cases, however, it is in markets that we see how prices are set.

A market sets the price for its product and that price influences the amounts bought and sold until, generally, the level is the same. Buyers join the market when they show demand for the product, and sellers offer their supply. These are called the *market forces* of demand and supply.

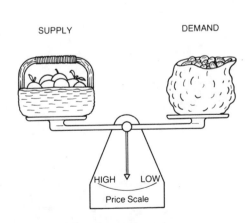

Supply and demand set price

more supply → low price ← less demand
less supply → high price ← more demand

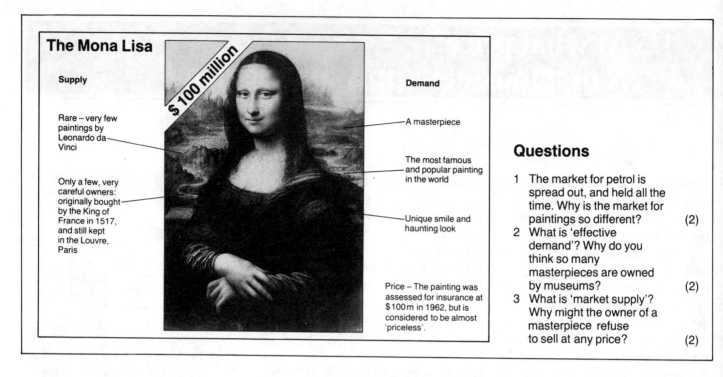

**The Mona Lisa**

$ 100 million

Supply

Rare – very few paintings by Leonardo da Vinci

Only a few, very careful owners: originally bought by the King of France in 1517, and still kept in the Louvre, Paris

Demand

A masterpiece

The most famous and popular painting in the world

Unique smile and haunting look

Price – The painting was assessed for insurance at $100m in 1962, but is considered to be almost 'priceless'.

**Questions**

1 The market for petrol is spread out, and held all the time. Why is the market for paintings so different? (2)
2 What is 'effective demand'? Why do you think so many masterpieces are owned by museums? (2)
3 What is 'market supply'? Why might the owner of a masterpiece refuse to sell at any price? (2)

# Demand and supply

*Demand* shows how much buyers want to buy of a product. You decide your demand for a number of things each day, but you cannot afford to buy everything you would like. No one has enough income to do that, because wants are endless. So you must choose between the different things you would like, and decide what to spend your money on. When you decide what to buy, and how much, that is your demand. We call this *effective demand* because it will have an effect on the market.

On your own, your actions make little difference to anyone else. Suppose you decide to buy more strawberries or fewer video games; if everyone else goes on buying as before then it will make no difference. You are just a very small part of a large market. But if everyone together starts to buy more or less that will make a difference. It may well change market price.

Higher demand generally leads to a higher price. If people think that a certain painting is a good investment or very rewarding to look at, they will pay more for it. The price of the painting goes higher. But there is only one copy of each 'old master' painting. In most other markets it is possible to make more, so that higher demand raises the amount sold as well as price. And lower demand cuts the amount sold, and sets a lower price.

Demand and supply set price together. *Supply* is the other half of the market and is made up of the amount that sellers wish to sell. They can only sell one of each old painting, but they can be more or less keen to sell. And oil firms can try to sell more or less petrol, for example, from time to time.

Higher supply generally leads to a lower price. If there is more petrol on offer, then petrol stations have to cut prices, or make special deals, to sell more quickly. The opposite is also true: lower supply generally leads to a higher price, and to less being sold in the market.

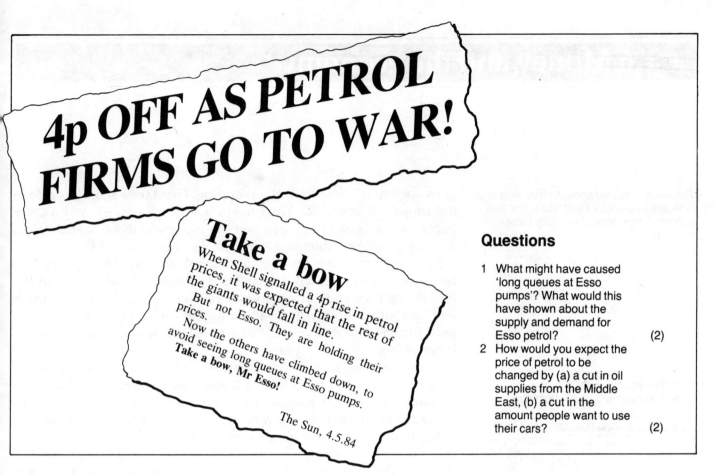

# 4p OFF AS PETROL FIRMS GO TO WAR!

## Take a bow

When Shell signalled a 4p rise in petrol prices, it was expected that the rest of the giants would fall in line.

But not Esso. They are holding their prices.

Now the others have climbed down, to avoid seeing long queues at Esso pumps.

**Take a bow, Mr Esso!**

*The Sun, 4.5.84*

### Questions

1  What might have caused 'long queues at Esso pumps'? What would this have shown about the supply and demand for Esso petrol? (2)
2  How would you expect the price of petrol to be changed by (a) a cut in oil supplies from the Middle East, (b) a cut in the amount people want to use their cars? (2)

## Price and value

What can price tell you? It cannot tell you how much something matters to you, for only you can decide that on your own. But it does tell you what it costs to buy one thing relative to another. It tells you how the market, made up of all buyers and sellers meeting together, values different things.

There is a lot of petrol around so its value and price is relatively low. There are only a few paintings by each old master, however, and their value and price is high. Changes in demand and supply mean that there is more or less around compared to how much is wanted. That changes value and price. We will see more about how this works in Part 4 of this book.

# 1.6 Money and the economy

The value of money changes from time to time, but so do output and jobs in the 'real' economy. How should we study these changes?

What can you buy with £5?
If inflation continues at 5% from now on...

Now – 100%
10 yrs time – 61.35%
50 yrs time – 8.73%

Let's say that it's time to do the shopping. First take a short bus ride to the shops – that's £1.50. Then buy a loaf of bread – £2, and a daily paper – £1. A book of stamps – you can use one of those new £5 coins. A short morning's shopping, and you can easily spend £100!

5 per cent *inflation* is not a lot. It means that prices rise in general by 5p in the £1 over a year. But what if this carries on for all your working life? By the time you retire to live on your savings and pension, prices will be much higher. They will be higher by 5p in the £1 after one year, but more than 60p in the £1 after 10 years, and be about eleven times as high after fifty years.

Things costing £1 now could cost you £11 by the time you retire. Each £1 you hold on to till then will only buy you a ninth of the things it could buy now. The value of money will have fallen. It may make sense to spend your money now rather than hold on to it till later.

But none of this may happen, of course. We may see a change so that prices fall as they did before the Second World War, instead of rising as they have ever since. A fall in the general level of prices is called *price deflation*. It means that each £1 buys more in terms of goods and services because prices for these things are lower. Thus the value of money rises.

This might seem a better prospect, but deflation in the past was more than just changes in prices. We talk of deflation these days when we see a fall in the amount of work, number of jobs and standard of living in the economy. Deflation seems to go with slump and even more unemployment. Your money may buy more but you have less money to spend if you become poor and earn no income.

## Finance

People use their money carefully. They try to protect the value of money they hold so that they can buy more with it. They lend, one way or another, to people and firms who wish to borrow. (We will see how loans are arranged in Part 5 of this book.) They watch the value of their money to see how it is affected by inflation. Will inflation make you better or worse off? It means that you can get less for each £1 of money, but you may also have more £1s to spend. Indeed, a rise in the general level of prices should affect you very differently from a change in the relative price of certain products, such as petrol or paintings.

A change in relative prices affects only those people who buy and sell those products. Other prices and other people should not be affected at all. In economics, we study these changes as they affect one market at a time, in what is called *micro-economics*. This covers individual choices made by producers and consumers, as we see in Parts 2, 3 and 4 of this book.

A change in the general level of prices is quite different, for it affects all prices together. All markets, all producers and all consumers are affected by this, and there are general changes throughout the whole economy. General changes such as this are studied in what we call *macro-economics*, as in Parts 5, 6 and 7 of this book. It explains also why the amounts of work, employment, production and trade change in the economy of the UK as a whole.

Inflation alone changes all prices together. Your pay is a price, and should rise as much as what you pay for in shops. Your income and your spending should rise together, so that inflation does not make you either richer or poorer. Only people who do not earn pay, or whose pay does not change as fast as prices, will lose out.

So what does make us all richer or poorer? How are the other general levels in the economy set – for work, employment, production and so on?

## Checklist – micro or macro?

Micro-economic questions are ones such as these:
● Why do one job and not another?
● Why make more of a product and not less?
● Why buy more and sell less of a product if its price falls?

Macro-economic questions are ones such as these:
● What causes mass unemployment?
● How can the government help to cut inflation?
● How well has the UK economy grown recently?

# Mr Shilling's motoring history

Since 1933 Mr Shilling has owned 11 cars. The table shows what he spent on each of them. Mr Shilling has always bought relatively cheap cars—between £3,000 and £5,000 at today's prices—so it is possible to compare costs between different periods. He has also "standardised" his costs, working out equivalent spending per day by assuming average daily journeys of 25 miles.

In 1934 it cost him 26p a day (or 5s 2½d, as it was then called) to keep his Ford Sports on the road. That is equivalent to £5.26 at 1982 prices. In 1982, driving his Ford Escort cost him only £2.59 a day, a fall in real terms of more than 50%.

Every component of his costs except petrol is smaller in real terms now.

● Road tax (road fund licence). Mr Shilling paid 46p road tax a day (at 1982 prices) on his first car, and 16p a day on his last, a fall of 65%. That decline took place in a period when there was a huge growth in the number of cars, and in the wider costs that go with

them: the economic costs of providing and maintaining a road system, and the social costs of accidents, congestion and pollution. The taxman is giving the motorist a much better deal these days.

● Repairs and service. These charges fell by 56% in real terms over the period. Remembering that labour costs have increased in real terms, this indicates the extent to which rapid technical progress has made cars more reliable and easier to maintain.

Petrol has been the exception to the rule—but less than you might think. Although Mr Shilling's bill was 1s 1d a day in 1934 and an average of £1.22 in 1979–83, that was a real increase of only 14½% over 50 years. And that is only because Mr Shilling's recent Escort used more petrol than his 1930s Ford Sports. Even after the rises of the 1970s, petrol was cheaper per gallon in real terms in 1979–83 than in 1933–35 (see the bottom line of the table). That cheap modern cars have been as thirsty if not thirstier than their 1930s

counterparts is the most surprising of Mr Shilling's discoveries.

### The pence that Shilling spent

Actual prices (1982 prices in brackets); pence per day assuming daily journeys of 25 miles

|  | May, 1933–March, 1935 | Feb, 1979–Jan, 1983 |
|---|---|---|
| Depreciation | 13.0 (261.6) | 76.0 (76.0) |
| Road fund licence | 2.3 (46.3) | 15.8 (15.8) |
| Insurance | 2.4 (48.3) | 17.1 (17.1) |
| Petrol | 5.3 (106.4) | 121.8 (121.8) |
| Repairs and service | 3.2 (64.3) | 28.1 (28.1) |
| **Total** | 26.2 (526.4) | 258.8 (258.8) |
| Cost of car (£) | 171 (4120) | 2910 (4460) |
| Miles per gallon | 37.4 | 30.6 |
| Petrol cost per gallon (p) | 7.9 (159.0) | 149.0 (149.0) |

The Economist, 12.11.83

# The 'real' economy

We see money as something different from the real goods and services we buy. No one wants money for itself, but only for what it can buy. Everyone wants food, clothes, personal possessions and other real products, because these make us all better off.

People work in the economy to produce goods and services. They put in real effort when they set their resources to work. They enjoy real goods and services when they buy as consumers. All this is what we call the 'real' economy.

We want the real economy to make as much as possible, so that we can be better off. We want there to be good economic growth and enough jobs to keep workers out of unemployment. We want the country to trade well with the rest of the world. These are our aims for the economy and we expect the government to help us reach them. We will see how the government can try to steer the economy in Part 6 of this book.

## Questions

1 What has been the change between 1933 and 1982 in (a) the general level of prices, (b) the general value of money? (2)
2 How has the price changed of (a) a new Ford car, (b) petrol? Is this more or less than prices in general? (2)
3 What do you understand by the phrase 'in real terms'. (line 17) Does it cost more or less in 1982 compared with 1934, in real terms, to (a) buy and (b) run a new Ford car? (3)
4 How do you think (a) cars and (b) road journeys have changed since the 1930s? Are these real or money changes? (3)

# 1.7 Good government

What is the government and why is it such an important part of the economy? What makes for good government?

## Questions

1 Which is run by (a) central government, (b) a local authority, (c) a public corporation? (1)

When you spend £1, over 50p ends up going to the government. When ten people go to work, around four of them work for the government in some way. When you lend £10, about £6 is borrowed by the government. Why is government so large and why does it affect the economy of the UK in so many ways?

There are different parts to the government, of course. Let's look at three activities; claiming social security, going to school, or posting a letter. Offices of social security are run by a department of *central government*. At its head is a government minister who must stand in elections and answer to Parliament on the way the department is run. Central government runs the armed forces, builds motorways and does much more besides. But in many areas it does not run government services although it pays for them. It raises money from taxation and loans, but then pays money over as grants to local authorities.

Some schools are owned and run privately, but most are run by the government through *local authorities*. People vote for their local council and pay rates to cover a share of its costs. But most money to run schools, the police, refuse collection and other local services comes to the local authorities from central departments. Your school is probably run by the council for your local area, such as Cornwall County Council or the London Borough of Brent.

Central departments and local authorities make up general government. But there are many other bodies which run services different from these. To post a letter you must use the Post Office, to buy electricity you must use the Central Electricity Generating Board, and to watch TV you must pay a licence so that money goes to the British Broadcasting Corporation. You pay for all these services to the firms that run them. These firms are called *public corporations* and are run separately from general government, although the government acts as their owner. It does this to act on behalf of us all as members of the public.

## Fair shares for all

What should government try to do for the economy? We expect it to help the poor. It runs the welfare state and aims to make sure that everyone in the country has a decent standard of living. It plays at being Robin Hood, and takes from those who are better off to give to those in need.

Everyone pays taxes but some pay more than others. The government tries to make up taxes that take most from people who are most able to pay. Income tax does this by taking a greater share from higher incomes.

## ENGLISH £195 WORSE OFF THAN SCOTS

The argument that Scotland suffers economically from her union with England and Wales was loudly proclaimed in the referendum campaign of 1978 about the proposed Assembly in Edinburgh.

But figures, for the year 1976–77, show that each Scotsman receives £195 more per head in public expenditure than his English counterpart.

He also receives a better return on his taxes paid than does the English or Welsh taxpayer. Inland Revenue receipts from Scotland in 1976–77 were £1,437·7 million; public expenditure on Scotland was £4,899·8 million.

These tax receipts ignore national insurance contributions, but taking equivalent figures, England and Wales receive 198 per cent. return on their payments to the Inland Revenue

while Scotland receives 341 per cent.

Breaking down figures made available to the Commons recently show that on housing, a Scotsman receives £25 more than his English counterpart (£112 per head to £87, in 1976–77); while on education he receives £28 more than an Englishman.

In agriculture, he is £23 per head better off; in health, £26 per head better off; in assistance to trade and industry and employment subsidy, he is £55 per head better off (£85 to £30).

### Scots cost more

His profit on roads is £13 per head (£55 to £42). Only on law, order and protective services is spending in England, Wales and Scotland on a par, and on Social Services the Scotsman costs £1 per head more than the Englishman.

To the Labour, Conservative, Liberal parties these figures are proof that Scotland has benefited rather than suffered from the Union.

But the Scottish Nationalists argue that the main reason for higher public expenditure per head on Scotland is that about one in three

employed persons work for the Government. "This is sad and unhealthy and a Scottish National Government will end it," a SNP spokesman said.

The Daily Telegraph, 15.9.78

### Questions

1 What is (a) public expenditure, (b) national insurance? (1)
2 According to the figures, how much extra did the government spend for each person in Scotland, (a) to support production of goods, directly, (b) to help children directly? (2)
3 What economic reasons may there be why it is 'sad and unhealthy' for 1 in 3 people to work for the government in Scotland? (2)

---

The government gives benefits to those in need. Social security benefits are paid to people who are poor, or out of work, or have children to support. State pensions are given to people who have retired, and are paid for by national insurance contributions from people who are in work and earning money.

The government runs basic and important services such as health, education and housing. You can pay for all these things and buy privately as well. But not everyone has enough income to afford private doctors and schools, or houses of their own. So the government offers health and education free or at low cost, and runs council housing at low rents. And it tries to put more of all its services into areas that are most in need. Poor regions of the country are helped more than areas that are well off.

# More for all

It is easier to give more to the poor if there is more around to give. We want the government to help the economy to run so that there is more production and more consumption for all. How can it do this?

The government aims to help the economy make the best use of its resources and to reduce waste. It gives facts and figures that help firms to run well. It aims to stop large sellers or buyers from controlling markets for their own ends at a cost to other people. It aims to stop people from harming the public as a whole.

We all act in our own interests, for individual and private reasons. But this can harm other people, for example when we throw litter away, leave gates open in the country, or start fires by accident in forests. The government aims to help the public as a whole by controlling what we do. It can tax or ban actions that are harmful. This helps put a stop to pollution by firms, or overcrowding in city centres, for example.

## Checklist – what makes for good government?

- if it changes the distribution of income to help those in need
- if it helps the economy to work well and stops individual people from harming society as a whole
- if it steers the economy well towards the aims of growth, high employment, low inflation, and balanced payments for trade

# Breaking the tobacco habit

The Royal College of Physicians says that at least 100,000 people in Britain die prematurely each year from smoking cigarettes. If the habit does not change, by the year 2000 another 1,700,000 people, equivalent to the combined populations of Birmingham and Glasgow, will have been killed by tobacco-related diseases.

Fortunately, the death toll which the college described as "an avoidable holocaust", is unlikely to be so high. Smoking is a dying habit which claims huge, but declining, numbers of victims.

In the past three years more than a million Britons have given up cigarettes, joining almost 10 million former smokers. Between 1972 and 1982, the proportion of adult males who smoke fell from 52 per cent to 38 per cent, while among women, the percentage dropped from 41 to 33.

Although between 16 and 17 million adults smoke, they have been a minority since 1976, a peak year for cigarette consumption. Then, male smokers had on average 129 cigarettes a week, and women smokers an average of 101. In 1982, the figures were 121 for men, and 98 for women.

Sales of cigarettes fell from 130,500 million to 102,000 million between 1972 and 1982, a 22 per cent decrease.

It seems likely that by 2010, less than 10 per cent of adults will smoke and Britain will be very close to being a smoke-free society.

Eventually it will be impossible for future generations to comprehend that millions of us smoked, knowing that we risked and suffered fatal disease in vast numbers as a result.

It will seem as useless a habit as we now consider the bleeding of people with leeches to have been a couple of centuries ago.

The decline of smoking, which began in the 1970s can be explained by several factors.

Taxation was increased five times in succession between 1974 and 1977, and sales dropped 10 per cent.

The emphasis on health hazards became much more emphatic. The Royal College of Physicians issued its initial warning report in 1965; the college issued it second report in 1971.

The tobacco industry feels it has been punish enough. It spends m than £100m a year in Bri on advertising, sales pro tions and sports and sponsorship. It contri almost £4,000m in t taxes in 1981.

The Times, 27.2.84

PACESETTERS DON'T SMOKE

HEALTH EDUCATION COUNCIL

## WHY NICK O'TEEN IS A WEED.

CIGARETTES LEAVE STAINS ON HIS TEETH, MAKE HIS BREATH SMELL AND HIS CLOTHES STINK.

HE CAN'T ESCAPE ME. HE SMOKES SO MUCH HE PUFFS AND PANTS LIKE A BROKEN DOWN STEAM ENGINE.

NICK O'TEEN IS A WRECK. IF HE HAD X-RAY VISION LIKE ME, HE COULD SEE THE DAMAGE CIGARETTES DO TO HIS HEART AND LUNGS.

## Questions

1 Why should the government aim to cut smoking? (1)
2 How has the government tried to cut smoking? (1)
3 How will the government (a) gain, and (b) lose if everyone stops smoking? (2)

The government aims to steer the economy as a whole so that it makes the most of its resources. It encourages firms to invest in new products and new resources so that there is more economic growth. It aims to keep inflation low so that people can trust money and plan how to use it well. It aims to help the country trade well with other countries, in the EEC and the rest of the world. It may try to change the payments for trade in and out of the country, and the exchange rate of the pound for other countries' money.

Unemployment wastes resources. People and machines stay out of work when they could be adding to production. The government tries to keep unemployment low and help people who are out of work. But there are problems in all this.

Sometimes the government achieves one aim only to lose another. Some people feel that the government may only make things worse by what it does. They say that the government is too large and has too much control of the economy. Free market forces might work better if left alone. To them, good government means less government.

# 1.8 The world's rich and poor

Have you ever thought of moving to a different country? Let us say that you could take your own lifestyle with you – your house, your money and all you own. In some countries you would stand out as you have so little. Incomes in Switzerland, the USA and West Germany are much higher on average than in Britain. There are many other parts of the world, however, where you would appear quite rich. With your cassette player, jeans and shoes you would have more than most people. Incomes are much lower in India, China, or Kenya on the whole.

Yet you would face many of the same economic questions wherever you lived. You would have to make the same sorts of choices – what to buy, how to work and what to make. The world's rich and poor must all go without some things to afford the things they want more. They must try to use resources in the best way because of the problem of scarcity.

## Scarcity

The main economic problem never changes. We all want more than we can have. First we want to eat potatoes, then take-away chips; first we want to drink water, then cold drinks; first we want material possessions, then less noise, worry and effort. Wants are endless. Rich and poor people may want different things but they all want more.

How can you satisfy your wants? You need producers to give you goods and services. Producers must use the country's resources to make what people want to consume. They must use your work and the work of other people. The more resources they use, the more they can produce. But resources are limited at any one time. There is only so much work and production that can be done.

How do different countries face up to the same economic problems? Why are there such differences between the rich and poor of the world?

## Checklist – how do different economies face the main economic problem?

| | Resources | Wants | Choice and scarcity |
|---|---|---|---|
| Planned economies | owned by the state for all its people together | the order and importance of wants is decided by government | choices are made centrally and planned by government |
| Free market economies | owned by private individuals for their own gains | private consumers decide what they want to buy and can afford | choices are made freely by individuals, to set up market forces |

So choices must be made about which wants to satisfy and which not. Producers must choose which products to make and how much of each. But will this satisfy wants in the best way? How is a country to make best use of its resources?

# What type of economy?

What would it be like to live in a country like Singapore, Japan or Brazil? You could work at any job you chose and help produce almost any product that people would buy. For these countries have economies that are based largely on free markets.

*Free market* economies are left to work with very little government control. Consumers and producers make their choices for their own private reasons with little need to mind how they affect the public as a whole. Consumers buy anything they want and producers make anything that sells. You can hope to get on well if you work hard, but if you cannot work you may suffer.

Countries like Russia and China are very different from this. There you would have much less choice about what work to do or what products to buy, for these are economies that are largely planned and controlled by government.

The government runs a *planned economy* to serve the public as a whole, and there is less room for private choice. Workers work for the country as a whole and producers make what the country needs, not what individual consumers wish to buy. But who knows what the country needs? This is for government to say, through careful planning.

Most countries in the world have free markets as well as government control. They are *mixed* economies, made up of private and public choices together. You work for pay, serving an individual producer, and buy what you want. But the government also acts as buyer and seller, takes in taxes and pays out benefits, and lays down rules to control people's actions.

# Why are incomes so different?

Why are some countries so rich and others so poor? The average income in Switzerland appears to be more than sixty times higher than that in India. Does one country have so many more resources than another? To an extent this is true, especially with man-made resources such as machinery and buildings. Some countries began to make these resources long before others and have built up great amounts of them.

It is also true that some countries make better use of their resources. They educate their people and learn how to manage production well. They learn about methods of production and take full advantage of new improvements. And, through trade, they share with other countries that have different strengths.

*International trade* allows countries to exchange what they make well for other products that they make less well. This has many different effects on an economy, as we shall see in Part 7 of this book. Some of

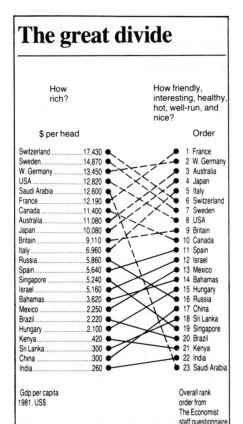

## The great divide

| How rich? | | How friendly, interesting, healthy, hot, well-run, and nice? | |
|---|---|---|---|
| $ per head | | | Order |
| Switzerland | 17,430 | 1 | France |
| Sweden | 14,870 | 2 | W. Germany |
| W. Germany | 13,450 | 3 | Australia |
| USA | 12,820 | 4 | Japan |
| Saudi Arabia | 12,600 | 5 | Italy |
| France | 12,190 | 6 | Switzerland |
| Canada | 11,400 | 7 | Sweden |
| Australia | 11,080 | 8 | USA |
| Japan | 10,080 | 9 | Britain |
| Britain | 9,110 | 10 | Canada |
| Italy | 6,960 | 11 | Spain |
| Russia | 5,860 | 12 | Israel |
| Spain | 5,640 | 13 | Mexico |
| Singapore | 5,240 | 14 | Bahamas |
| Israel | 5,160 | 15 | Hungary |
| Bahamas | 3,620 | 16 | Russia |
| Mexico | 2,250 | 17 | China |
| Brazil | 2,220 | 18 | Sri Lanka |
| Hungary | 2,100 | 19 | Singapore |
| Kenya | 420 | 20 | Brazil |
| Sri Lanka | 300 | 21 | Kenya |
| China | 300 | 22 | India |
| India | 260 | 23 | Saudi Arabia |

| Gdp per capita 1981, US$ | Overall rank order from The Economist staff questionnaire |
|---|---|

The Economist, 24.12.83

This is how 23 countries were placed by the income of their people (left), and by a poll of staff at The Economist (right). The staff were asked where they would like to live, for different reasons. Where would you choose?

## Questions

1 From the countries listed, find two that are largely (a) planned, (b) mixed, (c) free market economies. (3)
2 Why do you think that the richer countries are also more popular on a number of other counts, as shown by their overall order? (1)

**Where would you choose to live?**

|  | UK | Cambodia |
|---|---|---|
| How many people? | 56m<br>about 12 births and 12 deaths in every 1000 people each year | 8m<br>about 47 births and 19 deaths in every 1000 people each year |
| How much income? | about £2000 for each person in 1976; national output from many areas of production; about 30% traded. | perhaps £50 for each person in 1976; national output mainly rice and timber; about 1% traded, nearly all rubber. |
| How well off? | every 1000 people own about 400 telephones, 325 TVs, 260 cars, and 9 hospital beds. | every 1000 people own about 9 telephones, 3 TVs, 4 cars, and 1 hospital bed. |

(Source – 'The World in figures', The Economist, 1978)

## Questions

1 Use the figures to show how fewer wants are satisfied in Cambodia than in the UK. (3)
2 Use the figures to suggest possible reasons for the lower incomes of people in Cambodia than in the UK. (3)

these effects are not welcome, and lead countries to protect their home industries against trade. But the main effect is a good one, as countries become better off. People's incomes rise even faster in rich countries because they can gain even more from trade. Poor countries may have less to offer, and it can be difficult for them to start to close the gap.

# Part 2   Working

## 2.1 What's work?
## A guide to the factors of production

Nothing can be made without work, but there are different kinds of resources and production uses them all.

What do people do at work? They may sit at a desk, drive a bus or work a machine. In economics we look at work in a different way. We ask what they put into production of goods and services.

How do you know if you are working or not? It is not enough to feel tired, as if you have run a marathon, or written a ten-side essay. What matters in economics is your production, for you must add to the output of goods and services in order to be at work.

*Factors of production* are the resources used to make goods and services. They are hired by firms to work for a week say, or a year. And they are offered by people like you or me when we go to work. Production uses them all, together.

## Labour

There is one factor of production that we all know best. This is what people put into production from their own effort and ability and is called *labour*. Some people work more with their hands, perhaps chopping down trees or stocking shelves. This is manual labour. Others work more with their minds, using mental effort to add up figures or write letters to customers. This is called non-manual labour.

Some people work to control others and to manage the way a firm uses its resources. *Management* is a form of labour with special skills. Indeed, most labour is of different kinds. You study at school and college to try to improve yourself, and to change your type of labour.

How much labour is there altogether in the country? Clearly this depends on the number of people and how many are of working age. Some, like you, may be students and some may be retired. What matters is the level of population and how it is made up. We will see how in Sections 2.3 and 2.4

You can offer more labour or less depending on your hours of work. Perhaps you work eight hours a day and forty hours a week. There may be as many as 25 million people in the country altogether, doing the same thing. The total supply of labour is made up of all their work. This would add up to 25 million people × 40 hours = 1000 million *manhours and womanhours* of labour, each week.

## Land, capital and enterprise

People can work even by sitting at home in a chair. They can use their property and set it to work as factors of production. Perhaps they own some land that can be used to make goods and services.

Land can be used as a site on which to build a factory or an office. Land can also be used to grow crops like wheat or rice or to dig mines for coal or wells for oil. There is only so much land to go around until more is claimed from the sea or in space, but it can be used in better ways, with fertilisers for crops, say, and drainage for building.

Perhaps you have no land of your own, but you may own some *capital* now and even more in future. You can save money and lend it to a bank. The bank can lend to firms and so help to raise production. *Working capital* begins as money but is used by firms to buy materials and parts. Finally, it ends as *stocks* of goods and services made by firms and waiting to be sold.

Firms buy *fixed capital* as well. They have buildings and machines that are suited to certain types of work. People buy shares in firms and so own parts of this capital as their own property. They use it in production and earn income from it. This is called *private capital*. But some buildings and some equipment, such as bridges, roads and textbooks are owned by the government for us all.This is *social capital*.

Where do machines come from? They are all man-made by firms using resources to make more of this factor of production. The more capital they make, the more of everything we can make in future. This is *investment* in new forms of capital.

Labour, land and capital are all ways to work for someone else. But how can you work for yourself? You must take a risk. You must show *enterprise* and use your own money to hire resources and start up in production. You may lose the lot or you may do very well. That is how you know you are working for yourself, as an entrepreneur.

Many firms are too large for any one person to take all the risks. No one could afford to own businesses such as ICI or BP on their own. They take a share of the risk and own only a part of the business by serving as a shareholder.

## Checklist – what are the factors of production?

- *Labour* is work put in by people using their hands and minds
- *Land* includes sites for factories and offices, as well as the raw materials found on or under other sites
- *Capital* is fixed in buildings and equipment, and working as the money and stocks of firms
- *Enterprise* takes the risks of hiring other factors to produce goods and services

# Making a pet project pay

When Graham Brent-Jones from Lytham started looking after people's pets for a living he was 18. His venture has been going since September, thanks to the Government's Enterprise Allowance of £40 a week.

Says Graham: 'When people go on holiday they are not keen to use kennels and catteries, so I take care of pets in their own homes, I also water plants, draw the curtains, switch on lights, take in letters and act as a neighbour would.'

Graham has always been an animal lover. At school he worked on Saturday in a pet shop. His two full time jobs were in a pet shop and a boarding kennels.

Last year Graham was unemployed for four months, and heard about the Enterprise Allowance Scheme. He applied for it and went on a one-day seminar. Graham only had £400 in the bank, but his capital was boosted by a £1,000 loan from his mother. He points out that it was hard deciding what to charge clients. His basic rate is £3 a day for two visits, but it depends how far he has to travel.

Graham has used up more than half his savings on car maintenance and advertising. He says: 'It costs £12 every time I put an ad in the local paper. I paid £20 for 1,000 leaflets, which I distributed to vets, newsagents and private homes.
'I have to make ten visits a week to break even, that's at least £55 on running costs. I spend £15 on petrol, £15–20 on advertising, £5 on food, and I give my mother £20 towards the housekeeping.'

Graham hopes his enterprise will take off in the summer, when more pet owners go on holiday. By June he'll only be three months away from the end of his allowance.
Daily Mail, 21.3.84

## Questions

1 What factor of production did Graham offer in his Saturday job in a pet shop? How do you think his work would have changed if he had worked there full-time rather than just one day a week? (2)

2 What is Graham using as factors of production now in the way of (a) labour, (b) working capital, (c) fixed capital? (4)

3 Who takes the risks of setting Graham up in business? (4)

Why do factors of production change jobs, and what stops them moving as freely as we might wish?

When you were a small child, what did you think you wanted to be when you grew up:– a lorry driver, a model, a teacher, or all three? Your parents grew up expecting to do one type of work all their lives. You can expect to change your line of work several times in your working lifetime. You may choose to move from firm to firm in order to learn more, or just for a change. But you may also need to change your place of work. And the greatest change of all may be when you need to retrain, in order to move from one occupation to another. You must expect to be *mobile* if you wish to suit the jobs available.

## Factor mobility

Labour may move between occupations, or geographical areas:

Occupational mobility

Geographical mobility

MINE

FACTORY

BANK

## Why do people change jobs?

We take it for granted that people do different jobs. Some are farmers, others work in industry, and others are in shops and offices. Few of us would want, or be able to do all these different types of work. People specialise, as do all factors of production such as machines and land. We saw in Section 1.3 how strongly this specialisation has framed our modern economy.

Specialisation is needed in order to make the best use of resources and keep production efficient. And the pattern of specialisation is set by the pattern of production and by the ways that resources can be used. Some people change jobs because of luck or individual taste, but most major changes are caused by changes in production due to the supply and demand for products and factors.

Suppose the demand for a product rises; this may be because of consumers' tastes or rising incomes or some other market change. Its effect is to attract workers, machines and new businesses into the industry. Higher pay, better conditions of work and improved opportunities cause people to move from their old job to the new one. Changes in demand for a product affect all types of factors. They expand one industry at the cost of cutting another. Workers and machines are employed together in growth areas but are likely to become unemployed together in declining areas.

## Technical progress

There are other changes quite different from these. You may have to move from one job to another because you have been replaced by new machines. This factor-substitution is generally due to *technical progress*. Machines are built to make use of new techniques that cut the costs of production. Firms invest in this equipment and use it to replace labour.

But technical progress creates jobs as well. It allows firms to make new products and to improve old products. You may be needed to work with other factors to make these products. There may be fewer

## Checklist – why do factors move?

● changes in consumer demand for the products made by different factors
● changes in the tastes and situations of individual workers
● changes in methods of production using factors in new ways

Secretaries are poised to take over as the micro-chip transforms the office. . .

# Dear Boss, I've just got your job!

The silicon chip revolution is about to storm into Britain's offices with a vengeance. And the first victim of the assault will be middle management, *not* the secretary as we have all been led to believe.

Instead we are about to see a remarkable comeback in status as the golden age of the secretary returns to sweep junior bosses from their desks.

No more making tea, running errands, smiling meekly and typing the odd letter. . . to morrow's secretary will be a high-powered business-woman!

The great technological revolution which has already swept through America leaving five million desk-top computers in its wake—a figure expected to increase by 25 per cent each year for the next ten years—is poised to sweep through Britain.

'The introduction of new technology makes a secretary's job much more exciting,' says Anne Humphreys, head of training at St Godric's secretarial college. 'It takes away so much of the tedium and gives them more time to concentrate on executive decisions and organising the office. Her prestige is about to grow enormously.'

Tomorrow's secretary will be highly literate, will have at least one foreign language, be adept at summarising and separating important facts from different sources, and be fairly numerate.

Above all she will have to have been quick to seize the initial power her keyboard skills have given her over most middle managers.

## This will be your working day

8.30 Arrives at office.
8.45 Checks electronic mail system (letters sent from one computer to another).
9.15 Opens conventional mail.
10.00 A senior executive calls by cellular radio (system that interacts with telephone system on limited radio frequencies) to announce he'll be late. Secretary checks any appointment to be changed on computerised diary.
10.15 Secretary checks flight times of arriving overseas visitor via viewdata (information service run from a central computer via TV sets, e.g. Prestel) then reserves table for dinner using boss's credit card number.
10.30 Decides order of the day's work.
10.40 Works on agenda for afternoon's marketing meeting, using word processor. Agenda then transmitted electronically to those attending.
10.45 Starts to arrange meeting on new advertising campaign, using electronic diary which contains all executives' appointments and can work out most convenient time itself.

*For the ambitious secretary. . .the key to success is still at the keyboard*

10.55 Meeting arranged and entered on electronic diary.
11.00 Types general memo which she sends round by electronic mail—a low tone sounds at each terminal in the system signifying it has arrived. It can then be stored in computerised in-tray, or called on to screen.
11.30 The word processor reminds secretary it's time for statutory break to ensure her good health (eye strain and headaches limit efficiency).
11.45 Secretary prints out documents to be sent by regular mail by touching button on word processor. Letters sent to mailroom by battery driven mail robot, or transmitted immediately by tax machine to other cities or countries.
12.00 Secretary begins research for client presentation, using search and retrieve facility on computer. Then off to lunch.
2.45 Boss returns from lunch and asks her to prepare report on effect of lowering price on product.

2.55 Secretary starts report, using calculator section of her computer she bases calculations on data provided by company library and information stored in computer.
4.00 Secretary passes completed report to boss's terminal using alert tone so that he knows it's there.
4.10 Announces departure on intercom.

Daily Mail, 21.3.84

## Questions

1 What is the difference between occupational and geographical mobility? How is the 'technological revolution' likely to affect (a) the work secretaries do and (b) where they are able to do it? (4)
2 What abilities will 'tomorrow's secretaries' need apart from 'keyboard skills'? (3)
3 Explain how you expect the new office technology to affect each of the following:
(a) less skilled secretaries
(b) highly-skilled secretaries
(c) middle managers (3)

29

filing clerks and postmen, but there should be more electricians and computer salespeople.

If you are fully mobile between jobs and areas, you can adapt to these changes. The work you find may be even more interesting and better paid.

# Immobility

Most factors, however, are not fully mobile. You could not move a plot of land, a coal mine or a railway bridge from the north to the south of England. Neither could you use these resources in a different way, to produce computer games, for example. Factors of production such as land and much capital equipment are often *specific* and suited to only one type of work.

But surely people are more adaptable than this? You could become a lorry driver, model, teacher, or all three – or could you? Clearly, there are limits to labour mobility. We each have natural qualities such as strength, character and intelligence. We learn skills, study for qualifications, train at and gain experience in work. We have different attitudes and come from different backgrounds and areas. Perhaps if you decided at an early age to become a brain surgeon you would succeed. If you decide now you may have left it too late.

# An imperfect world

In a perfect world, factors would move freely between different lines of work. Jobs that became more attractive because of their pay, conditions or prospects would appeal to more people. Why is it that we do not all become policemen and policewomen the moment police pay goes up?

One reason is that we do not often know about such changes. You must begin your training as a doctor, for example, without knowing about job prospects in seven or more years' time when you will finally qualify. Another problem is in people's motivation. Entrepreneurs may have a clear purpose and aim for profit, but many of the people who sell factors such as labour, capital and land may be less hardhearted. They may wish to remain in their home area or the same line of business, whatever it costs them.

Finally, there may be restrictions that prevent the free movement of factors. These may be legal, for example, planning permission for land; or institutional, for example, being obliged to belong to a trade union (like actors' membership of 'equity'). Private house-owners must pay thousands of pounds to move, and tenants face waiting lists for council housing. But these difficulties are minor compared with the controls on working in a different country. For that you may need a passport, visa and work permit, and a new language!

The result of all this is that many factors are slow to move between jobs. Some, such as land and capital, may transfer only in the long term and be *fixed* in their short-term use. The supply of factors to different types of work may not adjust freely. It may, therefore, take time for you to find which job suits you, or for you to be able to offer your best work in it.

## Could you be a brain surgeon?

Are you clever enough to pass all your exams, for the next 10 years, at the top grade?

Are your parents brain surgeons?

Can you cut open a skull without fainting?

Can you stop your hand shaking, even on Monday mornings?

## Checklist – what makes factors immobile?

- they may not know about work opportunities
- they may not try hard enough to improve their pay or work satisfaction
- they may not be free to move job or area
- they may not be qualified for other work

# 2.3 How many mouths to feed? The level of population

How many mouths are there to feed in the UK? How many people need clothes, housing, health services and so on? We find out by counting *population*, for this measures the total number of people in the country.

Perhaps there are some people in the room with you now. If they stay still and wait for you to count them, it should be easy. But try to imagine doing this across the whole country. That is what a census of population does.

A *census* is an official count of population. Officials visit every home in the country to count the people living there, and to record if they are men or women, young or old, and so on. But this must all happen at the same time, in case people move and are counted twice. You can see why a full census is held only once every ten years.

The figures tell us that about 56 million people live in the UK. This number has grown at every census since the Second World War. From 1971 to 1981, however, the change was quite small. UK population seems to have reached a fairly constant level. Why is this?

## Births and deaths

The *birth rate* measures the number being born each year, as an average for each 1000 people in the population. In 1961 for example there were an average of nineteen babies born for each 1000 people. In the first half of the 1970s, however, the birth rate had fallen to only 14.

What affects the number of births? It depends on how many women are of child-bearing age, and also on how they live. People may marry later, and spend more years at work before starting a family. They may understand and use birth control better. They may choose to keep their family size down. And more babies may survive birth and the first months of their lives because of better health care.

In the UK we enjoy a high standard of health, and the number of deaths of young people stays fairly low. Fewer deaths in itself would clearly mean a rise in population. The *death-rate* measures the number of deaths as an average for every 1000 people in the population. This rate may fall over the years because of improvements in life-style and medicine, so that more people manage to enjoy their old age. Further changes in life-style, in eating habits, exercise and work, might do more to cut heart disease. Further discoveries in medicine might cut early deaths from diseases like cancer.

Births and deaths together set the rate of *natural change* of the population. Perhaps more are born than die in each 1000 people. Then, the population naturally rises. And if the death rate is greater than the birth rate, the population naturally falls. The UK now shows a low, *natural increase*, of around 1 or 2 per 1000 people each year.

How many people are there in the country? Why does population change, and why does it matter so much in economics?

31

## Factsheet – UK population

The number of people in the country has risen over the years, but is expected to stay fairly steady...

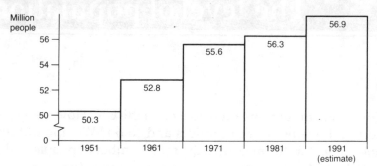

because more people are born than die...

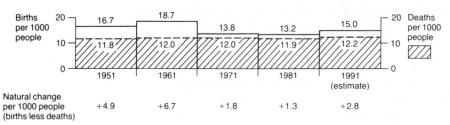

| | 1951 | 1961 | 1971 | 1981 | 1991 (estimate) |
|---|---|---|---|---|---|
| Natural change per 1000 people (births less deaths) | +4.9 | +6.7 | +1.8 | +1.3 | +2.8 |

and more people leave the country than enter it...

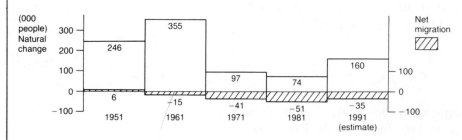

(Source – Social Trends, 1984)

### Questions

1  Find one year from the five shown in the data when (a) population is lowest, (b) population is greatest, (c) population grows fastest, (d) population grows slowest, (e) there is net inward migration, (f) there is a fall in the death rate. (3)

2  Use the data to suggest a reason for the expected rise in the natural growth of population in 1991. (2)

# Home and abroad

Perhaps you were born in the UK but will not die there. Perhaps you will die in the UK but were not born there. People can leave and enter the population when they *migrate* and change the country they live in.

Every year, emigrants leave the country and immigrants enter it. They may have family reasons for moving, or better jobs to move to. So population can either fall or rise, depending on the balance of numbers that move. Net migration figures measure the numbers entering less the numbers leaving the country. A positive figure shows that more come in than go out, and the population is raised.

Migration is high for the UK because of ties with other countries. Immigrants come from countries connected to Britain since the days of the Empire, and emigrants go to English-speaking, Commonwealth countries and others. On balance, UK migration is outward but only slightly so.

## Checklist – what changes the population?

- births – the birth rate measures the average number born each year for each 1000 people in the population
- deaths – the death rate measures the number who die each year for each 1000 people in the population
- migration – measures the number of people entering or leaving the country – net migration shows the balance of moves in and out

UK population is falling slightly because of migration, but rising more because of a natural increase, with births greater than deaths. On balance, therefore, there is a rise in the total number of people.

Things are very different in some parts of the world. Countries such as India, Kenya and Brazil have great natural increases in population. Improving health care, especially for babies and young children, means that many more grow old enough to start their own families. The birth rate in Kenya in 1980 was 55 babies for each 1000 people. The population was growing naturally by 40 for each 1000 people, or 4 per cent a year.

**Europe and Africa – what will the future bring?**

|  | Europe | Africa |
|---|---|---|
| Population 1980 (millions) | 372 | 470 |
| Birth rate (per 1000) | 15 | 45 |
| % of total population under the age of 15 | 22 | 45 |
| Death rate (per 1000) | 10 | 15 |
| % of total population over the age of 65 | 13 | 3 |
| Rate of growth of population each year (%) | 0.3 | 3.0 |
| Population 2000 (millions) (estimate) | 392 | 850 |

## Questions

1  Why is population expected to grow faster in Africa than in Europe? (2)
2  Use the data to suggest how these population changes will affect each economy differently. (3)

# Demand and supply

Why does it matter if there are more people around? They all want food, clothing, education and other things. More people means more wants to be met from production. Perhaps there will be different wants as well. More babies means more cots and, later, schools. More old folk means more health-care, perhaps, and pensions.

But will there be any more production to go around? Wants must be backed up by spending power if they are to count in economics. There may be more mouths to be fed, but no more to give them. This depends on resources and techniques of production.

Will the extra people be productive? Are they of working age and with the abilities needed for work? These are the questions we turn to in the next section.

# 2.4 Who are the workers? The distribution of population

Not everyone works. Why is this, and how does the number change from time to time?

Are you a worker? Not everyone is. Less than half the people in the country use their labour to produce goods and services. The others are too young or too old, or looking after a home or children; some are disabled and some are students; some are unemployed because they cannot find work.

So how do the people in the UK split into these different groups; what is the *distribution* of population? Suppose you are in a group of twenty-five people, perhaps the number of students in your class, that is typical of the whole UK population. How many of these are able to work? About six are younger than sixteen, and not allowed to work full-time, by law. Perhaps four are over the age of retirement. This is generally sixty for women and sixty-five for men, although many stop work sooner or later. These ten people cannot earn their own living. They are called 'dependent' because others work to produce goods and services for them. We are all 'dependent' as children or as the elderly, in our turn.

This leaves only fifteen in every twenty-five people at the right age to work, but how many of them do?

## Who wants to work?

I'M ECONOMICALLY ACTIVE TOO Y'KNOW!

There are many ways you can use your time. You can sit around or study hard or take exercise. These are all forms of activity, but none of them is economic activity. You must work to help produce goods and services to be *economically active*. Postmen and miners do this, but students and housewives do not.

Fifteen people may be able to work, but how many of them are willing to as well? One may be a student, and another two or three choose to stay out of work for other reasons. Most of these are married women looking after the home and the children, although twice as many of these now go to work as stay at home.

Around twelve people actively look for work out of the total of twenty-five. But not all of these find it. A number are unemployed. In 1984, these may have amounted to one or two of the group. Only ten or eleven out of the twenty-five people are paid to work full-time.

What does this tell us about the UK as a whole? The *working population* is made up of all those who can be economically active. But this workforce can be either employed or unemployed. From the total workforce of some 25 million people in 1984, only 21 million were in paid employment.

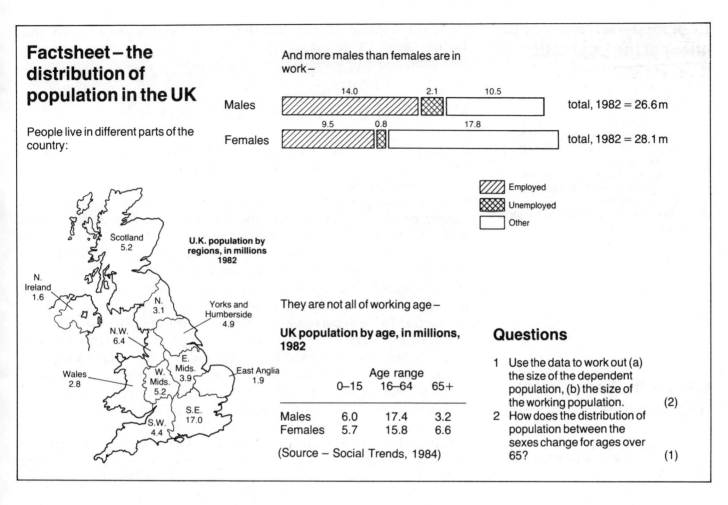

## Factsheet – the distribution of population in the UK

People live in different parts of the country:

And more males than females are in work –

| Males | 14.0 | 2.1 | 10.5 | total, 1982 = 26.6 m |
| Females | 9.5 | 0.8 | 17.8 | total, 1982 = 28.1 m |

- ▨ Employed
- ▩ Unemployed
- ☐ Other

**U.K. population by regions, in millions 1982**

Scotland 5.2
N. Ireland 1.6
N. 3.1
Yorks and Humberside 4.9
N.W. 6.4
Wales 2.8
E. Mids. 3.9
W. Mids. 5.2
East Anglia 1.9
S.E. 17.0
S.W. 4.4

They are not all of working age –

### UK population by age, in millions, 1982

| | Age range | | |
| --- | --- | --- | --- |
| | 0–15 | 16–64 | 65+ |
| Males | 6.0 | 17.4 | 3.2 |
| Females | 5.7 | 15.8 | 6.6 |

(Source – Social Trends, 1984)

### Questions

1. Use the data to work out (a) the size of the dependent population, (b) the size of the working population. (2)
2. How does the distribution of population between the sexes change for ages over 65? (1)

# What work do people do?

People work differently; they work in different parts of the country, in jobs where they need different abilities, in different industries. The workers who make up the working population are clearly not all the same.

The supply of labour is greatest in the south-east of England. Almost 17 million people live in this region compared with just over 5 million in the whole of Scotland. Greater London is more than sixty times as crowded as Scotland. More people live in towns and cities than in the countryside, although there are moves away from the centre of large cities – the 'inner city' – into outer areas and new towns. There are more jobs for them to do there.

What job could you try for if you left school at sixteen? Could you do much better if you went on to study in the sixth form or at college? You will join the workforce in the end, but with different abilities to offer. The country as a whole needs people who can do the work that is wanted. They want people able to learn quickly, to be skilled, and to write and think and talk and use machines as well. The workforce must be trained and retrained to be of good quality.

You can often use your training in different lines of work. Computer programmers can work for any firm that uses computers. This may be in industries extracting raw materials, or manufacturing goods, or providing services to customers. We saw in Section 1.3 where the jobs are now. But changes in industry mean that different numbers will work in

## Where do they all go at 16?

Each group of 100 typical 16-year-olds are occupied in these ways –

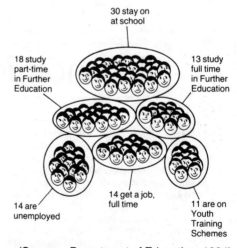

30 stay on at school
18 study part-time in Further Education
13 study full time in Further Education
14 are unemployed
14 get a job, full time
11 are on Youth Training Schemes

(Source – Department of Education, 1984)

### Question

1. How many 16-year-olds continue in education? Suggest 2 reasons why they do so. (3)

## Checklist – what cuts the share of the population that works?

- age structure – more children, students and pensioners means fewer workers
- sex structure – more women; if they look after the home and family instead of going to work
- education and training – prepares people for better work, but cuts the work they can do now
- unemployment – where people want to work but cannot find jobs

## What is the best level of population?

Suppose there could be 3 levels of population, and everything else about the country stays the same –

| Number of people (m) | 40 | 50 | 60 |
|---|---|---|---|
| Total output | 200 | 300 | 330 |
| Output per person (output/population) | 50 | 60 | 55 |
| so population is | 'too low', | 'opti-mum', | 'too high'. |

each field in future. There will probably be less work in manufacturing, such as car or TV production, but more in services such as entertainment and communications.

## What's the best number to work?

Are there enough people who can work in the country, or not enough, or too many? Perhaps we can never tell for sure, but we can at least know what to look for.

The *optimum population* is what economists see as the best number of people for a country at any one time. This is the number of people that makes best use of the country's other resources – its land, its machines and other capital, and its enterprise. Too many people will crowd those other resources and keep down the amount made for each person. Too few people will waste some other resources and also keep average production down. The optimum level of population is that which keeps production for each person in the country at the highest possible level.

The country can change its use of resources from time to time. Investment adds extra capital, for example, so the best number of people will change also, and rise as the amount of other resources rises.

It is all very well to know what the country wants, but what can it do to get the best number of people? The size of population and of workforce is set by forces that cannot be controlled at all well.

The total population may grow because of a rise in the birth rate or a fall in death rate. People may marry at a younger age or want more children. Health care may improve and help us all to live longer. These changes affect both the number of people and their ages.

Not everyone works, however. The workforce may have to produce for a rising population made up of more young or old people, who are dependent. Should more of the population be working, perhaps? This depends on the level of economic activity. The workforce grows as more married women go to work, but it falls as there is more education and earlier retirement. It depends on how people choose to live their lives.

# Economic 'time bomb' warning

"Time bombs" that will affect public spending are ticking away as a result of changes in the age structure of the population, politicians were told yesterday. Britain's population is likely to remain stable or to grow only slightly until the end of the century.

But the increase in the numbers of very elderly, the entry of children born in the 1955–65 "baby boom" into child bearing age, and a steep rise in the number of pensioners from the year 2010 when the "baby boom" generation start reaching retirement age, will all affect demands on health, social services, housing, education and pensions.

The labour force will at best grow only slowly or at worst decline early next century as the number of pensioners increases, so that there will be two workers per pensioner by the year 2030, against 2.75 at present.

That could mean a 60 per cent rise in pension contributions to a third of earnings.

In the shorter term, a threefold to fourfold increase in teacher training is needed to cope with the children to be born to the "baby boom" generation as they reach adulthood.

*The Times, 9.12.83*

## Question

1   A large number of babies were born around 1960. Explain the different effects of this on the structure of population and the demands for products (a) from about 1985–2000, (b) from about 2020–2050.   (4)

# 2.5 Unemployment

What are your chances of starting work at sixteen? Perhaps you have had enough studying and want to work full-time to earn money of your own. But for every sixteen-year-old in work there is another who is not. On average, your chances of being unemployed would be about 50-50.

What does it mean to be unemployed? You are willing and able to work, and you count as part of the working population. Probably you sign on at the Job Centre run locally by the Department of Employment. This office puts people who are looking for work in touch with firms looking for workers. It also counts the number of people, like you, who are looking for work. Altogether, these figures give the official number of *registered unemployed* in the country.

Probably, you claim money from the local office of the Department of Social Security. This money is often called 'the dole'. You can draw unemployment benefit if you have worked before, and paid enough in national insurance contributions. You can draw supplementary benefit if your income is very low. In this way, the government tries to stop hardship and poverty. You may be covered by this even as a school-leaver living at home. So you are paid benefits for not working – does this make unemployment worthwhile?

## What's wrong with unemployment?

Unemployment is a waste of time. People want to work and to earn pay. People look for work and apply for jobs they think they can do. But there are not enough jobs to go around, so they do nothing.

You may enjoy this for a while but most people do not. They find it boring and upsetting. They cannot keep up with family and friends who are in work. They cannot pull their weight.

This is a waste for the country as a whole. Part of its workforce is not being used, and some of its resources are wasted. National output is lower than it could be.

Nearly everyone is paid less on the dole than in a job. You are worse off if you are unemployed. But a small number of people may be paid more for their family, in extra welfare benefit. When they get a job they lose those benefits and may even be worse off. The 'poverty trap' means that they are paid more to be out of work than in it.

Most people want work and would be better off with it. So they look for jobs but do not find them. Why is this?

## Normal unemployment

Some unemployment is normal. You may leave school at sixteen, at the end of the year. Many other people may join you and look for work at

Unemployment is a waste of time and a waste of resources. So why are so many people out of work?

A day in the life. . .

9.00 Got up. Went to labour exchange. Walked there and back.
10.00 Arrive home – took child out for a walk.
11.00 Got back home, made cup of tea. Read daily paper.
12.00 Sitting on chair doing nothing. Radio on.
1.00 Made lunch. Bread, butter, jam.
1.30 Went to betting shop to see if luck was good. Walked to shop. Met friends, chatted for a while.
2.30 Arrive home. Sat down and did crossword in paper. Made tea for boys coming home from school.
3.30 Watch TV.
4.00 Tried to fix child's bike.
5.30 Had dinner.
6.00 Watched TV (news).
6.30 Helped boys with homework.
7.00 Settled down for rest of the night to watch TV.

'The Daily Life of the Unemployed' by Karen Trew and Rosemary Kilpatrick, Queen's University, Belfast, 1983.

## Question

1 What signs are there that this worker is upset at being out of work? (1)

the same time. Where are all the jobs to come from?

A number of jobs open up as older people retire and as others move up from one post to another. And in many types of work people leave their old job first and find a new job later. So it is quite normal for workers to be unemployed, now and then, for a short while.

This type of unemployment is called transitional or *frictional unemployment*. People are out of work for only a short time while moving from one job to another. Such unemployment is temporary, and shared by many different people at different times.

There are always some *job vacancies*. These are posts waiting to be filled, perhaps by people who have been unemployed for a time. Around one in three of these jobs is offered at Job Centres. So people come and go between jobs and unemployment, in a normal way.

Youth unemployment, however, is not like this. Your chances of a job at sixteen may be only 50-50. Many school leavers have to wait a very long time before they find work of their own. What causes this lasting unemployment?

# Structural unemployment

Would you like a job that pays £1000 each week and gives good holidays? It's yours if you are left-handed, can climb an oil rig upside down and live at the North Pole. Do you fit the bill?

There are many jobs that use certain abilities and are based in certain areas. Too often there are workers who do not match those abilities or areas. Workers lose their old jobs, in steel or mining perhaps, and do not fit the new jobs in computing or banking. So they become unemployed. This follows from changes in the structure of work and the work force, and is called *structural unemployment*.

You may look for work and try for a number of jobs. But you are unlucky and do not get anywhere. Why not? One reason could be that you do not have the right training. Most jobs are specialised. Postmen could not work as potters, for example, nor secretaries as nurses. Your training starts at school and college with the subjects you choose and the exams you pass. But then it goes on with job qualifications and experience in work. As well as all this, you have your own interests and abilities to offer to a job – you may be very helpful but not very good at organising other people, for instance.

You may have all the right qualities and still not get a job. Are you in the right place? Most jobs are lost from old, declining industries. These are found mostly in the north of the country or in the Midlands. New jobs are made by growth industries and by services, based more in the south and in regions where people are better off generally. You cannot easily move into these new regions when you look for a job. You may have family ties in your own area, or live in a house you are buying there or council property you rent. So you stay unemployed.

# Matching people to jobs

What makes it difficult for workers to match jobs? People can train at one kind of work and then retrain at another. We saw in Section 2.2

## Checklist – what are the main causes of unemployment?

- changing jobs – people leave one job before starting another. This is normal, frictional, or transitional unemployment
- structural change – technical progress and new consumer demands change the patterns of production and of work. People are unemployed in certain industries or regions.
- low demand in the economy as a whole causes mass, or cyclical unemployment for years at a time, in a national slump

# Factsheet – unemployment in the UK

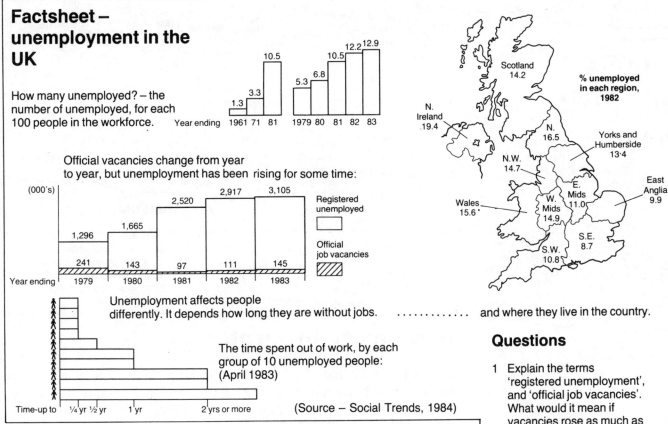

How many unemployed? – the number of unemployed, for each 100 people in the workforce.

Year ending 1961 71 81  1979 80 81 82 83
1.3  3.3  10.5  5.3  6.8  10.5  12.2  12.9

Official vacancies change from year to year, but unemployment has been rising for some time:

(000's)

| Year ending | 1979 | 1980 | 1981 | 1982 | 1983 |
|---|---|---|---|---|---|
| Registered unemployed | 1,296 | 1,665 | 2,520 | 2,917 | 3,105 |
| Official job vacancies | 241 | 143 | 97 | 111 | 145 |

Registered unemployed ☐

Official job vacancies ▨

Unemployment affects people differently. It depends how long they are without jobs. . . . . . . . . . . . . and where they live in the country.

The time spent out of work, by each group of 10 unemployed people: (April 1983)

Time-up to   ¼ yr  ½ yr   1 yr        2 yrs or more

(Source – Social Trends, 1984)

% unemployed in each region, 1982

Scotland 14.2
N. Ireland 19.4
N. 16.5
Yorks and Humberside 13·4
N.W. 14.7
E. Mids 11.0
East Anglia 9.9
Wales 15.6
W. Mids 14.9
S.E. 8.7
S.W. 10.8

## Questions

1 Explain the terms 'registered unemployment', and 'official job vacancies'. What would it mean if vacancies rose as much as unemployment? (2)

2 About what *number* of people had been unemployed for more than 1 year by April 1983? Why do you think some people are unemployed for less than 3 months but others for more than 2 years? (2)

3 Which 3 regions had the *lowest* unemployment rates? What else do you think those regions have in common? (2)

how this was important to make labour mobile between jobs. But we saw also how difficult it could become to make such changes.

Some people can change from old jobs to new ones quite easily. You may be young, clever and adaptable. You may have been taught how to make such changes in your way of life. But other people may have worked in one job for many years. They may say that it is too late for old dogs like them to learn new tricks. Firms may feel the same, and try to hire only young, well-qualified workers. Unions may try to block changes in old methods of work.

How much does it cost to change jobs? It might take years of studying to retrain. It might cost thousands of pounds to move house and family from the north, say, to the south. It costs even more to move a firm and its jobs to where it can find new workers. Government regulations may raise these costs, although government grants can help to make some changes.

These changes are difficult, but they happen more and more. The structure of work and of the workforce is changing quickly, because of *technical progress*. New machines, like computers and robots, come into factories and offices. This replaces old work but sets up new and different jobs. New products like pocket TVs and BMX bikes are bought, and make new jobs.

Do these new jobs help the unemployed? In many cases, of course, they do. But in many other cases they do not. People who are unemployed for a long time do not change easily to new types of work. They may be skilled in the wrong work, or be too old to retrain. They may live in areas where no new work is created. And there may not be enough new jobs to keep up with the number of old jobs being lost. Mass unemployment may grow.

# The young today— a Daily Mail inquiry

'I went on the dole as soon as I left school, and it really depressed me. I don't think many adults realise how awful it is leaving school with just nothing ahead.'
GARY FLEGG, 16, Mitcham, Surrey.

'There's no such thing as "the unemployment problem". People can get jobs—it's just they're too fussy or too lazy. I've just given up a job as a garage receptionist—didn't want to do it any more and I fancied a break. The fact is I know I can get a job at the Jobcentre the minute I decide I want to work again.'
PAUL TAULBUT, 19, London.

THE SPREADING stain of unemployment reaches its darkest point among Britain's young. Were it not for Government Training Schemes such as the Youth Training Scheme the unemployment rate for young people would reach 25 per cent, almost double the national rate.

In our survey school leavers were the hardest hit: three out of ten of those between the ages of 16 and 18 are unemployed, compared to only two in ten of those over 18. Not surprisingly, the highest unemployment rates are among working class kids.

However, the next most affected group, within our survey is, surprisingly, the most affluent – young people whose parents belong to the professional and managerial class. Perhaps upper middle class kids from a richer background than the rest can afford to be more choosy about the jobs they're prepared to take on.

'Choosy': I've found that word constantly cropping up when older people talk about unemployment problems among the young. The implication is that young people today have been encouraged by idealistic and woolly-minded teachers to feel they're too good for the great majority of boring, humdrum jobs: they'd rather live on the dole than soil their hands with uncongenial work.

Well, there's no evidence to support that view in our poll. The young *do* want jobs and happy loafing on the dole is *not* their preferred way of life.

In fact most young people would gladden the heart of Norman 'Get on-your-bike' Tebbit: Six out of ten of the unemployed say they'd willingly move to another part of the country to get a job.

Daily Mail, 26.1.83

## Question

1 Why do you think unemployment hits hardest at young people who are (a) school leavers, (b) 'working class kids', (c) from 'richer backgrounds'? (3)

# Mass unemployment

All the unemployment we have seen so far has been because workers looking for jobs do not match the jobs on offer. But what if jobs are not on offer? What if there is only one job vacancy for every ten people registered as unemployed, as in the first half of the 1980s? Then unemployment affects all types of workers in all parts of the country together. We can call this *mass unemployment*.

Mass unemployment is worse at some times than at others. It depends on how well the economy is growing. Growth means that firms make more output of goods and services. Generally they must hire more labour in order to do this. So growth brings more jobs.

Most economies seem to grow fast for only a few years at a time. Then they grow more slowly, if at all. There are trade cycles of booms and slump that last perhaps five or ten years. More jobs are made in good years, so that unemployment falls. But jobs are lost in bad years when unemployment rises. This is sometimes called *cyclical unemployment*.

Why should firms change their output and working methods all at the same time? We turn to these general changes in the economy in Part 6, but for now we must notice one main thing. It is the general level of spending in the economy that is most important. Spending leads firms to make goods and services, and to give jobs to workers. Spending sets the demand for firms' output. Low spending causes low demand, and so unemployment.

Spending may be too low for many reasons. Perhaps people choose to save their money instead of spend it, or firms choose not to risk buying new machines. Perhaps the government puts up taxes or cuts its own spending. We will see the effects of these changes in later sections.

Can we overcome mass unemployment? For a short time, at least, we can. The government can try to raise spending so that firms create jobs. But there may be a cost. Inflation may rise as a result and cut even more jobs in future.

# 2.6 What are workers worth? The pay of factors of production

Marlon Brando was paid over £1.8 million to appear in the film *Superman*, and he earned a further £7.5m from his share in the film's success later. Why does one person get paid so much? What are workers worth?

In economics we explain people's incomes by their work as *factors of production*. You can work as labour if you use your hands and mind to help make goods and services. You can put your property to work for you if you own capital equipment, money or land. You can take the risks in running a business if you show enterprise, hire other factors, and put them to work.

You can work in all these ways and earn an income. Your pay as labour is called *wages*. The pay on capital is called *interest*, as with the rates of interest paid on deposits in banks. Land is paid a *rent*, as with the farm land that tenant farmers rent from their landlords. And the *profit* made by a business, after all other costs have been met, is paid to its owners as a return for their enterprise.

Everyone earns their living by working in one of these ways. Some people work in more than one way. Marlon Brando was paid a 'wage' for acting in *Superman*, and he was also paid a share of the profits from the film. Perhaps he then went on to use his money in other ways, to buy land or to lend to businesses. He will then have worked as all types of factors of production.

Why is one person paid more than another for working? In economics we use supply and demand to explain levels of pay.

## Checklist – how are factors of production paid?

- labour is paid wages
- capital is paid interest
- land is paid rent
- enterprise is paid profit

## Supply and demand set pay

Why is pay high or low? The answer lies in supply and demand. Supply shows how much of the factor is offered for work. More supply means that the factor is more common, and generally leads to lower pay. Marlon Brando is one in a million – a great actor, who could offer special qualities to the people making the film of *Superman*. No one else could offer the same star quality. The film-makers wanted Marlon Brando to be in *Superman* very much, and they could pay to back up their wishes.

Demand also sets pay. Demand shows how much firms want a factor, and are willing to pay for it to work for them. High demand shows that the factor can do important work. Probably it helps to make a lot of output, and earns a great deal for the business. This is what Marlon Brando could offer in *Superman*. He could make the film more of a success by being in it.

Together supply and demand set pay. Low supply and high demand lead to high rates of pay. High supply and low demand lead to low rates of pay. So you can earn a lot of money when you go to work. But first you must become a rare and valuable worker that firms will want to hire. How can this be done?

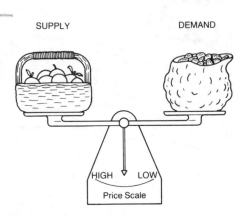

Supply and demand set price

more supply → low price ← less demand
less supply → high price ← more demand

## Five ways to improve your pay

```
┌──────────┐  ┌──────────┐  ┌──────────┐
│   Work   │  │ Work on  │  │Offer more│
│  harder  │  │  better  │  │ valuable │
│          │  │ machines │  │ abilities│
└────┬─────┘  └────┬─────┘  └────┬─────┘
     │             │             │
     └─────────────┼─────────────┘
                   ▼
     ┌──────────────────────────┐
     │ So raise your productivity,│
     │  and your employer's      │
     │   demand for your work    │
     └────────────┬─────────────┘
                  ▼
        £ PAY RISE £
                  ▲
     ┌────────────┴─────────────┐
     │ Show your employer how    │
     │ scarce you are, that there│
     │  is less supply of your   │
     │      type of work         │
     └────┬─────────────────┬────┘
          │                 │
┌─────────┴──────┐  ┌───────┴────────┐
│ Train, study,  │  │ Join a trade   │
│ or gain        │  │ union to       │
│ experience to  │  │ help limit the │
│ offer          │  │ numbers        │
│ specialised    │  │ who can do     │
│ abilities that │  │ your work      │
│ others cannot  │  │                │
│ match          │  │                │
└────────────────┘  └────────────────┘
```

# One in a million, or common as muck?

What type of work can you offer as a factor of production? Some types of factors are very special, because they are few and far between. Others are quite common and widely available. In itself, this makes supply either low or high, and sets pay to be different in each case.

Suppose you own a plot of land, for example. If your land is like all the rest – perhaps an old waste-tip, miles from anywhere – it will not be very valuable. But if it is in the centre of town, where there is little building space left, it may be worth much more.

The same idea fits your work as labour. You may leave school at sixteen and look for work. But without qualifications, training or experience, you can offer little more than many other people. You must study and train hard, and work well to learn your job, to have something special to offer. Abilities like yours will then be in limited supply and you can claim higher pay.

So, software-writers are paid more than secretaries, partly because of their extra training and skill. The best software-writers are paid even more, because there are few people who can offer their type of work. But it is never enough just to offer something special. Before you can be paid more, you must find someone willing to pay. Pay is set by demand as well as supply.

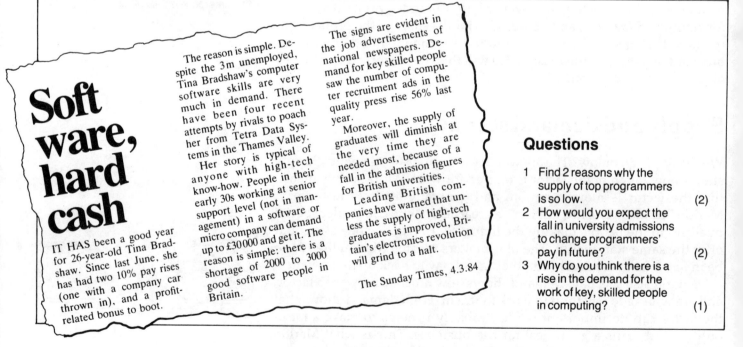

# Soft ware, hard cash

IT HAS been a good year for 26-year-old Tina Bradshaw. Since last June, she has had two 10% pay rises (one with a company car thrown in), and a profit-related bonus to boot.

The reason is simple. Despite the 3m unemployed, Tina Bradshaw's computer software skills are very much in demand. There have been four recent attempts by rivals to poach her from Tetra Data Systems in the Thames Valley.

Her story is typical of anyone with high-tech know-how. People in their early 30s working at senior support level (not in management) in a software or micro company can demand up to £30000 and get it. The reason is simple: there is a shortage of 2000 to 3000 good software people in Britain.

The signs are evident in the job advertisements of national newspapers. Demand for key skilled people saw the number of computer recruitment ads in the quality press rise 56% last year.

Moreover, the supply of graduates will diminish at the very time they are needed most, because of a fall in the admission figures for British universities.

Leading British companies have warned that unless the supply of high-tech graduates is improved, Britain's electronics revolution will grind to a halt.

The Sunday Times, 4.3.84

## Questions

1  Find 2 reasons why the supply of top programmers is so low.  (2)
2  How would you expect the fall in university admissions to change programmers' pay in future?  (2)
3  Why do you think there is a rise in the demand for the work of key, skilled people in computing?  (1)

# Delivering the goods

Whatever the work, you always work *for* someone. Firms hire factors of production in order to make goods and services. So you are in high demand if you can produce valuable goods and services. What matters is your productivity.

*Productivity* measures the output produced by a factor of production. One extra worker may raise a firm's output by two cars a year, say. If each car is worth an extra £4000 to the firm, this worker's productivity is £4000 × 2 = £8000 a year.

Firms often cannot measure the productivity of each worker as well as this. But they have quite a good idea of whether people are paying their way for the firm or not. Firms generally pay more for factors if they are more productive.

Here is an example. A firm must decide whether to borrow money and pay interest, to pay for investment in new trucks. How much of this capital should it use? The firm works out what it expects to gain by using the trucks in future. These are the returns from the investment, and show the productivity of capital. One truck is expected to be very worthwhile, and more than pays the extra cost of borrowed money. But the second truck has much less to offer. Its productivity is too low. It is not worth buying, except at a lower rate of interest. For the rate of interest is the payment made to capital.

What can you do to increase your value in production? You must show your boss that you can 'deliver the goods', that you can raise the value of whatever your firm does. Can you sell to customers, for example, or write good software programs? You may need to gain more training and experience, so that you can take on more work, or harder work. You may show your firm that you could do your boss's job as well as your own! Or you may find that the changes that matter most are out of your hands.

## Changes in pay

What causes changes in the supply and demand for factors? Some changes may affect just one worker rather than others, but important changes affect many at a time. Capital investment, for example, goes on all the time as firms buy new machines, buildings and stocks. This raises the supply of capital goods, but it also affects other factors. People working on better and larger machines can help to make more output. So investment raises the productivity of this labour. But the new machines replace other types of labour and put them out of work. So some people gain but others lose.

The demand for factors is set by the demand for products. If consumers buy more canoes, for example, firms raise their output of canoes. Workers, machines and other factors that are used to make canoes become more valuable as their productivity rises. Their pay is likely to rise as a result. So changes in pay can follow changes in consumer demand decided far away, for all sorts of reasons. Or sometimes there seems to be no reason at all.

Many lines of work do not fit the picture we have drawn. Not everyone has a productivity that can be measured, or faces a firm that hires to make a sellable product. The government may set its own demand for factors and change it with a special policy for incomes, say. It may set up regulations that control the amounts that firms can pay. Trade unions may try to change supply or demand to help just their own members. This is what we will study in the next section.

# The dentists who drill for gold

A GOVERNMENT Minister has demanded an inquiry into how two dentists have earned £250 000 a year between them.

Both have luxury homes and one has a 45 ft yacht, with two double bedrooms moored on the South of France coast.

No one is alleging anything illegal, but the painful thought is that some dentists can extract so much more from the Health Service than others.

These figures, and the lifestyle that goes with them, are bound to amaze the public and indeed, the vast majority of dentists whose earnings are nothing like this.

The average net income of a Health Service dentist is estimated at around £17 000.

So how can anyone go so far above that figure?

● Fillings are the most lucrative line. The more that can be slapped in at a single session, the faster the money rolls in.

● Another method that is a gold-plated form of raising income is the use of "painless" dentistry.

This plays on the patients' fear of the drill, and offers a drip knock-out anaesthetic as an alternative.

And they may charge you £10 or more for this.

"It is extremely easy just to drill teeth needlessly, and put in fillings that are larger than they need be," says Brian Lux, a member of the General Dental Council, and council member of the General Dental Practitioners Association, who wants to see rip-off dentists thrown out of the profession.

He points out that a small filling on a biting surface earns a dentist £3.10, but if he drills to extend it to the front and back surface, he earns £7.10 from the Health Service.

The national average for Health Service dental treatment is under £18, but Coventry's runs at nearly £24.

Daily Express, 5.6.84

## Questions

1 Show 3 ways in which dentists can earn more pay by doing more work (3)
2 Suppose that dentists succeed in ending tooth decay. How would you expect this to affect their pay? (2)

About 1 in every 2 workers in the UK is a member of a trade union. What do unions offer, and how do they affect people at work?

Let's say that you want to work at the local factory. You have all the right abilities and a good record. A job is waiting for you there – but you cannot have it. You are not a member of the trade union, that runs a *closed shop* in the factory! (See *Collective bargaining* below.)

Trade unions are bodies made up of people at work, who join together to help themselves. This help comes in a number of ways, but what we know best is the way unions try to protect the pay and the jobs of their members.

There are many different unions in the country. You may know the largest ones best. These are mostly *general* unions, such as the Transport and General Workers Union (TGWU) and the Amalgamated Union of Engineering Workers (AUEW). Their members come from many different industries, and do different types of work.

Some *industrial* unions are also well known. You may hear of strikes in mining, in teaching or on the railways, and guess that the National Union of Miners (NUM), of Teachers (NUT) or of Railwaymen (NUR) are involved. In most industries, however, there are a number of different unions, each with their own members. Some are small traditional *craft* unions, such as the Master Builders Association. Others are growing, newer, white-collar unions, such as the Association of Scientific, Technical and Managerial Staffs (ASTMS), whose members work in clerical and other service jobs.

What do all these unions do? Should you join so that you can work at the factory?

The smallest trade union in the UK is the London Handforged Spoon and Fork Makers Society, instituted in 1874, and now with a membership of 6.

(Source – Guinness Book of Records, 1984)

## Checklist – what are the different types of unions?

- general unions have members in many different industries and types of work, often unskilled
- industrial unions have members all in the same industry
- craft unions have members, often only a few, with specialised skills
- white-collar unions have members in services, clerical and administrative work

## Your friendly trade union

You may be surprised to see all the different benefits you can get by joining a trade union. Many unions were set up long ago, before there was much in the way of personal insurance, education or legal aid. They help their members, therefore, as forms of 'friendly' societies.

Unions collect money from their members – a little at a time, as regular subscriptions. Most of this money is kept in funds and used for social benefits. The union pays to members in need, perhaps because of sickness or injury at work. It helps members to pay legal costs, in law claims against employers, for example. Some unions even run their own holiday camps at the coast and pay for their members to study at college.

You often hear of union leaders meeting the government and talking about politics. This also follows from the way unions have helped their members over the years. They try to change government's policies to help their members. Many of them give support to the Labour Party, paying money to the party and supporting its campaigns. Some go further, and pay a salary to a sponsored Member of Parliament who can support, advise and represent the union in Parliament.

But would these be your reasons for joining? Probably not. You are more likely to join so that the union can protect your pay and your job at work.

---

## Factsheet – trade unions in the UK

**Unions**

In 1981 there were about 24.5 million people in the workforce, and 12.1 m of them belonged to unions – just 1 in 2. By 1984 the number had dropped to about 10 million.

Most members are in a few large unions –
TGWU is largest, with over 1.5 million
The top 11 unions have about 2 in every 3 members, the top 25 have about 4 in every 5.
Unions are changing – they are larger, and there are fewer of them.

**Strikes**:

The number of strikes in the UK is quite high, but most are short, and unofficial. About half those in 1981 and 1982 lasted less than 5 days. But they cost days off work – about half a day each year, for workers on average over the period 1978–82. Other days off work caused by sickness and absenteeism cost many more days than this.

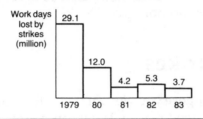

**Questions**

1 Explain the terms (a) trade unions, (b) unofficial strikes. (2)
2 Why do you think unions are growing larger? (1)
3 How could the rise in unemployment from 1979 to 1983 help to explain the changes shown in work days lost by strikes? (1)

---

# Pay and jobs

Suppose you work at the factory but do not belong to a union. What can you do on your own to protect your pay and your job? You can use your own voice to complain, but who to? You work for a firm that hires many people and has many more to choose from instead of you. You can be replaced. The employer who hires you is larger and stronger than you.

A trade union gets its members to join together and to act together for their joint benefit. Together you can make a claim for more pay or for better conditions of work. You can stand together to protect each other's jobs. You can try to stop the employer sacking workers, or at least make sure that people who are made redundant in this way are well paid.

Why is the union better at doing all this than workers on their own? It is because workers are stronger in a number. They can refuse to work until the employer does what they ask. The employer may replace one worker at a time, but cannot replace all workers at the same time, especially if there is a closed shop.

# Collective bargaining

A *closed shop* is where all workers at a work-place belong to the union. The employer cannot hire any worker who is not a member of the union. You have to be a member of the union Equity before you can act on stage or TV, for example. You have to be a member of the National Union of Journalists before you can write for a major newspaper.

Trade unions are stronger if they have a closed shop. They represent all workers in deals with their employer. But employers gain something as well. They can deal with all their workers, on pay or job conditions,

## Closed shops

Mr Leon Brittan, at the time Secretary of State for Employment, had this to say about closed shops, and why the government was bringing in laws to make workers vote to support, or end them:

"The closed shop has killed existing jobs and prevented new ones from being created. Those who use the closed shop to impose their own price on their own labour do so at the expense of the profits needed for tomorrow's investment and tomorrow's jobs. And they do so, too, at the expense of all those who might otherwise be employed if the rigid wage structures and restrictive practices which such unions enforce did not apply. That is why there is nothing fraternal about the closed shop."

17.12.83

## Question

1 What is a closed shop? What may be the advantages and disadvantages of closed shops? (3)

for example, simply through the union. There is clear, collective bargaining.

You bargain with your employer if you ask for a £10 pay rise and she offers you £5, or you ask for four weeks' holiday, and she offers you two. *Collective bargaining* works in the same way. The people selling and buying a certain kind of work bargain to reach a deal. Workers join together in trade unions, and employers may join together as well in an *Employers Association*.

Bargaining often works at two levels. Employers and unions collect into groups at national level to decide matters of pay and conditions of work for their industry as a whole. These terms are then taken by all firms and all workers together. But extra bargaining may also happen at local level. Union leaders may meet employers at the place of work, in the plant, or on the shop floor, to decide other details.

Sometimes the two sides agree a bargain quite quickly. Sometimes they do not.

## Strikes

Suppose you work at the factory for a while, and then you are sacked for no good reason. What can your trade union do to help you? It can take the matter up for you. It can talk to your employer and represent you at an industrial tribunal. This is a law court that deals only with legal matters to do with work. The union can also take industrial action against the employer.

Industrial action takes different forms. Your fellow workers may stop working overtime, or have a go-slow and do less work generally. They may work to rule and make production more difficult. They may strike.

The longest strike in the world was by barbers' assistants in Copenhagen, Denmark. It lasted 33 years.

(Source – Guinness Book of Records, 1984)

## The Miners' Strike 1984

About 20000 miners will lose their jobs in cuts announced yesterday by coal chief Ian Mac-Gregor.

As the industry stumbled towards an all-out strike, he revealed there would be a reduction in output of four-million tons this year.

That would mean job losses of around 15000, said Mr MacGregor. They could be shed through natural wastage and voluntary redundancy, he insisted, and would be enough to ensure that the Coal Board breaks even.

Pitmen in Yorkshire and Scotland have been called on to strike at the end of the week.

And there will be pressure at tomorrow's meeting of the miners' executive to call the first national strike for a decade.

Leaders of the union feel the time is approaching when the row over pay and pit closures must be brought to a head.

Nineteen weeks of an overtime ban have done nothing to shake the resolve of Coal Board chairman Ian Mac-Gregor.

He warned the union that a long and damaging strike could spell disaster for the industry.

"It would be a form of self-destruction," said Mr MacGregor.

Mr Scargill alleged the Government and Coal Board are eventually aiming to slim down the industry from 184000 workers to only 100000 miners in 100 super pits.

Mr Scargill warned the Coal Board: "We will do all in our power to stop it."

He urged the Coal Board to come back to the negotiating table and start serious pay talks.

But Mr MacGregor made it quite clear he will not increase his 5.2 per cent pay offer.

● SINCE the miners strike of 1974 72 pits have been closed – a fall of 29 per cent – and the number of miners has been cut by 66000 or 27 per cent. But coal consumption has gone down just 18 per cent in the same period. These are the details:

|  | Pits | Miners | Consumption |
|---|---|---|---|
|  | 246 | 246000 | 127.2m |
| 1974 | 219 | 232500 | 128.4m |
| 1979 | 174 | 180000 | 104 m |
| 1983 |  |  | Daily Express, 7.3. |

### Questions

1 What 2 forms of industrial action by miners are mentioned here? (1)

2 What did (a) the employers and (b) the trade union ask for in their collective bargaining? (2)

Workers *strike* by stopping all work for the employer. An official strike is called by the union, which then pays strike benefits to its members and their families while they are out of work. Unofficial strikes are often held locally without the full support of the rest of union members.

But will a strike work? This depends how much it harms the business of the firm, and how much it costs in lost production. The union tries to use the support of all its members – and the more members it has, the stronger it can be. It tries to win support from other workers and other unions. It sets up *pickets*, where strikers stand outside places to do with the firm's work, and try to persuade other workers to join the strike or delivery lorries to turn away.

Other unions can support the strikers in some of this. But the law now stands against strikes that are not against the strikers' own employers, and picketing that is not at the pickets' own place of work. Perhaps the Trades Union Congress (TUC) could help. This is the national body where unions meet together. Mostly it deals with the press and the government, but it also solves disputes between unions and arranges for unions to help each other.

How long do strikes last? They cost both workers and employers money, from lost wages and production, so it depends who feels these costs the most. Both sides will end up agreeing to a bargain one way or the other, but they may need help to do so. The Advisory, Conciliation and Arbitration Service (ACAS) is one body that can help. It can investigate the problem, and it can talk to both unions and employers to try to bring them together. This is called mediation or conciliation. If asked by both sides, it can decide a fair bargain for them. This is called arbitration.

# Pay or jobs

So trade unions can bargain with employers and help their members. They can push for more pay, better conditions and more jobs. But with what success?

Unions represent workers. They can change the supply of labour therefore by cutting the amount of work, or the type of work that their members are willing to do. But they can do little to change the demand for that labour. Demand is set by firms hiring workers to make goods and services for customers. All that unions can do here is make labour more important than other factors. They cannot often make the customers want more.

What happens if unions cut the supply of labour? Less work is offered, which in itself should lead to a higher rate of pay. Each hour of work is more scarce and more valuable to the firm. But this is because there is less work done. And, if it pushes up the price to the customer as well, there may be even less work to do. In itself this is likely to mean fewer jobs. Unions may raise wages but often only by cutting jobs. They must choose which matters most.

## Checklist – what do unions offer their members?

● social benefits such as accident insurance and social clubs
● collective bargaining to improve pay and conditions of work
● protection of jobs
● political strength in dealings with government and the general public

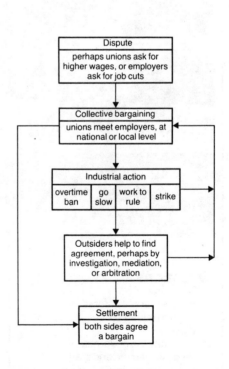

47

What can government do to help people work? How can it change what workers offer, or the jobs on offer to them?

How can the government help people into work? One way is to help workers match the jobs that are on offer. Education plays a part in this, and so does training.

At school you learn how to work, how to use your abilities, and how to learn new skills. In training you learn about a certain line of work – perhaps how to fly an airliner or run a restaurant. The government does much to help, by running schools and colleges, and by giving grants for people to go on with their studies. In these ways it can try to steer people towards the jobs which will be on offer to them.

Training takes time, however, and is difficult to do. Doctors may study for nine years, only to find that the supply of jobs has dried up. You may not be strong enough in maths to become a computer specialist. You may need to move to a new area to look for jobs you can do. The government can encourage this. It can suggest that you 'get on your bike' to look for work instead of staying 'on the dole'. But what more can it do?

# How Mark Watts escaped the dole queue and found soccer glory. . .

If the fates had been allowed their way Mark Watts would be just another unemployed youth.

But fortune, in the unlikely guise of a Government youth employment scheme, intervened. It led to a job and as from this week, a contract. And instead of watching Tottenham Hotspur, Watts spent last Saturday playing against them in his First Division debut for Luton Town.

"Last summer we thought about getting rid of him." said Luton's manager.

"We just weren't convinced that he was good enough."

And a club like Luton, unfashionable and with only the most limited of financial resources, could not afford the gamble.

The Government, however, still can. Under the Youth Opportunity Programme*, a youngster who is hired by any company – a steel works, a clothing business, a football club – will have his wages paid by the Programme for six months. So Mark was taken on.

Mark has now signed professional terms, coming off the Youth Opportunity Programme. His wages will go up from £25 to £75 a week.

*YOP was replaced by the Youth Training Scheme in 1984.

Daily Express, 21.1.83

## Questions

1  Why is there 'a gamble' in training young soccer players?  (1)
2  Why may the government take this gamble and start young people in work when firms do not?  (2)

What if there are spare workers in the north and spare jobs in the south? The government can try to move both to an extent. It can offer grants to help people pay for a move to the south. It can make it easier for people to exchange their council house in one town for another somewhere else. It can offer grants and other aid to help firms to take their work to the north.

The government uses its regional policy for this. It supports industry in regions of high unemployment, and helps new industry to settle there. We will see how this works on firms in Section 3.8.

# Cutting down the barriers

What if there are not enough jobs to go around? How can the government help firms to make more? One approach is to cut away any barriers that stop them doing so.

Trade unions may cause some of these barriers. They aim to save jobs but in some ways they make things worse. Suppose they push up the wage rates, for example. This may raise prices and make it more difficult for firms to sell. Output falls and jobs are cut, if not for union members, then for others in the industry.

The union may set up rules of work to stop other people from doing its members' work. These rules make it difficult for firms to change methods of production or to keep up with the times. Again, it is difficult to sell and jobs are cut.

So government can try to control unions, perhaps so that they affect only their own members and not other workers. It can help unions and employers to bargain evenly. Above all, the government can control the way that pay and jobs are set in its own area of work – the public sector.

The government's own actions can lead to other barriers against new jobs. Taxes can put up the cost of hiring extra people and official rules can make it too difficult for firms to risk taking on more workers. Also the government may help to price people out of work by setting a minimum wage.

# Can people price themselves into work?

A *minimum wage* is the lowest rate of pay that employers are allowed to pay their workers. In most cases this is agreed between unions and employers. In some businesses, such as shops and farming, however, there are Wages Councils set up by government to protect workers and to set minimum wages by law.

But what if workers are not worth that much to the firm? A very young worker may not know the job well, and others may not have much ability in the work. The product they are making may not be valuable to customers. All this makes productivity low, so that the employer cannot afford to pay a full wage to the worker. Either the firm takes on the worker and pays too much, or it leaves the worker unemployed. Some workers are bound to be left, and unemployment is higher because of the minimum wage.

Can people price themselves into work by taking lower rates of pay? In one way this makes sense. Firms should find that these people can pay for themselves in work through their productivity. As unions, government and workers accept lower wages, firms should accept more workers.

The minimum wage is set for a reason, however. It is set to give enough pay for a reasonable standard of life. Lower pay may mean more poverty. There may also be other changes in the economy brought on by the fall in wages.

Lower wages may allow firms to cut prices and raise output. There may be more goods and services for everyone to share. But lower pay may instead lead to lower spending, and so less output of goods and services. National production may fall and add to the problems of mass unemployment. These are problems for the economy as a whole.

## A letter to The Times –

Sir, You argue (leading article, December 20) that wages councils, which set legal minimum rates of pay for nearly three million of the lowest paid and largely non-unionised workers, "tend to price young people out of jobs" and should be abolished. . .

Look at the Young Workers Scheme (YWS), which is designed to cut the wages of young people: employers receive a subsidy of £15 a week for each young person they employ at wages of less than £42 a week.

But how successful has the scheme been in creating new jobs?

Last week the House of Commons Public Accounts Committee reported that 77 per cent of the jobs subsidised under YWS would have existed anyway and that the few new jobs created cost the Exchequer £5355 each. Most employers simply cut the wages of young people they already employ, or replace older workers with youngsters. . .

Yours sincerely,
CHRIS POND, Director,
Low Pay Unit,

December 20, 1983

## Young peoples pay – too high a price?

THE electricians' union has agreed to cut the starting pay of apprentices from £41 to £28 a week.

The idea behind the unprecedented 33 per cent pay cut is to create 8000 new jobs over the next three years.

Daily Mail, 7.1.83

## Questions

1 Why are apprentices in training not worth as much to employers as experienced electricians? (1)
2 Explain the terms (a) wages council, (b) minimum rates of pay. (2)
3 Explain why a cut in wages should make firms want to employ more workers. Why do unions usually try to stop this? (2)
4 Show two ways in which a fall in the wages of young people may affect other workers. (2)

# Part 3 Business

## 3.1 What do firms do? The business of production

Production is about how firms use resources to make goods and services. What are firms and what problems do they face?

Congratulations! Old Uncle Percy has died and left you his farm. You are now the proud owner of fifty cows and all that goes with them. What will you do now?

It is a dairy farm and the land is used to feed and keep cows which give milk. It is part of the agriculture *industry* that includes all producers in the same line of business. It extracts raw materials from the land and so is a part of primary production. But your milk goes on to be used by factories to make other products such as milk chocolate and biscuits. This is part of manufacturing, or secondary production. When these products are sold by shops to customers, this is part of the service industry that make up tertiary production.

You own a business *enterprise*. This is a company, set up in law to make its own deals, buying and selling with other people. What can you gain from owning an enterprise? You have money put at risk to run the business and you should expect a return. This return is called profit.

## How do you run a business?

Businesses are run mostly for profit. The government runs its businesses to help its customers or taxpayers, so that they gain the profit. Private businesses like your firm run to make profit for their owners. You may also want to help your workers, customers or friends. But, setting these aside, there is often just one clear aim left. You want the business to make as much profit as possible for you, the owner. So how should you run your firm?

*Firms* are units of production that use inputs of resources to make an output of goods or services. Should you hire a manager to look after the day-to-day business of the firm? You could pay him to make the right choices, and to run the firm in a profitable way. Perhaps you should use your resources in a number of different ways and divide the business up.

## Divide and rule

Your farm may be quite small but still have a number of different sites. It may have fields and shed on one side of a hill and buildings for equipment and housing on the other. You could choose to work these as different *establishments*, each with their own workers, land and machines.

Large firms usually run many different places of work. Shops such as Woolworths and banks such as Barclays have branches in each

### Factsheet – production in the UK

How much is made by each group of industries?

|  | (%) |
| --- | --- |
| Agriculture, forestry & fishing | 2.35 |
| Oil and gas | 5.68 |
| Other energy & water | 4.96 |
| Manufacturing | 23.08 |
| Construction | 5.51 |
| Distribution | 12.25 |
| Transport & communications | 7.01 |
| Banking & finance, etc | 11.86 |
| Property | 6.00 |
| Public administration, defence, etc | 6.83 |
| Education & health | 8.53 |
| Other services | 5.94 |

National output (Gross Domestic Product) in 1982 = £245 000m
(Source – Annual Abstract, 1984)

### Questions

1. What share of national output (GDP) is produced by (a) the primary sector, (b) services? (2)
2. Explain how a firm such as Marks and Spencer may be involved in more than one of these groups of industries. (2)

town, for instance. Ford has factories at Dagenham, Cardiff and Hailwood, but runs many smaller plants as well in the UK. This helps them to specialise and to cut costs, and to buy and sell across the whole country.

You could have different managers to run different parts of the business. One could run the milking, and another could run bed and breakfasts at the farmhouse. In this way, your enterprise would own a number of firms producing differently.

Large organisations go even further than this. They set up a number of different companies, perhaps with different owners for each. A holding company can keep overall control and own most or all of the others, which are called subsidiary companies. Multi-national companies can work like this, with subsidiary companies in many different countries. Ford UK, for example, is owned by Ford USA, who also own Ford Motor Credit and Ford of Germany, France, and so on.

**Firms and industries**

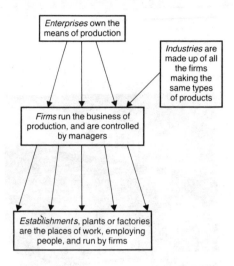

*Enterprises* own the means of production

*Industries* are made up of all the firms making the same types of products

*Firms* run the business of production, and are controlled by managers

*Establishments*, plants or factories are the places of work, employing people, and run by firms

# The Chilling Story of Marks and Spencer Chicken

**Resources:** M & S meet food suppliers, lay down rules about breeds of chicken and other meats, how live animals are to be fed, when and how to be slaughtered. . . 'an animal that is upset before it is killed makes tougher meat'

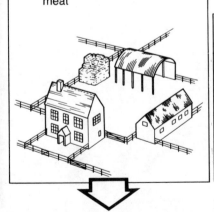

**On sale:** Within 24 hours of manufacture. M & S try out new products in about 20 stores and on staff in its canteens or at home! Beef stew and dumplings was tried out one November and up to 40 000 a week were selling by February.

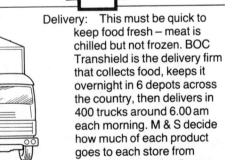

**Delivery:** This must be quick to keep food fresh – meat is chilled but not frozen. BOC Transhield is the delivery firm that collects food, keeps it overnight in 6 depots across the country, then delivers in 400 trucks around 6.00 am each morning. M & S decide how much of each product goes to each store from weekly sales figures.

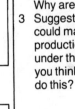

**Manufacturing:** M & S meet 350 food manufacturers, such as Riverside Pork Farms. Chefs make up new dishes. M & S lay down exact recipes – up to 24 pages long! Much care about clean production and good quality.

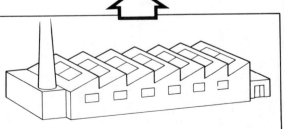

## Questions

1  Give an example of a firm that M & S deals with in (a) secondary (b) tertiary production.    (1)
2  How many establishments does BOC Transhield run for M & S? Why are there so many?    (2)
3  Suggest changes that M & S could make to put all stages of production more completely under their own control. Why do you think they have chosen not to do this?    (2)

# What must you decide?

You face a number of choices in running a business. Some of these are to do with your own work and problems only – which cows to sell, when to call the vet, how to get up early, and so on. But other questions are the same for firms in all types of production.

What are your aims? You want a profit, but do you want it sooner or later? To make more profit, you must expect to take on more risks. This may mean going into a new line of business and borrowing more money.

What should you make in your firm? For a while you have little choice. It takes time to change your machines, your land or your livestock, for example. But you could look for new products that might sell well. Given long enough, any change is possible if you run the firm in the right way.

How should you make your products? You will aim to keep your costs as low as possible, but first you need to know about methods of production and the best ways to fit resources together. You may need to move to a new location to find new land, new resources, or a better place to sell your products.

Lastly, you must choose how much to make. Should you keep output where it is, or raise or lower it? Again, it can take time to change the way the firm runs, including the greatest change of all: you may choose to close down altogether, sell off the farm, take the money and run!

McDonalds sold 50 billion hamburgers in 1984, in 8304 restaurants, in 34 different countries.

## Question

1  How many (a) enterprises, (b) establishments, (c) products?    (1)

# 3.2 Privately-owned business

What is the difference between BAC and BSC? BAC is the British Aluminium Company Ltd, and BSC is the British Steel Corporation. Clearly, one makes aluminium and the other makes steel. Also, one makes more profit than the other – BAC made £12 million and BSC lost £668 million from 1980 to 1981. Now we are close – who earned this profit or paid for this loss?

Private business is owned by private individuals like you or me. Profits are paid to the owners of the business. BAC is privately owned, by its shareholders, and so are ICI, Liverpool Football Club, and the Royal Ballet. BSC is a public corporation and part of the public sector of the economy. It is owned by the nation as a whole, and run by people chosen by the government. The Post Office, British Rail and the BBC are all similar.

## How can you own a business?

There is one simple way to own a private business. This is to set it up using only your own money. You can act as a *sole trader*. You have full control of all the firm does, and earn all the profits of the business. So this may be a good way to run a shop, say, or bed and breakfast accommodation.

What if there are no profits, however? You face all the risks of business alone. You have to pay all the bills of the firm out of your own pocket. You might do better to take on a partner. Doctors, solicitors and other professional people often choose this as the way to share the risks and the profits of their business. A *partnership* allows up to twenty people to own a firm jointly.

This can go well where partners work closely together. But all partners still have to pay business bills out of their own pockets. They may choose instead to set the firm up as a *limited* partnership, so that they may each lose only what they choose to put into the firm. Some partners may be active in running the business, while others act as 'sleeping partners', letting their money do all their work for them.

You can share a business in other ways as well. Shoppers, farmers and others can join up in buying and selling, for example. *Co-operatives* are firms owned jointly by a number of workers or customers, working in their common interest. You probably know best the Retail Co-operative Societies, which trade, often in large stores, in town centres. But there are wholesale co-ops and farmers' co-ops which work in the same way. The people who use the firm own it as well. They earn profits based on how much they use the firm.

Most large businesses are like none of these, however. Instead, they set up as joint-stock companies.

Most firms in the UK are owned by people privately, but in a number of different ways. What does each have to offer?

## Checklist – what are the main types of private business?

- sole-traders – owned by one person, for example local shops
- partnerships – owned by a number of partners, for example, solicitors or doctors
- co-operatives – owned by their customers
- private joint-stock companies – owned by a few shareholders with limited liability; shares traded privately
- public joint-stock companies – owned by many shareholders with limited liability; shares traded publicly, on The Stock Exchange

**People and business**

| *Shareholders* own limited companies and appoint . . . |
|---|

| A Board of *Directors* to be in charge of the firm that employs . . . |
|---|

| *Managers* and *workers* to run the business from day to day, and sell to . . . . . . |
|---|

| *Customers* |
|---|

# Buying a share in the news – Reuters go public

In 1851 Paul Julius Reuter began telegraphic transmission of stock market quotations between London and Paris via the new Dover-Calais cable. He had previously used carrier pigeons to deliver stock prices from Brussels to Aachen. Reuter soon extended his service between London and Paris to other European countries and expanded its content to include general and economic news. Although initially serving only financial institutions, by 1858 Reuter was supplying almost all leading European newspapers with general news.

The reputation of Reuter's service was enhanced by a number of scoops. The first of these came in 1859 when Reuter transmitted Napoleon III's Paris speech foreshadowing France's war against Austria later that year. In 1865 Reuter was two days ahead of any other agency in Europe with news of President Lincoln's assassination.

Paul Reuter retired as Managing Director in 1878 and was succeeded by his son, Herbert. Following Herbert's death in 1915, a small group headed by Mark Napier, the chairman, and Roderick Jones, formerly the company's manager in South Africa, bought the entire Reuter shareholding and in 1916 created a private limited company, Reuters Limited.

Reuters has been controlled by the press for nearly 60 years. By 1984 it was owned 42% by The Press Association, 42% by the Newspaper Publishers Association, and the rest by similar bodies from Australia and New Zealand.

The sale of shares in 1984 was expected to raise over £48 m that would be used to expand Reuters operations. The company offered 57 m shares for sale, and applied to The Stock Exchange for its shares to be admitted to the Official list.

(Source – Reuters offer for sale, 16.5.84)

## Questions

1  When was Reuters (a) a family business, (b) a private limited company, (c) a public limited company? (3)
2  Explain the terms (a) director (b) manager (c) shares. (3)
3  Why do you think Reuters chose (a) to become a limited company, (b) to go public, on The Stock Exchange? (4)

## Joint-stock companies

How could you raise more money for your business so that it could grow? One way is to ask a large number of people each to put a little of their money into the firm. If business is good, they earn profits from their share of the company. If business is bad, they stand to lose only what they put in. This is what happens with joint-stock companies.

*Joint-stock companies* are owned by a number of investors. These shareholders each own a part of the company when they buy some of its stock, its ordinary shares. The company is set up in law as a body on its own, and must pay its own bills. Shareholders stand to lose only what they have spent to buy their shares. This gives a limit to their risks, and offers *limited liability*.

You can be more willing to invest in business if you have limited liability. Companies can raise more money this way, and grow into very large businesses. The firm can carry on even if some of its owners lose interest or choose to pull out, because there are others who share the burden. But this works very differently for different types of company. It depends if the shares are bought in private or in public.

## Private and public companies

Joint stock companies are all owned by share-holders, and are all part of the private sector of the economy. But they are of two different types. Private companies are owned by between only two and fifty shareholders. Often the company is quite small, and its owners are members of a family or friends. This may be a good way to own a family hotel, for example, or a local football club. Shares can be bought and sold, but privately, with the agreement of the other owners.

Public limited companies (PLCs) are usually much larger. These have at least seven shareholders, but perhaps many thousands. Shares are offered to the general public, so that pensions funds, insurance companies, you or I can buy them if we wish. Shares are bought and sold second-hand at the Stock Exchange. People are more willing to invest in companies because they know they can sell out this way, quite easily if they need to.

Most of the national companies that we hear of – ICI, Unilever, the Prudential, Lloyds Bank and many, many others – are public limited companies. They have the resources to specialise and produce successfully. They hire experts and make a balanced range of products. But they do face problems in being so large.

The owners may be out of touch with the managers who run the business for them from day to day. Many shareholders are quite glad to leave such detailed control to the experts.

But there can be a gap between customers and owners, or even between staff and owners of the business. Large companies are not always the easiest, or the friendliest, ones to deal with.

# 3.3 Publicly-owned business

Do you know that you are a shareholder? You may not have any shares in private-owned companies, for you need your own private capital to be able to do that. But if you are a citizen of the UK you have a share, of sorts, in the companies run by the nation. Some of your taxes have been used to buy shares in, and to run, publicly-owned business.

*Public enterprise* is when a company is owned by the nation, and run by some part of the government. Government acts as the shareholders, setting the aims of their business and finding managers to run it well. But the government acts for you, as citizen and tax-payer, in this. So, you can have some stake in a large number of different businesses. Let's see what they are.

## What is the public sector?

The Post Office is one of the largest businesses in the land. It is a nationalised industry, and part of public enterprise. Other nationalised industries are also very large, and together they control important areas of business such as travel, power and communications. Rail, electricity, gas and coal are also state-owned.

These industries were *nationalised* some time ago, when the shares of private firms were bought by the government for the nation. More recently, a number have been *privatised*, British National Oil Corporation, Jaguar cars, British Telecom, for example, as the government has sold shares back to private investors.

Nationalised industries are run as *public corporations*. The government acts as shareholders for the nation, and chooses a board of directors to run the business. This board is in overall control of what the firm does, and chooses managers, staff, products and methods of production. The business is expected to work on its own and pay for itself, almost as private companies do.

There are other public corporations that run rather different businesses. Many of these work side by side with private firms – the British Broadcasting Corporation (BBC), for example, is public, but Independent Television is run by private firms.

Other public enterprises are run locally. These are cases of *municipal trading*. Your county council runs bus services and swimming pools, for example, and charges customers for their use. Local authorities set rents to pay towards the cost of council housing.

These are all parts of the public sector of business. You pay as you use each service, in the price of train or bus rides, for example. But tax payers are also charged to set up the firms in the first place, and to pay interest on loans used in that way. They may even pay for losses or investments, year by year. So do you get your money's worth?

What is public enterprise? What special problems are there in running it? Do we need it at all?

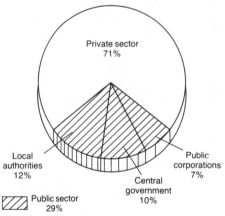

## Jobs in privately and publicly-owned business

Private sector 71%

Local authorities 12%

Public corporations 7%

Central government 10%

Public sector 29%

(Source-Economic Trends, March 1984)

## Checklist – how does a public corporation differ from private business?

- it is owned by the state for all the people and not by private shareholders
- the board that controls the firm is appointed by the government rather than by private shareholders
- it is run in the public interest for its customers and the nation rather than to earn profit for private shareholders

## A service for society

Steel lost £668 million in 1980–81 as a nationalised industry; Rail lost £634 million in 1980. What special problems does public enterprise face to cause such losses?

Private companies are run to serve shareholders and bring in profit. Public corporations are run to serve the nation, which can be very different. Suppose you live off the beaten track or are poor or elderly, for example. You still need transport and power and communication, but cannot afford to pay a profitable price for these services.

British Rail and local bus services do run to distant areas; the electricity grid and post service do cover the whole of the country. Nationalised industries have to run a service for society even if it costs more to run than they can cover with their charges. Some losses are bound to follow.

How to make the railways pay – cut tracks by ⅘, cut business by ½, cut jobs by ⅔: turn a £1 billion loss into a (small) profit.

(Source – Serpell Report, option A, HMSO 1983)

### Questions

1 BR is 'a public enterprise'. What does this mean? (1)
2 Show 2 changes that would help BR to make a profit. (2)
3 What are the differences between the services BR offer to 'passengers and taxpayers'? (3)

## THE CASE FOR KEEPING BRITAIN ON THE RAILS

IF British Rail wants to make a profit, all it needs to do is buy a few sets of buffers.

Buffers at the north end of Newcastle Central station, buffers at Bristol, buffers at Cardiff, buffers at Bournemouth, Edinburgh, Glasgow and Leeds.

Wales and the South-West, most of East Anglia and the whole North of Scotland would become trackless wastes.

Dozens of holiday destinations, tourist spots and sizeable cities would be without railways for the first time in a hundred years.

But cheer up. This plan will save you, the taxpayer, almost £1 billion. It will, according to the Serpell report on the railways, make British Rail a profit of £34 million.

Others believe BR would still make a loss. But that does not really matter, for the loss would be an insignificant part of the national economy.

*The railways would be equally insignificant.*

The plan was designed with passengers, rather than taxpayers, in mind.

In London and the South-East, where people are more tightly-packed than anywhere else, the railways remain by far the most efficient method of moving millions of people daily to and from their work.

There is little doubt that the gap between revenue and cost could be narrowed by raising fares (in the South-East) in real terms. However, this would have effects on road congestion and, possibly, employment.

When Dr Beeching in *his* report tried to save money on the system by lopping off its smaller branches, two things happened which the Serpell report does not cope with at all. . .

Bus services intended to replace branch lines failed to attract the same level of business and frequently died out within a few years.

The second effect was a loss of business on the main lines – because those who could not start their journey by rail saw no reason to finish it on a train.

The same applies to freight. If the branch line to a coal mine is closed, the coal is unlikely to be moved anywhere by rail.

If power stations lose their rail links, they too will have to receive all their supplies of coal by a road system which would rapidly become clogged.

Daily Express, 21.1.83

How are losses paid for? Some are covered by profitable services in other parts of a large nationalised industry. But it is not very fair if customers in the south pay more to help customers in the far north pay less. A better way may be for the government to give *subsidies*, that grant money to cover chosen social services. Taxpayers pay for this as a whole.

# Too big for comfort

Why else may there be losses? Could it be that industry does not work as well when it is nationalised? There are two reasons why this may be so.

Publicly-owned business cannot 'go bust' in the same way as private business. It is backed by the state, and the government can raise enough money from taxes and loans to pay almost any amount of loss. Managers and workers in private firms lose their jobs if their firms suffer a loss and 'go bust'. Managers and workers in the public sector feel saved from this. So they may try less hard to make their firms work well, to cut costs, and earn profits.

Many nationalised industries are protected in another way as well. They are so large they face no competition, but are the only firms selling in their own field. They are monopolies, so customers cannot choose to buy from other firms instead. Worse still, customers often cannot choose to go *without* the product either, for services such as power and travel are very important to us all.

Why does it matter if a firm is a monopoly? For nationalised industries it means that they can take less notice of what their customers want. Prices may be set too high, or products be of poor quality. There may be delays and bad service.

# How should public enterprise run?

There are problems in running public enterprise well, but many can be overcome. The government can find ways to help to cut costs and to serve customers and the nation in the best possible way.

The government can set clear aims for its businesses. It can make managers keep to those targets and replace them if they fail. It can raise the risks of competition, in the way nationalised industries sell against each other, or against firms abroad. Coal, gas and electricity, for example, must try to sell better than each other to the same customers.

There are 'watchdogs' to make sure that public enterprise works well. Parliament controls the government, and there is a committee of MPs to study the work of nationalised industries. Each industry has its own body to represent consumers and take up complaints from customers. The Office of Fair Trading can take steps to look into bad practice that follows from a nationalised monopoly.

Is all this enough? To some people it clearly is not. They feel that publicly-owned businesses will nearly always work less well than privately-owned businesses. They believe that state enterprise should be returned to the private sector, to cut costs and make profits.

But what of social services? These could still be offered, perhaps, if the government laid down rules asking for chosen services in certain areas. British Telecom, for example, has to keep open its network of phone boxes around the country. And what of monopolies? Public monopolies would become private monopolies with the power to raise profit at their customers' expense. Perhaps this could be controlled by the Office of Fair Trading, but perhaps not. This is the issue we meet more fully in Section 4.7.

# 'THIRD-RATE' STATE FIRMS

The public would not tolerate State monopolies in food. Imagine – nationalised food: no Sainsbury's, no Tesco, no Co-op, no neighbourhood grocer. Just one State-controlled concern.

In comparison with private sector companies the message is clear: Public enterprises perform relatively poorly in terms of their competitive position, use labour and capital inefficiently, and are less profitable.

Surveys of the customers of nationalised industries have discovered a pervasive discontent with declining standards while anecdotes recounting examples of poor service from nationalised industries are legion.

My judgment is that the nation cannot tolerate a third-rate performance for a significant proportion of its productive capacity.

Mr John Moore, Minister in charge of the Government's privatisation policy, in a speech to City stockbrokers, 1.11.83

## Questions

1 Explain the term 'state monopoly'. Why do you think the public 'would not tolerate nationalised food'? (2)
2 Give 2 reasons why public enterprises 'are less profitable than private sector companies'. (2)

Firms use inputs to make their products, but at a cost. Why do costs change, and how does that affect output?

How do you make something even as simple as a plastic kit bought from a toy shop? You use the parts, glue and instructions with your own labour and that of the people you call for help. These are *inputs* of resources used in production. You end up with an *output*, which is the finished product made from the resources. You have a boat, plane or horse, say, or some strange mix of all three if you go wrong!

All production works in the same way. Firms hire resources to work for them as factors of production. They buy inputs of materials, labour and machinery. They put materials together in the best way they know how, perhaps to make something simple such as a clay pot or complicated such as a car.

We know that firms face choices along the way. They must choose what to make, how to make it, and how much of it to make. They end up with an output they can supply to their customers, but at a cost. Inputs must be bought and output must be sold at a price to cover the firm's costs. What are these costs?

## What are a firm's inputs?

What must you use to make a plastic kit toy? Clearly there are parts and your own time. But in economics we see inputs in terms of factors of production. Land is the space used for production, but also the sites that are used to find raw materials. The materials you buy in a kit are like the materials that most firms buy – they have been made by other producers using other factors. Even crude oil is a product, extracted from the ground using machines, labour and so on.

Capital is tools and equipment, stocks and money. Labour is the human effort put in with your hands or by using your mind. Enterprise is the last factor used, to take the risk of hiring land, capital and labour, and to fit them all together knowing that plans might go wrong.

All inputs have a cost. Most are hired, by paying the people who own factors of production. You expect to be paid, for example, if you work as labour. Land is paid rent, capital is paid interest, labour is paid wages and enterprise earns profit. But even where no money is paid there is still a cost. You could have done something else with your time instead of building a kit. Workers could do things other than work for one firm. There is an opportunity cost when a firm hires them because they give up doing something else.

## Millions from under the sea

It seems fantastic, but oil is now being extracted by Britain from the North Sea at the rate of over £54 million A DAY.

Only the United States, Saudi Arabia and the Soviet Union produce more than our output of 2.5 million barrels a day.

Of course the weather has a great effect on profitability in one of the most difficult oil fields in the world but, tremendous sums of money are being generated off our shores – and are also being spent in extracting the oil.

As most of us might guess, drilling for oil is expensive. A well should take around 70 to 90 days to drill, costing up to £5.25 million.

But in a business where profits seesaw so do costs. Take sophisticated, new-design rigs. Suddenly there are too many of them on the hire market, so charges have tumbled. Rig-hire now costs just over £14 000 per day, compared with over £52 000 early last year.

You may have 160 men on a rig at any one time, with another shift standing by on shore. Only the men offshore are paid.

A skilled driller earns £12 per hour. He is paid 12 hours a day, seven days a week while on the rig or platform (a rig floats).

The men's laundry and breakfasts, main meals and light refreshments (tea, coffee, milk, fruit juice is always available free) costs up to £18 per man per day.

There are 66,746 men now working with North Sea oil.

A supply boat costs £2000 to £3000 per day depending on the size. And when you use helicopters a 44-seater Chinook is £555 per hour.

But all these costs are nothing seen in the context of the sheer volume of oil coming up.

Daily Mail, 5.3.84

### Questions

1  List 4 inputs that a firm must buy in order to drill oil from the North Sea. (1)
2  Work out, as best you can, the cost of drilling for oil for one extra day. (2)

# How do firms measure costs?

How much does it cost a firm to hire its factors of production and make its output? There are different ways to measure this, and each of them is used for a different reason.

How much does it cost to buy all the inputs used by the firm over a certain period of time? This is measured by *total cost*. Suppose the firm buys twice as many inputs, perhaps doubling the size of its factory. As long as each input's price is the same as before, then total costs double. But how much does it cost to produce each *part* of output? For this we need different measures.

*Average cost* measures the cost of making each product. Say it costs £100 to make ten kits, then the average cost of each kit is $\frac{£100}{10} = £10$.

In general we find average cost by dividing total cost by the total level of output. This tells us how the firm has done overall, but does not give any clue to the cost of making one more product. This extra cost may be either higher or lower than the average.

*Marginal cost* measures the extra cost of making one extra product. You may be very tired of making kits so that it takes you longer to make one more. Marginal cost may rise to £15, perhaps. Each part of production has its own cost, and it is the sum of those marginal costs that makes up the total cost of production. The rise in total costs at each stage, when one extra product is added to output, is how we find marginal cost.

These measures may be difficult to understand until you get used to using them. Firms use them all the time. They measure total costs to see how much they are spending on inputs. They use average cost to see how much they must make from selling each unit to pay for its cost of production. If they fail to cover average cost with price, they 'go bust'. But it is marginal cost that helps to show if they are making too much output or too little. It allows them to set what they gain from sales against the extra cost of making extra output.

**Drilling for oil – production from the North Sea**

## Checklist – how to measure costs?

● total cost measures payments for all inputs – those that are fixed for a time and those that are variable, and change with output
● average cost measures the payment made to produce each unit of output, on average
● marginal cost measures the extra payment made to produce one extra product

# Why do costs change?

Is there any way a firm can cut its costs?

There are a number of ways it can, but some are more sensible than others. Every firm wants to cut its costs by buying inputs as cheaply as possible and using them in the best way. It aims to make its output for as low a cost as is possible, given what it knows about methods of production. So all measures of cost take the lowest possible cost for that level of output.

Output can change, however. A firm can hire less inputs and make less output. This usually cuts costs. But payments for overheads take time to change and are *fixed costs* in the short term. Payments for materials and labour are more changeable and make up *variable costs*. These cause total costs to fall and rise with output. But how much? Output may have to fall a lot or a little in order to cut total costs.

Suppose the firm stays the same size but tries to change its output. Inputs such as buildings and machinery are kept the same, but inputs such as labour and materials are changed. At low levels of output the firm needs extra factors to gain from specialisation, and total costs rise more slowly than output. At high levels of output the extra factors will crowd things, so that total costs rise faster than output.

But what if the firm changes output by changing its size and use of all inputs together? Small firms may gain by growing because they find economies of scale. Firms that are already too large become difficult to control and suffer diseconomies of scale. We will see how this happens in Section 3.6.

Costs may change for other reasons, of course, that the firm cannot help. The prices of factors are set by supply and demand, from many different workers and many different firms. A fall in price helps all firms to cut costs, but a rise puts costs up. So costs change from time to time even if output does not.

---

## Measuring costs

A firm measures its total costs at four levels of output, each week –

| Output | Cost |
|--------|------|
| 0 | £100 |
| 1 | £150 |
| 2 | £180 |
| 3 | £240 |

- fixed costs cover the rent of buildings, rates and other overhead expenses. These are shown by the £100 it costs to make nothing at all.
- variable costs rise as output rises, at first by less because of division of labour, but then by more as inputs do not work together so well.
- average cost is found from total cost over output – the average cost of making 2 products, for example, is

$$\frac{£180}{2} = £90$$

- marginal cost is found from the rise in total cost when output rises by 1. The extra cost of making the second product, for example, is

$$\frac{£180 - £150}{1} = £30$$

### Questions

1 Suppose fixed costs double. What is the new level of total cost for making 2 products? (1)
2 From the table shown, what is the variable cost of making (a) 1 (b) 3 products? (1)
3 Similarly, what is the average cost of making (a) 1, (b) 3 products? (1)
4 Similarly, what is the marginal cost of making (a) 1st, (b) 3rd product? (1)

# How do costs affect output?

What could lead you to make up kits for a living? Someone would have to offer you a price which more than paid for the cost of production. It is so with all firms.

Firms produce for profit. They make profit if they earn money from sales, called revenue, that more than covers costs. If revenue covers costs, then the firm can stay in production. If revenue does not cover costs, the firm should think of closing down. So a rise in costs, for whatever reason, is bad news. At the same level of price it makes production more difficult. It might make some firms go bust and make others cut their output. A fall in costs should do the opposite and raise output. You might even try to make up more kits for sale if you could make extra profit by doing so.

**'The world's biggest bankrupt'**
In 1978 Mr William Stern, a property dealer, was declared bankrupt. He owed £100 million, but had only £10 070 with which to pay. As the judge said, 'this bankruptcy has been described as the world's biggest, but really it is a very ordinary bankruptcy with noughts at the end.'

(Source – Stephen Pile, The Book of Heroic Failures, Book Club Assocn. 1980)

## Houseplant industry wilts under growing costs

The decision by one of Britain's largest growers of potted plants to close its 25 acres of glasshouses in Hertfordshire's Lea Valley this autumn has sent shivers down the spines of other horticulturists.

"Tom's weeds" was the title given to the Rochford venture by *The Tatler* in the early days after the war when potted plants began appearing in sitting-rooms all over Britain.

However, for the next 30 years or so the market boomed, and Rochford, with an annual production of between 3 000 000 and 4 000 000 plants at its peak, was ideally placed to take advantage of this growth. By last year it shared about 10 per cent of the total market.

In the last three years or so, however, while the number of potted plants sold has continued to rise steadily, profit margins have fallen so low that many growers are barely making a profit. Rochford and Sons, whose houseplants business accounts for roughly three-quarters of the group's £4.7m annual turnover, has accumulated a loss of more than £1m since 1981.

Costs have risen, of course, with inflation. But one of the greatest problems for Rochford and other potted plant growers has been the stagnation in wholesale prices.

In December 1979 the wholesale price of a home-grown African violet was 42½p. In 1984 the price was only slightly higher at 44p. It sells in the shops at between 75p and 95p.

British growers blame a combination of factors for the levelling-out of prices. They include increased competition from Continental producers, principally the Dutch, as well as negotiated deals at rock-bottom prices by multiple stores, such as Marks & Spencer and Tesco, which tend to set the level for other retail outlets.
The Times, 8.5.84

### WINDOW-SILL ECONOMICS

**HOW THE PRICE (WHOLESALE) OF HOUSEPLANTS HAS REMAINED STATIC** Typical African Violet in 9cm pot

1979 42.5p
1980 42p
1981 36p
1982 43.2p
1983 43.3p
1984 44.2p

**BREAKDOWN OF HOUSEPLANT COSTS**

75–95p

MARKETING 15% Plastic sleeve, label, packaging, transport

MATERIAL Compost, stock 10%

35% ENERGY Heating, lighting –usually oil

30% LABOUR Potting up, spacing out, preparing for market, labelling

OVERHEADS 7% Glasshouse depreciation, maintenance, water, pesticides, fertilisers

PROFIT 3%

## Questions

1  What share of houseplant costs appear to be variable? (1)
2  Explain why Rochford and Sons houseplants business went bust. (2)

# 3.5 Big or small – the growth of firms

Why do some firms stay small while others grow large?
How do firms grow anyway?

**The scale of manufacturing industry**
In every 10 firms typical of manufacturing industry in the UK:

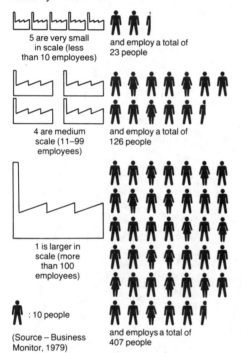

5 are very small in scale (less than 10 employees)

and employ a total of 23 people

4 are medium scale (11–99 employees)

and employ a total of 126 people

1 is larger in scale (more than 100 employees)

: 10 people

(Source – Business Monitor, 1979)

and employs a total of 407 people

## Question

1 Explain why you would expect (a) a local shop (b) a national bank, to be small or large in scale. (1)

## Checklist – how can firms grow?

- internally by using their own resources, or externally by joining up with other companies
- horizontally at the same stage of production in the same industry
- vertically to a different stage of production of the same products
- diversifying to produce different sorts of products as parts of different industries

Imagine you were looking round for a job. There might be jobs available in a small newspaper shop nearby, or in the local garage, selling and servicing cars, or in a factory in town. Would you prefer to get a job in a small firm where you would know all the others working there, or in a large one with many branches and different activities?

Let us look at ten typical manufacturing firms which have vacancies for you.

The first five firms are very *small in scale*. They each employ ten or fewer people and have little in the way of machines and buildings. You would work closely with all the other employees, probably on one site only. You would probably offer an individual service to your customers in a small area. Less than twenty-five people work for these five firms all together.

The next four firms on your short list employ between eleven and ninety-nine people each. These are *medium-scale*. They might run a number of different operations, and you might work in any one of a number of sections. Work would be more specialised and opportunity somewhat greater, for these four firms offer 126 jobs in all.

The last firm on your short list employs one hundred or more people, in what we call *large-scale production*. This is likely to involve mass production of a range of widely-sold goods, such as cosmetics, kettles or lager. Your own section of the firm may be quite small but you are likely to feel part of a large organisation.

You may be more remote from both customers and the owners of the business but have a better chance of finding work that suits you best. More than 400 people work for this one firm, and it also owns more equipment and buildings than the other nine smaller firms together.

It follows that most firms are small in scale, but that most jobs (three-quarters of the total in manufacturing industry) are in large-scale units. Your chances of working for the tenth firm on the short list are much greater than for the other nine.

## Internal and external growth

How would a firm that you work for expand and grow? It would need more workers, more machines and more land to increase the scale of production. But what would be the best way to buy them?

Should the firm grow internally or externally? Internal growth comes when a firm uses more factors of production in its own operations. 'More' might mean taking on extra workers or buying more machines, or it might mean using better quality factors such as more highly skilled workers or more modern equipment. For example, a car firm might employ extra workers on a new production line in order to launch a new model it has designed. A firm can make a clean start this way, using the newest machines and the latest methods. There are risks, however, for it takes time to start production and it is not easy to break into markets dominated by other firms.

External growth comes when a firm merges with or takes over another firm. A *merger* is where the owners of two firms agree to join together to form one bigger company. A *takeover* is when owners of one firm buy control of another, to include it as part of their own operations. External growth can be fast. It can get a company involved in a large number of new products and new sales areas, or it can strengthen what it is already doing.

# Vertical, horizontal and diversified growth

In which direction would you want your firm to grow? There are different stages in production, as raw materials are made into products that are sold to consumers. There are also many different types of products each made by different industries. A small firm is likely to be working on only one stage of production in one industry. Should it grow by producing more of the same product or take on more stages of the same production, or branch into a completely different industry?

*Horizontal integration* is growth at the same stage of production and in the same industry. A merger of two chains of petrol-selling stations is of this type. It gives the firm a larger share of the market and, it is hoped, a chance to sell its product more successfully.

*Vertical integration* is growth to a different stage of production of the same good or service. An oil-refining firm that opens its own petrol-selling stations grows forwards in this way, towards the consumers who buy its product. If the same firm then opens its own oil fields it grows backwards towards its source of raw materials. Vertical growth gives a firm more security, a chance to cut costs and to sell more successfully.

Growth may be neither horizontal nor vertical. A firm may enter a quite different field of production to *diversify*. A petrol service station grows in this way if it opens a café or sells toys. A cigarette manufacturer may diversify into food retailing. An oil company might buy an American coal-mining firm. This sort of growth is known as *conglomerate growth*.

# Why grow?

The growth of a firm affects its customers, workers and shareholders in different ways. Customers might lose the personal service they had grown used to, but gain a greater choice of products and outlets. Workers might lose some involvement, personal contact and range of work. They may gain, however, if there are more opportunities for specialisation and promotion within the larger firm – or even lose their job in a resulting 'shake-up' or 'rationalisation' within the firm. These are the matters you would need to consider in choosing the size of firm you want to work for.

But it is the owners of a firm and the managers they employ who must

## The Story of Morris

**1912 – Morris**
William Morris makes his first car, the Morris Oxford. Buys in components from other firms, even engines from the USA, and assembles them at Oxford. Output grows.

**1951 – BMC**
Morris merges with Austin, but keeps separate models and dealer networks.

**1961 – BMC**
BMC merges with Pressed-Steel Fisher who make most of their car bodies.

**1968 – British Leyland**
BMC merges with Leyland trucks, 'Morris' cars kept as the name for more standard, basic cars for company use.

**1984**
The last car with the Morris name – the Ital – stops production.

## Question

1  What sort of growth did Morris cars show (a) at first, after 1912, (b) in 1951, (c) in 1961? (3)

## Checklist – should a firm aim to grow?

- large firms may spread the risks of business, control their markets, and gain economies of scale
- growing firms may be more flexible or profitable
- but small firms may be more specialised and make better local or personal contacts

decide whether the firm grows or not. What can they gain from making their firm larger?

Growth may reduce risk. A company which diversifies is not so dependent upon its success in one market. If one market declines it can still sell in other markets. A company which grows vertically can gain greater control over buyers and sellers, making these operations serve its needs rather than the needs of others. A company which grows horizontally can gain greater control over its market.

Once a firm starts to grow it may do better and better. It may be able to grow even faster in the future. It may see growth as a way to increase profit.

---

## Bouquets to last for ever

'MY forte is creating a very special personal gift or memento,' says Jean Gilbert, explaining why she is not intent on expanding her business.

Her main job of pressing, preserving and framing bridal bouquets.

Her prices for a framed bridal bouquet design range from £40 to £350. At the top end of the range the frames are finished with real gold leaf. All of them carry an inscription in gold leaf, a skill Jean went on a course in illumination to perfect.

Jean now advertises more widely, and has also branched out with a couple of other projects, including gifts for bridesmaids, jewellery, and a do-it-yourself flower picture kit, production of which she started with the aid of a £5000 bank loan.

'Feeling that I offer rather a luxury service, I wondered if orders would begin to drop off as a result of the recession, and thought it might be wise to diversify a little,' says Jean.

Her fears were groundless, however, and she finds she is dealing with as many as 100 weddings a month in the peak season.

Jean's business has expanded to the extent that she now employs between three and seven people mostly on a part-time basis, and new premises had to be found last year.

But the business is still relatively small. Jean estimates that turnover for the year ending in May 1984, will be around £40000.

'I could make more money going out to work as a secretary,' she says. But she wouldn't get half the satisfaction.

Daily Mail, 8.2.84

### Questions

1 What do you understand by the terms (a) expanding a business, (b) diversify? (2)
2 Jean Gilbert's business is still small. What are the advantages of this (a) to her, (b) to her customers? (2)
3 How might the business gain from further growth? (2)

---

Renault lost nearly £50 m when they bought a new process for making instant coffee, and 2 new factories to use it. The process did not work, its 'inventor' disappeared, and Renault made not one bean of profit!

## Why stay small?

Why then do firms that start small often stay small? One reason is that it may be difficult to sell any more. Size depends on the state of the market. The firm may sell to customers who are all in different areas. The product may be difficult to carry very far, or customers may not want to travel to buy it. Shops selling fruit and vegetables or newspapers are like this.

Customers may demand specialised and individual service. They may want to choose what and where they buy from a wide range. Hairdressing and high fashion clothes are like this.

Some markets are suited to mass production and others are not. Batteries are standard products, and can be made and sold in large numbers. Antique furniture is different – customers are not pleased to see a number of 'unique' pieces just like theirs!

Some firms do not wish to grow too large. Their owners may enjoy being in full control or in everyday contact with all their staff and customers. They may not want to take on the risks and change that come with growth.

Lastly, there are many areas of production where small firms can be as efficient as large, and produce at the same, or even lower cost. Growth may raise the cost of making each product if there are diseconomies of scale. It can be true that 'small is beautiful' in production.

Mabel and Doris run a cake stall in the market. Once a week they make ten or twenty cakes in Doris's kitchen and sell them at the market. Now they have an order for 100 a week from the tea shop in town. Should they take it on?

They would need more mixing bowls and other equipment and somewhere larger to work. They would have to increase their *scale of production*.

But they could afford to buy a bigger and better food mixer and a new large oven with special features. 'If we make 100 cakes instead of ten each one will cost us less. We will make more money,' they think.

*Economies of scale* come when a firm cuts costs by growing larger. The scale of operation rises because there are more of all factors of production together. Total costs rise, but not as much as output. The cost of making each product, therefore, is less. Production becomes more economical, and this cuts the costs of making each unit of output. Double the output causes costs to rise by less than double. This changes the average cost curve of the firm.

## Why do average costs fall?

Let us say that the average cost of making each cake in a batch of ten is 100p. Double the output, to twenty, causes average costs to fall, perhaps to 90p for each cake. Economies of scale cause average costs to fall over the long term as shown in the figure. At an output level of 100 cakes average costs are lower still – at only 60p each. (See figure 1.)

Large-scale production allows a firm to keep costs down in many different ways, depending on the situation of the firm. It is helpful, though, to take five main forms of economies. All of these can help Mabel and Doris and most other producers in the economy.

First there are *technical economies*. Mabel and Doris would hope to use more and better equipment. Many machines cannot be divided into smaller parts – they must be bought as one large item to make a high level of output or not at all.

Tools need to be used together, and to fit in well with the work load. It is costly to leave an expensive machine standing idle, perhaps because there are not enough smaller tools to load or unload it.

The returns from using large machines and buildings rise faster than the cost of running them. A large oven costs little more to buy or to heat than a small one, but it can hold much more at one time. The same idea explains why there are large oil tankers, gas holders and discount warehouses.

Next there are *marketing* economies. Doris knows that the prices of materials are nearly always lower for bulk. You can buy packets of several chocolate bars at a time at a reduced price. You can get a season ticket for less than all the daily fares added up.

What are economies of scale? What makes firms more or less able to gain from them.

**Think big, and cut costs**

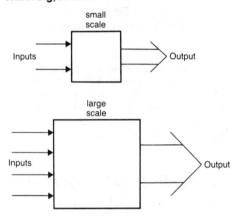

Large machines and organisations can work better – double the inputs can lead to *more* than double the output.

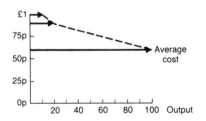

*figure 1 – economies of scale cut average costs*

| Output (per week) | Average cost (£) |
| --- | --- |
| 10 | 1.00 |
| 20 | .90 |
| 100 | .60 |

**Where cows make way for machines**

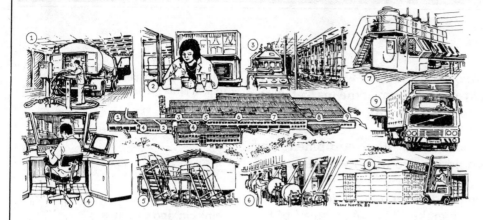

Kallhäll Dairy in Stockholm – one of the newest, and largest in Sweden.

1) Milk reception area – computers monitor deliveries from 34 tonne tankers, 350 000 litres a day. Milk is checked and put in 8 cold store tanks.

2) Laboratory – to help find new milk products, such as milk and fruit juice, or yogurt for stomach ache. New products can take years to develop.
3) Processing – 4 automatic production lines making 25 different products – milk, cream, yogurt, sour cream, and so on.

4) Computer control centre – computers cut the workforce from 260 to 220, but are kept as different machines, to be simple and flexible, to allow for changing tastes and products.
5) 6) 7) 8) Packing into paper cartons – 4500 an hour made automatically from rolls of card, and carried by robot trucks and overhead conveyors.
9) Dispatch to customers – workers sort, and check deliveries.

Financial Times, 18.6.84

## Questions

1 What are economies of scale? Show how this dairy gains an economy of scale in (a) milk reception, (b) its laboratory and (c) packing. What type of economy is each? (3)
2 How might a larger scale of production bring diseconomies of scale? (3)

## Checklist – what gives economies of scale?

● technical advantages from large and balanced use of machines
● marketing gains from bulk buying and selling
● financial advantages in spreading risks
● managerial advantages from the use of experts
● research and development – where costs and risks again can be spread

It takes almost as much work to arrange a sale of 100 cakes to one buyer as it does to sell one. But selling costs can be shared across much more output.

Large firms gain from *financial economies* because they can borrow money and use it better than some small ones. They are more often secure because they can spread their risks. They invest in a number of different operations and if any one of them fails the firm can still rely on the others.

*Managerial economies* come from the use of experts. Large firms can hire specialists such as lawyers or accountants full time.

The same holds with *research and development*. It costs a great deal to set up and to run a research organisation. Firms must be large if they are to afford to do so.

## Internal and external

All of these gains from scale come from improvements within the firm. They are *internal* economies, because the firm makes better use of its own factors of production. Some firms are likely to gain much more than others in these ways.

Other advantages are possible as a firm grows, but they are *external*. All firms in an industry gain at the same time as the whole industry grows. Usually this is caused by the *concentration* of one industry in a certain area, as we see in the next section.

Clothes shops are often set close to one another in a town centre. As you walk down the High Street you see many different stores – Dorothy Perkins, Richard Shops, Chelsea Girl for girls, Burtons, Hepworths, Horne Brothers for men. These shops compete with one another and yet choose to be near to each other. Why is this?

They gain more than they lose from concentration. They are well placed for both customers and staff, who know where to find them, for the best choice of clothes or work. Specialist services are set up to work for all these shops together. Window cleaning, security collections of takings, and perhaps deliveries of materials, are made easier.

# Diseconomies

Can firms ever grow too large? Is there some high level of output at which economies of scale begin to be replaced by diseconomies?

For most firms the answer is yes. More and larger machines carry a risk that they may break down or become out of date. Large supertankers are an efficient way to carry oil, but are very costly to maintain in a recession, when there is no longer work for them to do. An expensive specialised production line builds cars as cheaply as possible, but can be stopped by a strike of workers at any stage. It may also be difficult to adapt to new work if consumers do not wish to buy its products.

More important still is the problem of management. Larger organisations are more and more difficult to control. Resources begin to be wasted and mistakes are made. Other problems can usually be avoided – a good factory design can be repeated, in small and separate units. But the problem of fitting all units together, and managing them in the best way, often remains.

*Diseconomies of scale* may and do arise. They raise the cost of making each unit of production. They cause average costs to rise, but only when a firm becomes too large.

Figure 2 shows a firm that can produce a wide range of output. As output rises, average costs fall at first due to economies of scale. At output level 0 they are as low as possible. Above that output level there are diseconomies of scale and average costs begin to rise.

Concentration brings external economies of scale.

## Questions

1  Many clothes shops are run by multiples. Show 2 internal economies of scale that they can gain from. (2)
2  Why may it be difficult for shoppers to gain from bulk buying? (2)

# The optimum size of a firm

The firm tries to produce each output level as cheaply as possible, and to choose the one and only output level at which profit is greatest. But in another sense, output level 0 is the best of all, not to the firm who is interested only in profit, and therefore must compare cost to revenue, but to the nation as a whole. We need each firm to use resources in the best way, and to produce as cheaply as it can. In terms of the national interest, output level 0 is the *optimum size* of the firm.

What is this size in the different parts of UK industry? Clearly it must vary a lot from case to case. British Leyland made almost 700 000 vehicles in 1979, but was perhaps still below its optimum size. Toyota of Japan produced four times as many to gain fullest advantage from economies of scale. But production of specialist vehicles like Rolls Royce or Morgan sports cars needs to be limited. This keeps up standards of finish and meets the market demand for an exclusive product. Chateau Latour discards up to a third of its wine each year to maintain the quality of the little it sells. The optimum size of a great vineyard is really quite small.

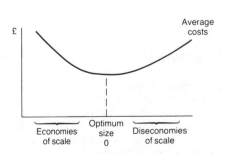

*figure 2 - too big or too small?*

# 3.7 Where to set up shop? The location of production

How do firms first choose where to set up in production? It is largely a matter of costs – the costs of getting resources, and of supplying customers.

**Who built Heathrow airport's new terminal?**

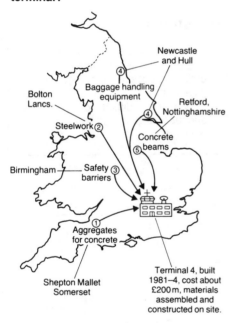

Terminal 4, built 1981–4, cost about £200m, materials assembled and constructed on site.

## Questions

1 Suggest a possible reason why gravel for making concrete comes from Somerset but safety barriers come from Birmingham (2)
2 Suggest 2 reasons why the UK's main airport is at Heathrow, in West London. (2)

Is it better to do business in the north or the south? In a city or out of town? We can see how a firm chooses its *location* as the best place to produce. Let's say that James Brothers have invented a new product – disposable scissors. Now they must set up a small new factory, but where should it go?

They are very like other firms and hire factors of production nearby. They must try to put together land, labour, capital and enterprise to make their output as cheaply as possible.

Location makes a big difference to costs. If the firm sets up on a good site then costs will stay low. But if James Brothers choose badly and set up in the wrong place then costs may be too high and the firm may go bust. Once they have set up it may be more difficult to move again. The firm owns or rents a site and has its machines set down there. Workers live nearby and both customers and suppliers may come from the local area.

So James Brothers are lucky to choose from scratch. They can find any site in the country for their factory. Most firms cannot, but are tied down by the work they do already.

## Supply of materials

Should James Brothers put their factory close to its sources of materials? Every firm must buy inputs such as steel, plastics or packaging. These all have to be delivered, and the firm can cut its transport costs if it goes closer to its suppliers.

It may make little difference where the work is sited – in Glasgow or Guildford. Good roads and railways make for fast and easy transport to most of the larger industrial sites. Electric power, post and phone services are available throughout the country. But the cost of land and other resources may differ greatly from place to place. Also there are many firms that need to be close to their raw materials. Coalmining must be on coalfields, farms must use suitable land, fishing boats must use ports and get to the best fishing areas at sea. Primary industries as a whole are based where they can extract their raw materials from land or sea.

Heavy manufacturing industries may be the same. Steel-making uses great heat, so its firms are often found near coalfields, in South Wales and Sheffield. Perhaps James Brothers could make their disposable scissors in one of these steel-making areas? It depends how much it costs the firm to have its raw materials delivered. There may be other costs that are more important.

# Workers and services

A firm does not only buy raw materials for its inputs. Where are the workers to come from, and people to service the machines or to advise the business? Sometimes these are all quite specialised and difficult to find except in certain parts of the country.

What could James Brothers find in a steel-making area, for example, to help them make disposable scissors? There would be workers used to steel-work, with the right skills and background. There would be other firms to act as back-up, to keep machines working well, to give advice in the special problems of the business, or to find buyers interested in steel goods. There are gains, therefore, if firms in an industry group together. They gain *external economies* of scale, that cut the costs of them all.

Suppose the needs of the firm are less specialised? Then it may wish only to find the right number of workers at the right cost who can do the work. Perhaps it should choose an area of high unemployment. But will this be the best place to sell from?

# Finding customers

Clearly a firm must find customers for its product if it is to make money. But there are delivery costs in transporting the finished product to its customers. There are also costs in telling people about the product and making them interested. People will not buy disposable scissors, for example, unless they know about them and see them to buy. So should the firm go close to its customers?

Selling costs may be much greater than the other costs of the firm when it collects its inputs. If so, it makes sense to find the market, the place where customers buy the product. The firm can then set up shop close to the market. But will this be in just one place?

## Checklist – how do firms choose the best location?

- aim to keep costs as low as possible
- so keep close to their supplies of materials
- but also keep close to their buyers
- and take account of the wishes of people in the firm, and the effect of government policies

---

## COMMODORE MOVES TO CORBY

COMMODORE, one of the world's leading manufacturers of personal computers, yesterday confirmed its decision to establish a mass production plant in the steel-closure town of Corby, Northamptonshire.

The Canada-based multinational, which is producing 150000 microcomputers a month from its advance factory in Corby, will increase capacity to 350000 units a month when the permanent plant opens in September. This will make the UK its main manufacturing base for personal computers.

Production of the company's two biggest selling machines – the VIC 20 and the Commmodore 64 – will be transferred to the new plant from Braunschweig, West Germany. The German plant will concentrate on computers for business. Two-thirds of the UK output will be exported.

The company hopes to be employing 600 people by the end of the year, and this figure is expected to rise to 1000 in two years' time. The present factory is already employing more than 200, 70 per cent of whom are under the age of 25.

Mr Howard Stanworth, general manager of Commodore Business Machines UK said government grants were a significant factor in attracting Commodore to the UK. He added that he thought Britain was the best place to be for microcomputer production.

Mr Kenneth Baker, In-formation Technology Minister, said he was delighted with the project, which involves an initial investment of about £6m rising to £20m by 1986.

"This is not a minor involvement, but a major one," Mr Baker said. He claimed the UK's attitude towards free trade had played a significant part in persuading the company to expand its UK operations. "First they were selling here and now they have decided to manufacture here."

Commodore claims to have sold more than 800000 computers in the UK, and sales grew about threefold in the second half of last year.

Financial Times, 21.3.84

### Questions

1. Find 2 reasons why Britain may be the 'last place' for producing personal micro computers. (2)
2. Much of the computing industry is concentrated in the Thames Valley. Suggest a reason for this, and for Commodore setting up well away from there, at Corby in the Midlands. (2)
3. How would you expect Commodore's decision to affect the people of Corby and the type of firms based there? (2)

Some markets are *concentrated* because customers are found all in one place or nearby. The work of the City of London, for example, is often like this. People buy some specialised services in and around just one building. So if you sell shipping, you should be close to the Baltic Exchange; if you sell commodities such as rubber or jute, the London Commodity Exchange; if stocks and shares, the Stock Exchange; and if insurance then Lloyds of London.

Concentrated markets attract *subsidiary* firms. These sell different products that are useful, perhaps as inputs, in the main market. Disposable scissors may sell best in areas of office blocks, where most paperwork is done, or close to schools. It is more likely, however, that people will buy disposable scissors wherever they live or work. Customers may be scattered far and wide across the country.

*Scattered* markets are spread wide because customers buy products in many different areas. This is so with many personal services, for example. People use hairdressers, post offices and builders, close to wherever they live and work. Local shops sell to local people, so newsagents, greengrocers and bakers are scattered across the country.

There is another reason for this, however. Some products, such as scissors, can be stored and carried from place to place. But foodstuffs may not last longer than a few hours or days. Hairdressing, cafés and take-aways have to do their work at the shop. These products are not durable and cannot wait while the firms try to find customers. So they must be sold locally.

## North or south?

James Brothers must now decide. They can set up their factory in the north, close to other steel firms and to their materials. Or they can set up in the south close to where more people live and work, and where they expect to sell most of their product. Which should they choose?

In both places they have good roads that put them in touch with materials, or customers, only a few hours' driving time away. Technical changes give them better machines and methods of production. No longer do firms need workers with traditional skills, nor do they have to work in just one place. But once set up, it is difficult to change. Only a small number of firms move to new areas. Most work with fixed buildings, sites and equipment. So poor areas with weak industries seem to stay like that. They may even become worse if firms move out to set up closer to customers in richer areas.

James Brothers may feel like this. The owners and managers may want to work in just one area, perhaps the one they know or like best. They may be guided by government in a big way. The government cuts the cost of working in some areas, and puts firms off setting up in others. This can become the most important cost of all to firms. We see how in the next section.

Why are some industries concentrated, and others scattered?

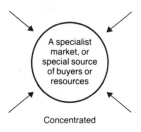

Concentrated

Scattered

# 3.8 Government, industry and the regions

Do you live in the south-east of England, or in one of the regions to the north and west, or in Wales, Scotland or Northern Ireland? Over the last twenty years the government has paid about £1000 for each worker in the UK to the poorer regions of the country. Do you know anyone working in the steel industry? The government paid for losses worth over £5500 for each worker in the industry in 1980 to 1981. Why does the government spend money in these ways – what problems is it trying to beat?

The regional problem is one of differences in incomes and unemployment which are too great between different regions of the country. Regions such as Northern Ireland and the north-east of England are much worse off than the south and south-east. Inner-city areas such as Toxteth in Liverpool are much worse off than suburban areas on the outskirts of cities.

What is it like to live in an area with regional problems? Your chances of finding a job are low. Whatever your abilities, however keen you are to work, there are very few jobs you can try for and too many other people who also want them. Once you have a job, the money you earn is not likely to be very good. Many people try to leave the area to find somewhere better, but not everyone is free to move. It is the young, able and well-qualified people who move most easily, because they have most to offer.

How can government help with the problems of poorer regions and of industry? Does it aim to offer a comfort or a cure?

| Rich and poor regions in the UK in the 1980s | | | |
|---|---|---|---|
| | South-east England | North-east England | Northern Ireland |
| Expected population change, 1981–2001 | +5.3 | −4.1 | — |
| Unemployment % rate (1983) | 9.5 | 17.3 | 21.5 |
| % of those unemployed more than 1 year | 35 | 45 | 51 |
| % of employees in manufacturing (1981) | 15 | 21 | 11 |
| % of employees in services (1981) | 74 | 62 | 71 |
| average dwelling price on new mortgages (1982) | £30 000 | £18 000 | £20 000 |
| average earnings per week (full-time male, April 1983) | £185 | £159 | £151 |
| income (GDP per head, 1981) | £4180 | £3420 | £2720 |

(Source – Regional Trends, 1984)

## Question

1 Use the data to describe the problem of great regional differences for consumers and producers. (3)

71

# How can government help the regions?

The government can help the regions rather as you would use a carrot and stick to help a donkey climb a hill. The government's 'carrot' is to help firms bring more business into the regions by cutting costs there. It gives grants to cut the cost of land and capital, and cuts companies' tax bills. This is often done more in some areas than others, and changes from time to time. More business should mean more jobs, one way or another.

The government tries to get firms to hire more workers in the regions. For a time it paid a subsidy to cut the wage cost of each person in work. It also helps with building and retraining, houses, roads, parks and other facilities. All this is meant to encourage people to set up new business and live in the regions.

There is a 'stick' as well, which the government uses to stop business from settling in richer areas that are already too crowded. Firms must ask if they can build offices and factories over a certain size. The

# Mean street... easy street

**WORKINGTON, Cumbria**

POPULATION: 27000 and falling
INDUSTRIES: steel, paper, vehicles

UNEMPLOYMENT: 17.8% School-leavers 42%

DISTANCE FROM LONDON: 326 miles

COMMUNICATIONS: By road – A66, A595, A596. Rail – W Coast main line connection at Carlisle (34 miles); link to Barrow. Nearest major airport – Newcastle (93 miles)

HOUSING: average 3-bed terraced – £15000

REGIONAL AID: development area status allowing 15% grants on new plant and machinery; enterprise zone status allowing businesses 10-year holiday from rates

IN boomtown Wokingham they have a message for firms eager to set up shop in the heart of the M4 computer corridor: please go somewhere else. Pressure on space is such that companies are actually turned away, so that Britain's Silicon Strip can control its headlong development rate.

Just 256 miles north, in work-starved Workington, however, it's the army recruiting office that's turning people away. Even this traditional escape route for youngsters eager to avoid the dole queue has a six-to-12 months waiting list.

**WOKINGHAM, Berkshire**

POPULATION: 24000 and rising
INDUSTRIES: services, electronics, software, light engineering
UNEMPLOYMENT: 7.3% school-leavers 5%

DISTANCE FROM LONDON: 32 miles

COMMUNICATIONS: By road – M4 (five miles), M40, M3, M25. Rail – London-Bristol connection at Reading (eight miles); link to Gatwick Airport. Nearest major airport – Heathrow (22 miles).

HOUSING: same house – £35000

REGIONAL AID: none.

Wokingham is in the vanguard of the new information revolution which is changing the face of Britain just as much as the industrial revolution did 150 years ago. Then, Workington prospered mightily as the steel industry mushroomed; now the vast majority of the youngsters leave school with little prospect of work. One local head reports that morale is surprisingly good, though last year just 6.6% of the school's leavers found jobs. Grades in exams are higher as children try to equip themselves as well as possible for the bleak world outside. Computing skills are taught, though the head recognises that "there aren't many computing jobs in the area".

Wokingham has at least 25 electronics companies, ranging from Hewlett-Packard with over 1000 employees to small software companies like Control-C-Software, with half a dozen employees.

The whole of Wokingham appears to be switched on to high technology. Over half the jobs advertised in a local employment agency require some computing skills. Schools are busy churning out computer-literate children. Michael Cole, the head of St Crispin's School was amazed when he asked his pupils at assembly to raise their hands if they had access to a home computer. Nearly half did.

The service sector is the careers officer's trump card in coping with this year's crop of school leavers. Not many will find work in the small electronics companies, but secretaries, office staff and shop assistants are all needed. A new Safeway supermarket, for example, may mean an extra 100 jobs. By this process, nearly 70% of local school leavers are able to find a job without too much trouble.

The Sunday Times, 18.12.83

## Questions

1 The economies of Workington and Wokingham are working with very different success. How is this explained by their different (a) locations and (b) industries? (4)

2 What is 'regional aid'? Show 2 ways in which the government is trying to help Workington. (3)

government can say no, or say 'look elsewhere first'.

All this is for firms owned privately. But much business is part of the public sector, owned by the nation and run by some part of government. This business can also be led into the regions. Tax offices are based in Portsmouth or Dundee, for example, and car licensing is run from Swansea.

## A comfort or a cure?

What does government offer the regions – is it a comfort or a cure? On the one hand it is right that the government should help people on low incomes. It does this across the country as a whole. Spending more in inner-city areas and regions may be part of the same idea. But can it do more and beat the problems as well?

What would you do if you were given money by the government? Probably you would spend it, and the same happens in the regions. Some spending gives business to firms outside the region, especially for goods such as TVs, maybe, or cassettes or petrol. But it makes more jobs and more income inside the region as well. Shopkeepers, cleaners, postmen and teachers all have more work to do.

This may not solve the real problem, however. People in poor regions have low incomes and are unemployed because of the problems of their industries. Often industry is in decline and cannot change to make things better.

## The problems of industry

Would you do better to work in steel, paper or vehicles, or in services, electronics and software? Some industries grow and do well because demand rises for their products and because of technical improvements in their production. Other industries decline as their products are replaced by different ones, or by firms working in different countries.

What can the government do to help? It can give grants to cut the costs of weaker industries and to subsidise their production. This keeps their output up and unemployment in those industries down at least for a time. Where declining industries are concentrated in poorer regions of the country, this clearly helps those regions. But for how long and at what cost?

How can government change industry and the regions?

Some changes must come, and new industries or locations must replace old. The government may do better if it helps new and growing industries instead of the old. It can help workers to retrain and move to new industrial sites. It can help new firms to set up by cutting their costs and their tax bills. Some people feel that these changes will happen anyway, and easily enough. They say that government can help most if it stays apart from business and lets firms get on with the job.

Other people say that the problems of industry cannot solve themselves. One in every three jobs in the manufacturing industry were lost between 1966 and 1984. One in every two jobs in British Steel and British Leyland went between 1977 and 1984. Output has fallen as well, though not as much or in as many industries. Government may need to control industry much more fully – perhaps with public ownership, perhaps with controls on trade – to beat this problem.

# Part 4 Buying and selling

## 4.1 Buyers and sellers – distribution and markets

How do sellers find buyers? What is the work of distribution and markets in this?

Here is the easiest question you will ever be asked in economics:
Where would you go to buy a record?

A   To a shop in town
B   To the record factory
C   To the City of London
D   To your friends

The answer is most probably A, of course. You buy records at a record shop in town. The shop puts record buyers in touch with record sellers. Shops do the business of distributing records.

*Distribution* is an important stage in production. Manufacturers use raw materials to make goods, often in large and specialised factories. Other firms then take over and specialise in finding customers for those goods and selling to them. Distribution is when finished goods are sold to the final customer who consumes them.

You are a consumer when you buy records, soft drinks or magazines. Mostly you buy these things from shops.

## Retailing

Would you buy a record at the local corner shop, at W. H. Smith's in the main street in town, or at a hypermarket on a large site away from the town centre? These are all shops and are part of retailing. Retailers are firms that specialise in buying products that they sell to the general public. But some businesses are much larger than others.

Most shops are small businesses. These *single outlet retailers* are often owned and run by just one person or one family. You meet them when you buy from the 'shop on the corner' or 'down the road'. They offer a local and individual service, perhaps staying open long hours. They are easy to get to, and sell everyday goods such as fruit, bread, newspapers and sweets.

Most business is done by larger shops, however, such as Boots, W. H. Smith, Tesco and Marks and Spencer. These are all *multiple retailers* that run chains of shops selling the same things in the same way, but in many different places. They sell most of what people buy for the house, and food and clothes. You are likely to buy your record from one chain-store or another. Why do they do so well?

Multiples cut their costs by running as large firms with economies of scale. They buy in large amounts and sell quickly. Customers feel that they know the shop, where to find it, and what it sells, in all parts of the country. The firm can afford good advertising, expert staff, and the best town centre sites. Costs and risks are spread between its many branches.

W. H. Smiths opened their first bookstalls at railway stations in 1848. By 1900 they had around 800 such outlets. They began selling in the High Street only in 1905.

# What's the best way to buy?

Even so, you might not buy your record there. Your local town may have a *department store*, which has a section selling records alongside many different types of goods. There may be a co-op – a retail *co-operative* society – that runs in the same way but is owned by its customers. Or you may buy on *mail order* – choose from a shop's catalogue and get your record by post.

Which would be the best way to buy? Different shops have different things to offer, and retailing has changed a great deal in recent years. People now make less use of department stores, even when they are variety chain stores like Woolworth's. Specialised shops can offer a greater range and perhaps better prices.

Customers now travel more to look for the best buy. There are more supermarkets and hypermarkets. Supermarkets are large shops such as Safeway or Tesco that sell from one large site. They cut costs by selling quickly from a number of pay outlets and by asking customers to serve themselves. About half of all groceries are sold in this way.

Hypermarkets are larger still. These sell a full range of household goods as well as food. Most customers drive to them and park in large car parks. They are found well away from the town centre, where there is more land to use. You may find a range of records there, selling at good prices. The shop passes on some of its gains from economies of scale. But what else helps it to keep prices down?

# Wholesaling

Where do you think *shops* buy from? Suppose you asked the people running a record shop, 'Where would you go to buy a record?' They might answer 'To the record factory' or they might not. They might use a wholesaler.

*Wholesalers* generally buy from factories and sell to retailers. They buy large quantities from a number of different producers. They then have a range of different products to offer retailers. Retailers choose what they want to have on sale in their shops and buy the smaller amounts that they wish to handle. But they must pay a price for doing so. Wholesalers buy at one price and sell at a higher one to cover their costs and make a profit. Why do retailers agree to pay this extra cost?

Many, of course, do not. More retailers, and especially the larger chains of stores, buy from the manufacturer directly. But they may then do their own wholesaling, using warehouses and delivery trucks to serve all their shops. This can cut the costs of delivery if, say, only one load goes to each shop instead of a different load from each factory. It may allow products to be packaged or presented better for 'the point of sale' in the shop. It may allow retailers to ask the wholesaler about his products, as an expert, or to buy on credit and pay for goods later when they have been sold.

Wholesalers can act as specialists, therefore, in the chain of distribution from producer to consumer. They work in the middle, helping retailers to distribute products to consumers in the best possible way and to put buyers in touch with sellers. They work to make markets.

## Factsheet – retailing

Most businesses are small

Small multiples 13%
large multiples 1%
Single outlet retailers 86%
Total number of retail businesses = 228 000 in 1980

but a large number of shops are run by multiples:

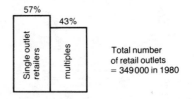

Single outlet retailers 57%
multiples 43%
Total number of retail outlets = 349 000 in 1980

and large multiples employ most people and do most business:

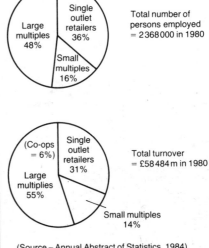

Single outlet retailers 36%
Large multiples 48%
Small multiples 16%
Total number of persons employed = 2 368 000 in 1980

(Co-ops = 6%)
Single outlet retailers 31%
Large multiples 55%
Small multiples 14%
Total turnover = £58 484m in 1980

(Source – Annual Abstract of Statistics, 1984)

## Questions

1. Explain the difference between (a) single outlet retailers and multiples, (b) co-ops and other large multiples. (2)
2. What are economies of scale? Large multiples employ 48% of all workers but do 55% of all business; suggest possible reasons for this. (3)

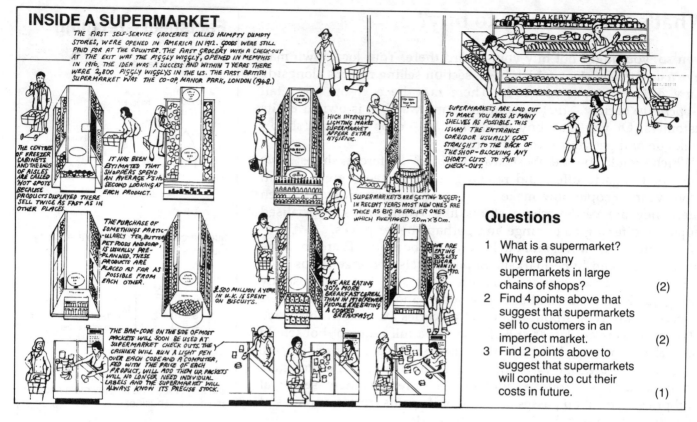

## INSIDE A SUPERMARKET

THE FIRST SELF-SERVICE GROCERIES CALLED HUMPTY DUMPTY STORES, WERE OPENED IN AMERICA IN 1912. GOODS WERE STILL PAID FOR AT THE COUNTER. THE FIRST GROCERY WITH A CHECK-OUT AT THE EXIT WAS THE PIGGLY WIGGLY, OPENED IN MEMPHIS IN 1916. THE IDEA WAS A SUCCESS AND WITHIN 7 YEARS THERE WERE 2,800 PIGGLY WIGGLYS IN THE US. THE FIRST BRITISH SUPERMARKET WAS THE CO-OP, MANOR PARK, LONDON (1948.)

THE CENTRES OF FREEZER CABINETS AND THE ENDS OF AISLES ARE CALLED 'HOT SPOTS' BECAUSE PRODUCTS DISPLAYED THERE SELL TWICE AS FAST AS IN OTHER PLACES.

IT HAS BEEN ESTIMATED THAT SHOPPERS SPEND AN AVERAGE 1/5th SECOND LOOKING AT EACH PRODUCT.

THE PURCHASE OF SOMETHINGS PARTIC-ULARLY TEA, BUTTER, PET FOODS AND SOAP, IS USUALLY PRE-PLANNED. THESE PRODUCTS ARE PLACED AS FAR AS POSSIBLE FROM EACH OTHER.

£500 MILLION A YEAR IN U.K. IS SPENT ON BISCUITS.

THE BAR-CODE ON THE SIDE OF MOST PACKETS WILL SOON BE USED AT SUPERMARKET CHECK OUTS. THE CASHIER WILL RUN A LIGHT PEN OVER EACH CODE AND A COMPUTER, FED WITH THE PRICE OF EACH PRODUCT, WILL ADD THEM UP. PACKETS WILL NO LONGER NEED INDIVIDUAL LABELS AND THE SUPERMARKET WILL ALWAYS KNOW ITS PRECISE STOCK.

HIGH INTENSITY LIGHTING MAKES SUPERMARKET APPEAR EXTRA HYGIENIC.

SUPERMARKETS ARE GETTING BIGGER; IN RECENT YEARS MOST NEW ONES ARE TWICE AS BIG AS EARLIER ONES WHICH AVERAGED 20m × 30m.

WE ARE EATING 30% MORE BREAKFAST CEREAL THAN IN 1970 (FEWER PEOPLE ARE EATING A COOKED BREAKFAST)

WE ARE EATING 35% LESS SUGAR THAN IN 1970.

SUPERMARKETS ARE LAID OUT TO MAKE YOU PASS AS MANY SHELVES AS POSSIBLE. THIS IS WHY THE ENTRANCE CORRIDOR USUALLY GOES STRAIGHT TO THE BACK OF THE SHOP-BLOCKING ANY SHORT CUTS TO THE CHECK-OUT.

### Questions

1 What is a supermarket? Why are many supermarkets in large chains of shops? (2)
2 Find 4 points above that suggest that supermarkets sell to customers in an imperfect market. (2)
3 Find 2 points above to suggest that supermarkets will continue to cut their costs in future. (1)

# Markets

You go to buy records at the local record shop, but there are a large number of such shops selling to customers all over the country. Together these make up the *market* for records, because shopping puts buyers in touch with sellers. We saw in Section 1.5 how a market is any arrangement that makes buyers and sellers meet to exchange goods and services.

If you want to buy or sell company shares, or diamonds, or rubber, you can use the specialist markets in the City of London. Why does this not work with records? Clearly, there are many different people who wish to buy records. They live in all parts of the country and come from the general public. This is a mass market, scattered and dispersed. But the City of London, a centre for finance, deals in specialist markets. Buyers and sellers are usually certain firms, and are concentrated so that they all gather at a certain time and place.

Now, suppose that you want to sell your own records second-hand. How is this market different? Now you can buy and sell with your friends, at school or at home. There may be some shops you can go to, or you can arrange deals of your own. But would you and your friends know what you were doing?

*Perfect markets* are where buyers and sellers know all they need to know in order to make their plans. They know about prices, for example, and they know just what they are dealing in. They act freely and sensibly to do what they think best. But most markets are not like this – instead they are *imperfect*. You will find it difficult to know who might want to buy your records, or at what price exactly. Your friends cannot tell how badly you have treated your records. There are usually some difficulties around to make markets work less than perfectly.

## How to distribute products?

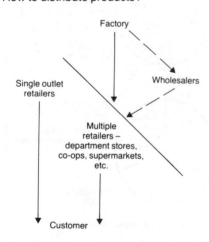

Factory

Wholesalers

Single outlet retailers

Multiple retailers – department stores, co-ops, supermarkets, etc.

Customer

## Checklist – what makes a market perfect?

● perfect knowledge by all buyers and sellers of all they want to know
● perfect freedom for buyers and sellers to act as they wish
● perfectly sensible actions by all buyers and sellers to do just what they think is best

How many packets of crisps do you buy each week? Let's say usually it is three. Why should this ever change, so you choose to buy more or less? We can tell only by looking at your consumer demand.

*Demand* measures the amount of any good or service a consumer chooses to buy. We saw in Section 1.5 how demand and supply are both important in setting price. High demand and low supply lead to a high price, for example. But what sets demand to be high or supply to be low in the first place? We will look at how sellers set supply in the next section, and here we look at how buyers set demand.

No doubt you would have your own reasons for buying crisps. You buy when you feel hungry or notice them in the shop, perhaps. You may buy just for fun, or for no real reason at all. But in economics we look at this in a different way. We deal only with people buying things for sensible reasons, because they want them and choose to spend money that way rather than any other. They buy to get satisfaction. *Utility* is used by economists as a measure of that satisfaction.

So what makes people choose to buy more or less from one week to another? There must be a number of reasons, but the first one we look at is to do with *price*. A fall in price usually makes you want to buy more, and a rise in price makes you want to buy less.

Your *demand curve* shows the different amounts you plan to buy at different levels of price. This may be difficult to measure when you go shopping, because you usually see only one price for each good at a time. We want to measure demand for a certain time only, as with the crisps you buy each week. And we want to see how price changes demand on its own. Other changes may also affect you from time to time, but are kept to one side in what we do now. So we must imagine changes in price while everything else stays the same. How could we measure this for crisps?

## Drawing up a demand curve

Suppose you buy three packets of crisps each week, and their price is 20 p for each packet. Your demand is for three, when the price is 20 p, but what if price goes higher – to 30 p? Then you might buy less, perhaps only two packets each week. And if price goes lower to 10 p, you might choose to buy more, perhaps as many as six.

We can show all this in a table of demand, how three different prices set three different amounts. We can also draw a chart to show prices and quantities together, as in figure 1. Price rises from the bottom to the top of the chart, and the amount of demand rises from left to right. We can join up points on the chart to show a demand curve. Falling prices raise demand, so the curve slopes downwards from left to right.

What makes you want to of something? These are the ideas that explain market demand and the demand curve.

The cosmetic group Noxell paid £652 000 in 1979 for 5 years rights to the face, eyes and lips of model Cheryl Tiegs. 'Though God makes models, he makes very few'.

(Source – Guinness Book of Records, 1984)

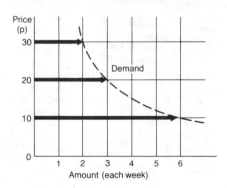

*figure 1 – a demand curve*

| Price of each packet of crisps | Amount you wish to buy each week |
|---|---|
| 30 p | 2 |
| 20 p | 3 |
| 10 p | 6 |

(all other things stay the same)

77

- price – higher price usually means lower demand
- other prices – of substitutes, and joint goods – affect demand in opposite ways
- income – more income usually means more demand
- tastes – people may want more or less for their own reasons

You expect a rise in price to cut your demand and a fall in price to raise your demand. This is shown on the chart. The change in price causes a *move* along the demand curve. A rise in price causes a move up and to the left, and a fall in price causes a move down and to the right.

## What changes demand?

What else could make you want to buy more crisps? Perhaps you have more money you can spend one week. People's *incomes* set how much they can afford of all goods and services, and their *budgets* show how much they plan to spend altogether. People may earn more from their work, or choose to save less or to borrow more. More income usually means more spending on one thing or another. Lower incomes usually lead to less spending.

You may always choose to spend on different things – such as on crisps, soft drinks or biscuits. Some you buy instead of each other, because they are alternatives and *substitutes*. You could buy biscuits instead of crisps, for example. But why should you choose to? It can depend on prices, for a fall in the price of biscuits may make them a better buy than crisps. A fall in the price of a good cuts demand for its substitutes to some extent; a rise in price raises demand for substitutes.

Sometimes goods are bought together. You may like crisps and soft drinks together, for example, and have *joint demand* for them. They are

# Why Britain's coal industry may be booming by the year 2000

The future of coal as an energy source in Britain depends on the action of two men.

They are the chairmen of two other nationalized industries, the Central Electricity Generating Board and the British Gas Corporation.

The NCB now depends on the electricity supply industry for its existence. The CEGB takes more than 70 per cent of the NCB's output, although its present chairman is a firm enthusiast for nuclear power.

He is still convinced, however, that the power industry will increase its reliance on coal. "The development of a viable coal industry in the UK, producing coal economically is

something as dear to my heart as it is to the coal board. Cheap coal means cheap electricity."

British Gas, having had the good fortune to find natural gas on its doorstep, abandoned coal as an input, but had continued its research into the making of synthetic natural gas from coal and now claims a world lead in this.

Synthetic natural gas is far removed from the poisonous town gas made from coal until the mid-1960s, and the British Gas Corporation's research into its manufacture from coal is based on the need to show the oil companies in the North Sea that it is not entirely dependent on them and that when North Sea

gas runs out there is an alternative ready to be pumped into the national network.

In addition to this the industrial demand for coal may treble by the year 2000.

The Monopolies Commission has suggested that a small amount of this increase will come from existing customers and that the majority will come from industry moving to coal for the first time.

Industrial demand for new coal-fired boilers, however, will increase only when existing oil or gas-fired boilers need replacing.

It is little surprise that the NCB takes the view that industrial coal consumption must be stimulated and has the vision to look beyond

the present glut of oil to the time when British coal will be among the world's major and cheapest energy sources.

*The Times, 20.3.84*

## Questions

1  Which firm (a) sells coal, (b) makes up most of the market demand for coal, in the UK?                                    (2)
2  What is a demand curve? How would each of these changes affect the demand curve for coal?
(a) an increase in the amount of nuclear power on offer
(b) improved production cutting the price of coal
(c) government grants to help industry buy new boilers
(d) new findings of cheap oil      (5)
3  Find three reasons above why the demand for UK coal 'may be booming' by the year 2000.                         (3)

*complements* to each other, and your demand changes in the same way for both. A rise in either price cuts demand for both, and a fall in price raises demand.

How much do you like crisps? You may grow to like them more, or buy more in hot weather, and so choose to spend more money on them each week. You may be led into this by the firms making crisps, because their advertisements are so good or because they make exciting new flavours or shapes. Changes in tastes can change demand for all sorts of goods one way or the other. This also makes you want to buy more or less than before, even though price has not changed.

# Demand curves new and old

Changes in income, in other prices or in tastes change the conditions of demand. We draw a demand curve while those conditions stay the same. A change in demand conditions changes the whole demand curve.

Suppose you enjoy a rise in income, and so want more crisps each week. Other improvements in the conditions of demand would work in the same way. Before, you chose how many packets to buy at each price and drew a demand curve of those choices. Now you will choose more at each price level, and there will be a new and different demand curve.

Let's say that you now want to buy one extra packet of crisps at each level of price. Your old and new choices are shown in figure 2. The new demand curve shows up to the right of the old, so that you choose three instead of two when price is 30p and so on. We say that the demand curve *shifts* to the right when it changes from its old to its new level.

Other changes in conditions of demand may change the demand curve by more or by less, and to the left or the right. But they all cause shifts from an old to a new curve, to some extent. It is sometimes difficult to work out how these changes would appear on the chart. It is helpful to ask if demand will be more or less, at each price level. More demand means a shift to the right.

# Market demand

Your demand is set by prices and how you respond to them, by your income and by your tastes. Other people's demand is set by their own conditions of demand, but in the same way. Together, people set the demand for goods and services in markets as a whole. Market demand for a good is made up of the demand of all individual buyers who want to buy that good, added up.

How could this work for crisps? You are a very small part of this market because so many other people buy crisps as well. But all together, you make up the whole market. Suppose that there are just ten other customers who each work out their demand as you have done. You can add how much you would buy to the amounts they would all buy, at each price level. This gives the market demand curve; figure 3 shows how this might be done.

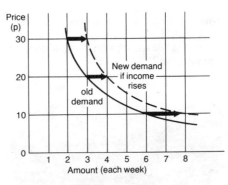

figure 2 – a shift of demand

| Price | old demand | new demand, if income rises |
|---|---|---|
| 30p | 2 | 3 |
| 20p | 3 | 4 |
| 10p | 6 | 7 |

(all other things stay the same)

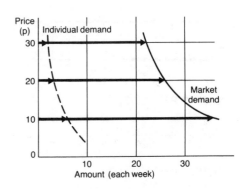

figure 3 – individual and market demand

| Price | Your demand | Everyone else's demand | Market demand |
|---|---|---|---|
| 30p | 2 | 20 | 22 |
| 20p | 3 | 23 | 26 |
| 10p | 6 | 30 | 36 |

(all other things stay the same)

# 4.3 How much to sell? The supply of products

What makes firms change the amount they want to sell?
How does this set market supply and the supply curve?

Fords produced the car of the decade in 1957 – The Edsel. It was one of the biggest and most expensive cars ever built, at a time when people wanted economy cars. Half of the models sold went spectacularly wrong – doors wouldn't close, paint peeled, brakes failed, and so on. Time magazine called it 'a classic case of the wrong car for the wrong market at the wrong time'.
(Source – 'The Book of Heroic Failures,' 1980)

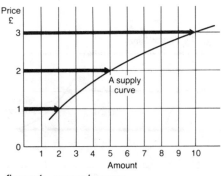

*figure 1 – a supply curve*

| Price of each record | Amount you wish to sell |
|---|---|
| £3 | 10 |
| £2 | 5 |
| £1 | 2 |

(all other things stay the same)

It's all very well making up your mind about how much you want to buy – of crisps or anything else. Consumers everywhere can do the same, and so set their demand. But how much will be on offer? Will there be enough for everyone to buy what they want? This depends on supply.

*Supply* measures the amount offered for sale at a certain time. Producers everywhere choose how much they want to sell of the goods and services they make. But they may choose more or less from time to time. Why is this?

Let's suppose that you choose to sell some of your records second-hand. You could offer just one to your friends or the whole collection to a second-hand shop. How do you choose what to do?

## Price, and the supply curve

'Everything has its price' is an old saying. It fits well in economics. If someone offers you the right price for your records then you will sell them. Too low a price and it is not worth your while to sell. But as price rises higher, you are likely to want to sell more and more. Price sets supply.

Let's say you have ten records you could sell, although you will let some go sooner than others. How many would you want to sell at a price of £1 each? You may like your records still and for most of them it is not worth selling. But there are two you are less keen on. You offer to sell those two at £1 each. If people offer higher prices, however, you will choose to sell more. Let's say that you will sell five at a price of £2 each, and all ten at a price of £3 each.

These plans make up your supply curve. A *supply curve* shows the amounts offered for sale at different price levels. It shows only price differences because anything else that affects supply is made to stay the same. It shows supply for a certain time, such as a day or week.

We can draw up your supply curve in the same way, as with the last section. Figure 1 shows the list of different prices and the amounts supplied at each. It also shows a chart where higher prices lead you to offer greater amounts for sale. The supply curve slopes upwards towards the right. (It slopes in a different direction from demand.)

Supply works in the same way for other goods and services sold by other people. There is one important difference, however. Most sales are made by firms selling products they have made rather than things they own and like. They sell for profit, not for fun. It becomes even more likely that 'everything has its price'.

80

## Christmas gobbledegook

The turkey is one of the biggest success stories that the food industry has ever seen.

In the mid-1950s, Americans ate fewer than 20m birds each year and the British only 1.5m.

This year, 165m turkeys will be eaten in America and 28m in Britain – more than one turkey for every family each year.

The bird itself has changed almost out of recognition. It has lost its natural dark feathers, which left blotches on the skin, and is now bred anaemically white. Hens lay eggs all year round (without which fertility the business could never have taken off). They live in barns kept at constant spring temperatures, which trick the birds into thinking it is breeding time.

The "factory" hen lays about 100 eggs each year instead of the natural 14 or so.

Heavier cock turkeys now balloon to 35lb in a mere 24 weeks. This has been achieved by selective breeding of the fattest birds. Twenty years ago, they took six months to reach about 20lb. Male turkeys are now so fat they cannot mate, because they fall over and squash the hen. Some males grow so fast that their legs cannot bear their weight.

Feeding a turkey accounts for nearly 70% of the cost of raising it. The 40% rise in US corn prices last year put up the cost of producing a turkey by as much as 6 or 7 cents a lb.

Producers are already cutting back. In the first six months of this year 4% fewer turkeys will be born in America (because 4% fewer eggs were laid in the second half of last year.)

Turkey producers hope that the bird will become one of the world's most important food-stuffs in the next century.

This may not be gobbledegook. Think about animals simply as machines that convert vegetables into meat. The turkey is one of the most efficient of such machines. Stuff 2½lb of feed into him and he will convert it into about 1lb of meat.

In poultry farming only the chicken is more efficient than the turkey at converting feed into saleable flesh. But turkeys, being larger can be raised more cheaply, so prices are lower per lb.

As the world struggles to feed its hungry millions next century, the turkey could change from being the diet of the self-indulgent rich to being the staple of the poor.

The Economist, 24.12.83

### Questions

1 By how much has the supply of turkeys changed in Britain from the 1950s to the 1980s? Find 2 changes in methods of production that have helped to cause this change. (3)
2 What is 'a shift of the supply curve?' Explain how the change in the cost of corn in the USA affected the supply of turkeys there. (4)
3 Explain why producers are likely to turn to rearing more turkeys in future instead of alternative forms of food. (3)

# What changes supply?

Your supply curve shows how price changes supply. A rise in price, from £2 to £3 brings a rise in the amount you wish to sell from five to ten records. This is shown in the chart as a move along the supply curve from one point up to another. Other price changes cause other moves along supply curves in the same way.

What else can change supply? We draw a supply curve only while things other than price stay the same. But there are other reasons why you want to sell more or less, and these change the supply curve altogether. There may be changes in costs, in other prices, or in your tastes. These set the conditions of supply.

You have few *costs* in selling your records. Most firms pay much more for resources to produce their output of goods and services. Let's say that you must advertise your records for sale, however, and that this costs you money. The more it costs, the higher the price you need to make it worth selling each record. To look at this another way, the fewer records you will try to sell at each price.

Firms pay costs to produce, and face changes in costs for two main reasons. One is that factors of production such as labour or capital may cost more or less. The other is that all factors of production may be used more successfully, through technical improvements. New methods of production may cut the cost of making each of a firm's products.

Sellers can always choose to sell one thing or another, to some extent.

## Checklist – what sets supply?

- price – higher price usually means more supply
- other prices – firms can supply other goods instead, or joint goods as well
- costs – higher costs of production usually cut supply
- tastes – firms may choose to sell more or less for their own reasons, or because of the weather, etc

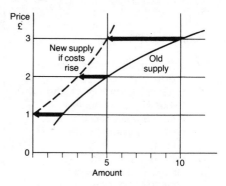

*figure 2 – a shift of supply*

| Price | old supply | new supply if costs rise |
|-------|------------|--------------------------|
| £3 | 10 | 5 |
| £2 | 5 | 3 |
| £1 | 2 | 0 |

(all other things stay the same)

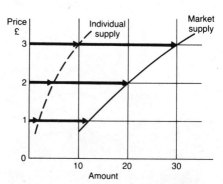

*figure 3 – individual and market supply*

| Price | Your supply | Other supply | Market supply |
|-------|-------------|--------------|---------------|
| £3 | 10 | 20 | 30 |
| £2 | 5 | 15 | 20 |
| £1 | 2 | 10 | 12 |

Perhaps you could sell your books or your tapes instead of your records? Perhaps you could sell your record player as well? Your supply is changed by the prices of these other goods.

Some goods are sold instead of each other as alternatives or *substitutes*. A farm may rear cattle for milk or beef, for example. Other goods may be sold together, as by-products or complements, in *joint supply*. Cows for beef give hides for leather-making. A rise in the price of one good raises its supply and the supply of joint products, but cuts supply of substitutes. A fall does the opposite.

Do you still like your records? You may be less willing to sell if this is so. You will be more willing to sell as you grow tired of hearing the same music. Supply is often changed by the *tastes* of producers, or by changes in the weather, or other outside influences.

How do changes in costs, other prices, tastes or other conditions of supply affect the amount people wish to sell? There can be a rise or a fall, by more or less, depending on how things have changed and how sellers respond. This is shown as shifts of the supply curve to the right or to the left.

Suppose it now costs you more to sell your records. Perhaps you have to pay to advertise, and are therefore less willing to sell. At each price level you now plan to sell less. Perhaps you now sell five records for £3 each, and so on, as shown in figure 2. Your supply curve shifts to the left, showing a drop in supply.

The same idea works for all sellers in all markets. Changes in the conditions of supply shift the supply curve from an old to a new level. We can work out where this will be by asking one question: do sellers offer more or less at each price level?

# Market supply

You may not be the only one trying to sell old records in your area. Some of your friends may join in, and together you will make up a local market. How is market supply different from just your own?

Clearly you offer more for sale as a group, altogether, than you do on your own. Market supply is the sum of all sellers' individual supplies, added up. You can all work out your own supply curves as we have seen, and then put them together to find the supply curve to the whole market.

Suppose the others offer twenty records for sale at a price of £3, and so on. Their offers are added to yours as in figure 3 to give the overall supply curve to the market. As we would expect, it still shows that more is offered for sale at higher prices. And as before, there are shifts from old to new supply if any of the conditions of supply change.

Some changes may affect only one or two sellers at a time. These have little or no effect on the market as a whole. You face strong competition now in selling your records. But other changes, such as a rise in the price of all new records, or a ban on selling records in school, may affect you all in the same way and at the same time.

Would you jump off the Severn Bridge for £1000? Would you pay £1000 to see your best friend jump? Perhaps not, but you might change your mind at a certain price. How much of a change in price would it take?

In economics, we often ask how demand and supply are affected by changes in market conditions. We expect a rise in price to lead to less demand and more supply. We expect a rise in income to raise demand, and a rise in costs to cut supply. But these changes may be large or small. It is useful to measure how much one thing affects another. That is when we use *elasticity*.

*Elasticity* measures the effect of changes in market conditions, such as prices and income, on demand and supply. It measures how much demand and supply change as a result.

Suppose that the price of packets of crisps rises, but only a little; other conditions stay the same. You are likely to choose to buy fewer crisps, but how much? A large change suggests that your demand is elastic, a small change suggests that it is not, but is inelastic instead. Elastic demand changes more than inelastic demand, and elastic supply changes more than inelastic supply.

## Elasticity and curves

We usually want to use elasticity much more exactly than this. We want to have a measure, often as a number, of how much things change. Elasticity does this. When its value is zero, this means that demand, or supply, does not change at all. When its value is as high as possible, at infinity, it means that they change as much as they possibly can. We can use this with demand and supply curves that show the effect of changes in price when other conditions stay the same.

Suppose you choose to buy just the same amount even if price rises or falls. You buy less or more of other goods in order to pay for a fixed amount of this one. Demand does not change at all and is totally or *perfectly inelastic*. The value of elasticity is 0, as shown in figure 1.

The same idea can work with supply. Firms may plan to sell just the same amount at high or low prices. Perhaps it is all they have to sell and they need the money, however much it is. Supply does not change at all and is totally or perfectly inelastic. Elasticity measures 0.

What is the most that demand and supply can change? A rise in price may lead you to cut the amount you want to buy down to nothing. It may raise the amount you want to sell to an infinite amount. A fall in price may raise demand infinitely and cut supply to nothing. In all these cases the measure of elasticity is as high as it can be. The demand and supply curves appear as flat lines such as those shown in figure 2. Demand and supply are totally or *perfectly elastic*.

How much more do you buy of something when its price falls? This and other changes are measured by elasticity, for demand and supply.

## Why No Stampede When Banks Cut Rates

Consumers are finally getting a break on interest rates – but without much effect so far.

In early October, a number of big-city banks reduced interest charges on consumer loans.

The new-car loan rate has been cut to 14 per cent from 19 per cent over the past six months, "it hasn't made any difference," says a bank official. "People have no confidence in the economy, and cars still cost too much."

US News & World Report, 1.11.82

### Question

1 What does elasticity measure? Is the demand for bank loans elastic or not in this case? Explain your answer. (5)

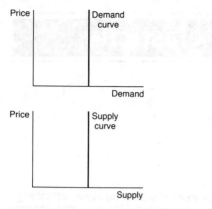

*figure 1 – demand and supply may be totally inelastic*

demand and supply do not change at all as price changes – price elasticity = 0

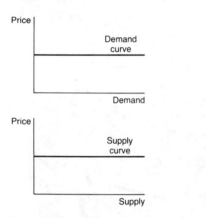

*figure 2 – demand and supply may be totally elastic*

demand and supply change totally as price changes – price elasticity is as high as it can be, at infinity

## Checklist – what does elasticity measure?

- price elasticity of demand measures how much price changes demand
- price elasticity of supply measures how much price changes supply
- income elasticity of demand measures how much income changes demand
- cross elasticity of demand measures how much *other* prices change demand

# How easy to change?

Would it bother you much to have only two packets of crisps a week instead of four? Perhaps not, for this is a good for which it is easy to change demand. You can adjust quite easily to price or income changes, so demand is more likely to be elastic.

But what about potatoes? It might be much more difficult for people to cut by half the amount of potatoes they eat. They may see potatoes as basic food, that is quite cheap anyway. Demand may not be easy to change if prices or incomes change. Demand may be inelastic as a result.

Suppliers also need to change, but in their case the amount they offer for sale. They may keep stocks ready for sale and use those more or less quickly. But otherwise they must change production and hire different amounts of factors of production to do so.

It is easy to change some lines of business – such as home decorating, perhaps – because spare workers, materials and equipment are widely available. It may be very difficult in other businesses, such as launching satellites into space, because resources are very specialised and difficult to find. So supply is more elastic if it is more easy to change production. It is less elastic if production cannot easily be changed.

Each good is sold in its own market, and has its own level of supply and demand in that market. Some are more easy to change than others, and elasticity differs, for both supply and demand, from case to case. All changes are easier to make as more time goes by, however, so supply and demand are often more elastic over a longer time. The measure of elasticity usually falls somewhere between 0, where there is no change at all, and infinity, where the change is total. What do different values of elasticity tell us?

# Price elasticity

What happens to your spending when price changes? A rise in price means that you pay more for each product you choose to buy, but you can choose to buy fewer of them. You pay more *and* you pay less. You can end up spending more money or less – it depends how your demand changes. This is measured by elasticity.

The price elasticity of demand shows how much a change in price causes a change in the amount people choose to buy. Low values of elasticity show that demand changes little, so a rise in price brings a smaller fall in demand. Total spending rises as a result. High elasticity shows the opposite.

But what is 'low or high'? The all-important value is *one*. Values less than 1 show low elasticity because demand changes less than price. Values above 1 show high elasticity because demand changes more than price.

Supply is measured in much the same way. Suppose people try to buy more plums, and the price rises as a result. For a day or so there are no extra plums in the shops, so firms can sell no more. Then they buy extra plums from wholesalers and farmers' stocks, so sales rise. But still the rise in supply is likely to be less than the rise in price. The price elasticity of supply shows how much a change in price causes a change in the amount firms choose to sell. Its value here is less than 1.

Much later, farmers can grow extra plums and send them to market. Perhaps next year there will be a larger rise in the number on sale than the rise in price. Supply is elastic, and the value of elasticity is greater than 1.

# Waiting for a mineral tidal wave

Mineral water producers are bracing themselves for a tidal wave of business if the water workers strike.

Cadbury Schweppes, which bottles "Malvern" water at Colwell in the Malvern Hills and has 8 per cent of the mineral water market in Britain, says it would be possible to treble its production rate. Aqualac said it could easily increase supplies of its sparkling Perrier water.

The Times, 21.1.83

**Question**

1 What does price elasticity of supply measure? Does supply appear to be more elastic or inelastic in this case? Explain your answer. (5)

## Income and cross elasticity

How would you spend a million pounds if you had it? How do people tighten their belts in a time of economic slump? These questions are to do with how income affects demand. We expect a rise in income to bring a rise in demand for most products, but not all. Some, such as first class fares or Rolls-Royces, may be bought only by the rich, so demand rises greatly as income rises and demand is elastic. Other goods such as potatoes or socks may be bought at about a fixed amount even if income rises, so demand is inelastic.

These changes are measured by income elasticity of demand. This shows how much a change in income causes a change in demand.

People may choose to buy one good rather than another, not only if their incomes change. They may also respond to changes in other prices. A rise in the price of one good, such as butter, may cut the demand for some others such as bread, and raise the demand for others such as margarine.

Cross elasticity of demand measures how much a change in the price of one good affects demand for different goods. Its value is positive if goods are bought instead of each other, as substitutes, but its value is negative if goods are bought jointly as complements.

Market price is set by supply and demand. How does this work, and how can we use it to explain price differences?

Why does one gold chain cost more than another, and why does the price of tea change from time to time? Prices may appear to be set by shops and firms, but only at what people will pay. Market price depends on supply and demand together.

The market is a place or an arrangement that brings buyers and sellers together to exchange each product. *Market price* is the price set by buyers and sellers for each good and service, through what we call the *market forces* of supply and demand. How does all this work?

You do most of your buying in shops that sell goods and services. Here it is the seller that makes the first offer by setting an asking or *bidding price*. But you can take or leave that price. Other customers do the same. Sellers sell all they have only at a price that buyers will pay. Buyers can buy what they want only at a price that sellers will take. There must be a match of supply and demand together.

## Matching supply and demand

Let's say that you arrange to sell some of your old records to some friends. You work out how many you want to sell at each level of price, and they work out how many they want to buy. Together you make up a market, with your supply and their demand.

You want to sell up to ten records, and that is the number they are willing to buy – but at different prices. We see this clearly in figure 1.

You start by asking £3 for each record, because at that price you will be pleased to sell all ten. But they only want four at such a price, so there is no deal. Instead they offer a price of £1 each for all 10, but at that price it is only worth your while to sell two.

| Price of each record | Supply = the amount you offer to sell | Demand = the amount they want to buy |
|---|---|---|
| £3 | 10 | 4 |
| £2 | 5 | 5 |
| £1 | 2 | 10 |

(all other things stay the same)

At price £2 the supply of 5 records matches demand. At other prices there is no match. A total of 5 × £2 = £10 changes hands.

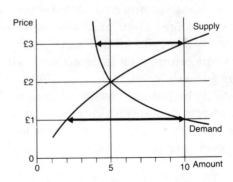

figure 1 – matching supply and demand

In the end, you agree a price of £2 for each record. You want to sell five records and they want to buy the same five at that price. Your supply matches their demand, and market forces set market price to be £2.

The price that matches supply to demand is called *equilibrium price*. Once this price is set there is no need for buyers or sellers to make any different offer. The chart in figure 1 shows how the amount sold matches the amount bought. Price is set on the chart at the level where the supply curve crosses the demand curve.

How much money changes hands? You can sell five records at £2 each. The total payment is therefore 5 × £2 = £10. This is seen on the chart as the 'box' drawn by price, and the amount sold.

## All clear

What is wrong with other prices, as far as you the seller and they the buyer can see? Price may be too high, as at £3. A high price causes high supply but low demand. You offer more for sale than they want to buy, so some goods go unsold. There is *excess supply*. In this case ten are offered buy only four are wanted, so six go unsold. This is shown on the chart as the gap between supply and demand when price is £3.

What if price is too low, as at £1? Now there is more demand at ten than supply at two. Buyers go without goods they want and would pay for. There is *excess demand* in this case, of eight. We can see this gap on the chart in figure 1 at price of £1.

The equilibrium price matches supply and demand to each other. There is no gap, because any excess is cleared away. Market price *clears* the market.

We can see how market forces work in this case, but most markets are much larger and more complicated. Still, the same ideas hold. If anything, price becomes more important. Buyers meet sellers only to agree a price that suits them all. It may take time for markets to clear perfectly, and shops may find that they get an excess of stocks on their shelves, or of customers to be served. But after a while they can give special offers, hold sales and change price to balance things up.

## Why may price be high or low?

Why should the price of gold bracelets be twice as high in one shop as in another? It may look the same, but it must be being sold in a different market. Supply and demand must be different in each case, because it is market forces that set market prices.

It can cost more to make one bracelet than another. Perhaps one is made with more gold than the other, or with more workmanship from skilled labour. But this is not the main difference here. High street jewellers put a '100% mark-up on manufacturers' prices' – they double the cost of making each bracelet when they set its price. This covers selling costs such as the rent of shops, and holding a wide range for customers to choose from. Discount jewellers sell a few lines, in bulk, perhaps by mail order. They have economies of scale and cut down on selling costs.

Costs affect supply. A firm with lower costs can sell its goods at lower

**What makes price rise?**

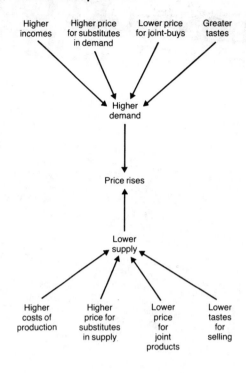

Higher incomes | Higher price for substitutes in demand | Lower price for joint-buys | Greater tastes

→ Higher demand

→ Price rises

↑ Lower supply

Higher costs of production | Higher price for substitutes in supply | Lower price for joint products | Lower tastes for selling

# DON'T GET CAUGHT IN THE GOLD RUSH

OLD jewellery makes you feel rich, but price has put a lot of it beyond our pockets until recently.

Now some firms are selling gold ingots, bracelets and chains by mail order and at discount prices.

"Solid gold at up to, near and under half price," say Green and Symons, of Piccadilly Circus, London, in their adverts.

*So just what sort of savings do we get from discount jewellers? And what kind of value?*

I bought the top-selling nine carat gold three-bargate bracelet at both discount and High Street jewellers.

I paid £16.95 at Green and Symons but at H. Samuel's branch in Cheapside, London a virtually identical bracelet cost me £42.50.

*Why is there such a huge difference in price?*

The managing director of Green and Symons, Mr Sidney Symons says: "High Street jewellers have a very slow turnover, so the customer has to pay for the time an item sits in the shop taking up space.

"We cut our profit margins and increase turnover, so we can offer much lower prices.

"And as we only offer a limited selection of jewellery, we don't have to carry a big stock you find in a High Street jeweller's shop."

H. Samuel merchandising manager Alan Lowe says: "The discount jewellery is very good value for money.

"We simply cannot compete with the discount jewellers. They are able to buy in bulk from manufacturers in a way that we can't – even though we have 250 shops.

"We have to pay the rent and rates for our shops all over the country, a staff of 3000 employees and make a profit for our shareholders. And that has to be paid for out of the cost of the jewellery.

"We offer a much wider range of jewellery than the discount houses, and we think we offer a better service."

The secretary of the National Association Of Goldsmiths, Mr Harry Wheeler, says: "Most of our members put a 100 per cent mark-up on manufacturers' prices.

*The Sun, 17.2.78*

● THEY look alike. They weigh almost the same. But there's a tremendous difference in the price. One bracelet costs well over twice as much. The one from H. Samuel costs £42.50. The one from Gerrards, a discount house, £16.95.

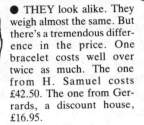

**Spot the difference**

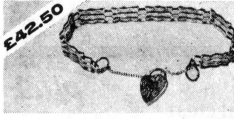

£42.50

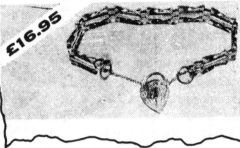

£16.95

1. Demand is greater and supply is less in the High St, so price is higher at £42.50.
2. Demand is less and supply greater from discount stores, so price is lower at £16.95.

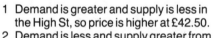
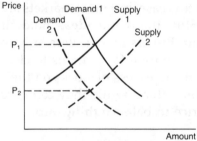

*figure 2 – a high or low price for gold?*

## Questions

1. What do you understand by the terms (a) discount prices, (b) bulk buying? (2)
2. Refer to figure 1. Suppose there is a change in this market: what will be the new level of equilibrium price if (a) new sellers join the market and sell 8 records for whatever price they can get, *or* (b) buyers plan to buy an extra 5 records from you at each price level. (4)

prices. At each price level it can afford to offer more for sale. This is shown in the supply curve in figure 2. Supply is greater at each price level from discount jewellers. The same bracelet sells for a higher price from High Street jewellers.

But who pays this higher price? There must be a demand from customers who agree to pay the shops' asking price. People buy from discount jewellers if they want good 'value for money'. They go to High Street jewellers if they want to choose from a wide range, and have the income and 'taste' to pay extra. The chart shows that discount customers choose to offer less money for the same sort of bracelet and offer lower demand than High Street shoppers.

Together supply and demand set price. Here there are two markets, two levels of demand and of supply, and two market prices. We can show all this on the same diagram, and find why one price is higher than another. We can do the same in other cases. But then there may be other reasons why demand and supply are different – perhaps different prices of substitutes, or the tastes of buyers or sellers.

# Why does price rise or fall?

Why do prices change? Why should the price of tea rise when the prices of coffee and of other goods and services do not? Again, the answer lies in supply and demand and how they set price. A fall in supply or a rise in demand lead to a rise in market price. A rise in supply or fall in demand cuts market price.

We can use the chart of supply and demand curves to show how; figure 3 does this for the example of tea prices. Why did the price of tea rise from 28p to 42p a pack in just a few months? Was it supply or demand that changed?

In this case, it was supply. India cut the supply of tea for her own reasons, so that less was offered for sale to the world. We show this on the chart as a change from the old to a new supply curve, with less on sale at each price level. This new supply meets demand and sets a higher market price, at more than double the value.

Changes in costs and other prices can also change supply in this way. Changes in consumers' incomes or in other prices can change demand. The result in each case is found from market forces and how they set equilibrium price and the amount bought and sold.

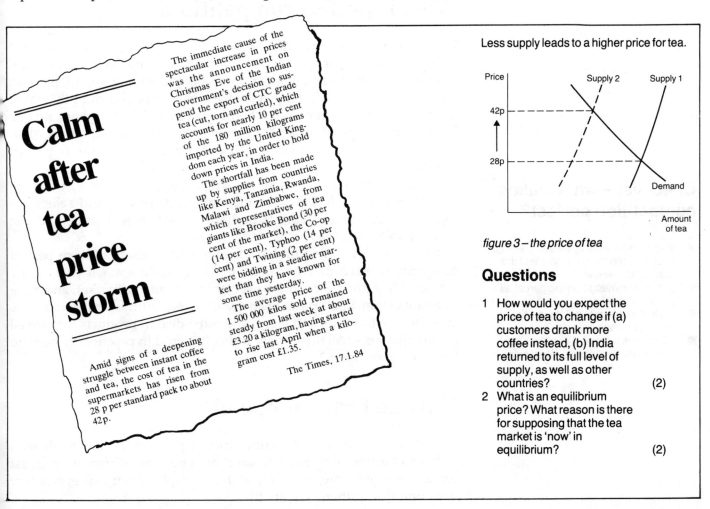

## Calm after tea price storm

Amid signs of a deepening struggle between instant coffee and tea, the cost of tea in the supermarkets has risen from 28 p per standard pack to about 42p.

The immediate cause of the spectacular increase in prices was the announcement on Christmas Eve of the Indian Government's decision to suspend the export of CTC grade tea (cut, torn and curled), which accounts for nearly 10 per cent of the 180 million kilograms imported by the United Kingdom each year, in order to hold down prices in India.

The shortfall has been made up by supplies from countries like Kenya, Tanzania, Rwanda, Malawi and Zimbabwe, from which representatives of tea giants like Brooke Bond (30 per cent of the market), the Co-op (14 per cent), Typhoo (14 per cent) and Twining (2 per cent) were bidding in a steadier market than they have known for some time yesterday.

The average price of the 1 500 000 kilos sold remained steady from last week at about £3.20 a kilogram, having started to rise last April when a kilogram cost £1.35.

The Times, 17.1.84

Less supply leads to a higher price for tea.

figure 3 – the price of tea

## Questions

1 How would you expect the price of tea to change if (a) customers drank more coffee instead, (b) India returned to its full level of supply, as well as other countries? (2)

2 What is an equilibrium price? What reason is there for supposing that the tea market is 'now' in equilibrium? (2)

# 4.6 Competition

Firms compete with each other to find buyers that they can sell to.
How do they do this, and how does it help you, as a consumer?

How do firms *compete* with each other to find customers for their products? You are a consumer yourself, probably for a large number of different goods and services. When you buy a magazine at the local shop, a record in town or stamps at the Post Office, what sort of deal do you get?

Some markets are less competitive than others. Some markets are supplied by only one firm. Customers have no choice but to buy from that firm or not at all. This is called *monopoly*, because there is just one seller in the market. Other markets are made up of many different sellers, but only one buyer. This is called *monopsony*. We look at monopoly in the next section.

Most markets are made up of a number of different firms. Firms try to attract customers to buy their own products and not their competitors'. But how many firms are there, and what forms of competition?

## What is perfect competition?

When do you have most choice as a consumer? Imagine that you want to buy a daily newspaper or a box of matches. You can buy from any number of different shops, or from people selling on their own, perhaps in the street. So much choice means that you can buy where it's cheapest. If one shop asks a higher price than all the others, no one buys there. If one shop asks a lower price than all the others, then everyone tries to buy there and it quickly sells out. This is perfect competition.

*Perfect competition* is where no single buyer or seller can change market price by what they do on their own. Buyers and sellers act together, without knowing it perhaps, to set market price and the amount sold.

It takes a very large number of buyers and sellers to have perfect competition. Each of them must make up only a small part of the market. They must each know everything about the market, and have free movement to all parts of the market. New firms and consumers must be free to set up and leave, and must deal in products that are all exactly the same. All this is very difficult to find in practice. So how do firms really compete?

## Checklist – what makes competition perfect?

● a large number of buyers and sellers each of them too small to affect the market as a whole
● perfect knowledge on the part of all buyers and sellers
● perfect freedom to act, to join the market or leave it
● all firms sell identical products, so there is the same price taken by all

## How do firms compete?

A market is made up of the same types of product, usually made by a number of different firms. You can choose between different breakfast cereals, or toothpaste, or cat foods, for example. What makes you buy from one firm rather than another?

Price is usually important, to some extent. If goods are exactly the same in all other ways, price is all that matters. You choose to buy the product with the lowest price, and so do all consumers. This is the case in perfect competition where there is nothing else to make products different. Everyone tries to buy the cheapest product, so that no one can sell at any price above the cheapest. All goods are sold at the same low price, which is 'perfect' from the buyer's point of view.

---

**Pepsi or Coke?**

| | **Pepsi** | **Coke** |
|---|---|---|
| |  |  |
| Invented by | C B Bradham in 1893 as a cure for peptic ulcers | John Pemberton in 1886 as the ideal brain tonic |
| How many sold in the world | 221 m a day, in 145 countries | 279 m a day, in 147 countries |
| Value of sales in UK | £100 m | £220 m |
| Backed by Presidents | Nixon | Kennedy/Johnson/Carter |
| and super-powers | USSR | China |
| Contents | mostly water and sugar, plus cocoa leaves, cola nuts, and secret ingredients | |

**Questions**

1  What is perfect competition? How perfect is the competition in the market for cola drinks?  (2)
2  Suggest 4 ways in which Pepsi and Coke compete to sell more of their own brand of drink.  (2)

---

But price differences do happen in many markets. You do not always look out for the cheapest, but often for the best buy instead. What else do you look for besides price?

It depends on what you are buying, of course, but there are three other ways in which firms sell to you. You may buy your chosen product because it is of better quality than the others, or better advertised, or because more shops offer it for sale.

Firms know this. They know that these other forms of competition are often more important than price. They sell more clothes, for example, by having good designs, making them well, and selling in as many good shops as possible. They sell cars by making them work well and look good and keep their value.

# Is competition good for you?

Small firms may not gain fully from economies of scale, and may not be able to make the best products or to sell them in the best way. But competitive firms do have much to offer.

Customers can buy more cheaply and choose from better products that are more widely available. The competition amongst supermarkets to sell their groceries, for instance, has kept prices down and sales standards up. Firms are kept on their toes. They must produce at low cost and sell as well as they possibly can, otherwise they may 'go bust'. This is the result of close competition.

So competitiveness can help to make firms offer consumers the best possible service. It can also lead to costs, however. Advertising may become very costly and do more than simply inform customers. It may stop new competitors from being able to set up in a market. Firms can use this as a way to cut competition, as we see in the case of monopoly in the next section.

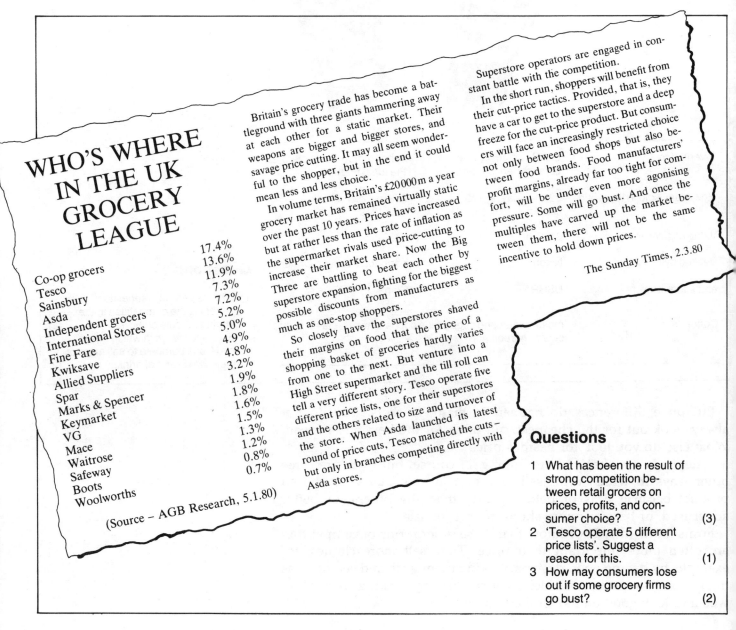

## WHO'S WHERE IN THE UK GROCERY LEAGUE

| | |
|---|---|
| Co-op grocers | 17.4% |
| Tesco | 13.6% |
| Sainsbury | 11.9% |
| Asda | 7.3% |
| Independent grocers | 7.2% |
| International Stores | 5.2% |
| Fine Fare | 5.0% |
| Kwiksave | 4.9% |
| Allied Suppliers | 4.8% |
| Spar | 3.2% |
| Marks & Spencer | 1.9% |
| Keymarket | 1.8% |
| VG | 1.6% |
| Mace | 1.5% |
| Waitrose | 1.3% |
| Safeway | 1.2% |
| Boots | 0.8% |
| Woolworths | 0.7% |

(Source – AGB Research, 5.1.80)

Britain's grocery trade has become a battleground with three giants hammering away at each other for a static market. Their weapons are bigger and bigger stores, and savage price cutting. It may all seem wonderful to the shopper, but in the end it could mean less and less choice.

In volume terms, Britain's £20000m a year grocery market has remained virtually static over the past 10 years. Prices have increased but at rather less than the rate of inflation as the supermarket rivals used price-cutting to increase their market share. Now the Big Three are battling to beat each other by superstore expansion, fighting for the biggest possible discounts from manufacturers as much as one-stop shoppers.

So closely have the superstores shaved their margins on food that the price of a shopping basket of groceries hardly varies from one to the next. But venture into a High Street supermarket and the till roll can tell a very different story. Tesco operate five different price lists, one for their superstores and the others related to size and turnover of the store. When Asda launched its latest round of price cuts, Tesco matched the cuts – but only in branches competing directly with Asda stores.

Superstore operators are engaged in constant battle with the competition.

In the short run, shoppers will benefit from their cut-price tactics. Provided, that is, they have a car to get to the superstore and a deep freeze for the cut-price product. But consumers will face an increasingly restricted choice not only between food shops but also between food brands. Food manufacturers' profit margins, already far too tight for comfort, will be under even more agonising pressure. Some will go bust. And once the multiples have carved up the market between them, there will not be the same incentive to hold down prices.

*The Sunday Times, 2.3.80*

## Questions

1. What has been the result of strong competition between retail grocers on prices, profits, and consumer choice? (3)
2. 'Tesco operate 5 different price lists'. Suggest a reason for this. (1)
3. How may consumers lose out if some grocery firms go bust? (2)

# 4.7 Monopoly

If you want to post a letter you have to use the Post Office; if you want to work as an actor you have to join the actors' trade union called Equity. In these and other cases you have no choice. There is a *monopoly* in these markets because only one seller sells postal services, and the work of actors.

## What makes a monopoly?

One firm may take over its competitors by merger or take-over. One firm may make up a new market and be the only seller in it. We all know hoovers and biros after the firms that first led the way with those products. But other firms can catch up unless something stops them. A firm needs *barriers to competition* to keep its monopoly.

The government can make strong barriers by passing laws of one kind or another through Parliament. The Post Office may be the only firm allowed to carry letters nationally, for example. Patents are set up in law to protect new inventions and allow firms to produce new products, without any close copies, for a number of years. This helps firms who have done the hard work in making new products.

Firms make up other barriers to competition on their own. A large monopolist may gain economies of scale and cut costs so that it can sell more cheaply than any small, new competitor. It can undercut its competitors' prices till they 'go bust', and then raise prices as much as it wants. A firm can spend heavily on advertising, so that customers keep on buying its own products instead of competing ones. Again, small firms cannot match these costs. There is very heavy advertising of washing powders and pet food, for example. All the main brands are made by only two firms in each market.

Why do paperback best-sellers cost the same wherever they are sold? Why do the building societies all offer the same interest rate to their savers? Sometimes firms make agreements with each other that limit competition. *Restrictive practices* may stop retailers from selling a firm's products at different prices, or stop producers selling in the same line of business, or stop firms selling at different prices. A *cartel* is an agreement between suppliers all to sell a product at the same price.

## Is monopoly a dirty word?

What sort of deal do you get from the Post Office and other monopolies, as a customer? Some do a very good job. They use their size to gain economies of scale, to cut costs and to sell at lower prices. They

What stops sellers competing with one another? What is monopoly, how does it affect you as a consumer, and what can be done about it?

The first upright vacuum cleaner was made in 1908 by W. H. Hoover, a New Berlin harness maker

The first ball-point pen was patented in 1943 by Lasala Biro, a Hungarian hypnotist.

### Question

1  Both Hoovers and Biros were patented. What is a patent? How does it lead to monopoly? (2)

## What are barriers to competition?

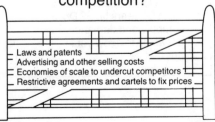

Laws and patents
Advertising and other selling costs
Economies of scale to undercut competitors
Restrictive agreements and cartels to fix prices

## The OPEC Price Cartel

In 1979, OPEC (the Organisation of Petroleum Exporting Countries) could control world oil. It sold most of the free world's oil, and held reserves that could last 70 years. It used this power to push the price of a barrel of oil up from about $15 to about $30 in 1980. OPEC's income from oil rose from around $200 bn to almost $280 bn as a result.

By 1984 the position had changed. The oil price was under $30 despite inflation. OPEC's income was down to $160 bn in 1983. Other countries, such as Britain and Mexico, now supplied more of the world's oil, and OPEC sold only 43%. Some OPEC members wanted to break the cartel, and sell at lower prices. No longer could OPEC keep output down and price up as it did before.

**Market shares in the free world**

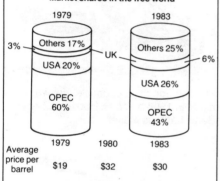

| Average price per barrel | 1979 | 1980 | 1983 |
|---|---|---|---|
| | $19 | $32 | $30 |

The Sunday Times, 15.7.84

### Questions

1  Suggest a reason why some members of OPEC might want to sell their oil at lower prices. (1)
2  What is a cartel? What does a cartel aim to do, and why? (3)
3  Suppose that OPEC countries began to use up their reserves of oil more quickly. What would be the effect on oil prices (a) now, (b) in 50 years time? Draw 2 supply and demand drawings to show your answer. (4)

plan ahead, bring in better products and better methods of production. They serve their customers well. But others can be very different.

Let's say that you are the only one in school who knows how to do the homework. You could choose to help all your friends and show them how to do it, or you could use your monopoly power. You are the only one who can offer the right answers. You chould choose to swap or sell them at a price.

Monopolies have the power to set how much they sell and how many customers they allow to buy. The less they sell, the more customers compete with each other to pay a higher price. Lower amounts sell for higher prices. In this way the monopolist can make as much profit as possible. But customers lose out. Some pay a higher price and others go without.

# How much power has a monopolist?

This depends on how many customers choose to go without rather than pay the higher price. Demand may fall more or less than the rise in price. We know that this is measured by price elasticity of demand. A firm has more monopoly power if it sells to consumers with less elastic demand.

Some monopolists are able to make the most of their market power by selling at different prices to different customers. They choose which price to charge which buyer, and stop buyers from switching from paying one price to another. This is called *price discrimination*. British Rail, for example, charges very different fares for the same journey to people going to work, shoppers, students and the elderly.

# Consumer protection

Firms can use monopoly power to make more money out of their customers than under competition. They may also feel safe from competition and the risk of going bust. They may not bother to cut costs or to improve products or to serve their customers well. Can consumers do anything about it?

On your own, as a consumer, you have no power to affect big businesses. But consumers can work together through the government. The government has a policy to improve competition and to stop monopolies acting badly. It looks at restrictive practices, finds most to be against the public interest, and bans them. It has a monopolies commission to look at monopolies and see if they are working well or not. It asks the same body to look at important mergers to see if firms plan to cut competition this way. It controls its own businesses in the public sector of industry to try to serve consumers in the best way. And it sets up rules and appoints officials to protect consumers from unfair practices by shops and factories.

# 4.8 Government and the market

Who builds up butter mountains, creates food coupons, and makes black markets? One way or another, these are all down to government, and follow from the ways government tries to steer markets. Suppose the government wants to raise the amount of butter sold by farmers. It can buy more butter itself until it has mountains left over; or it can give out free coupons that people use to buy extra butter; or it can fix the price and amount of butter and other foods so that markets no longer work freely. But why should it want to? What's the point of government trying to steer markets?

It's a hard life being a farmer, so they say. Your income depends on what you manage to produce from your land. This can be cut right back by bad weather or disease, however hard you work. But the more you all produce, the lower your prices. You can end up with less money from a good year of high output than from a bad year. And there always seem to be cheaper imports from other countries that do you out of business. Surely the country needs its farmers to feed the people!

So the government helps farmers. It tries to change output and price in many other areas as well, often for the same sorts of reasons. It helps groups of producers and workers to keep their incomes up, in mining and car production. It helps the country to keep up production of important goods, such as steel and arms. It tries to steer people away from goods and services that may be harmful, such as tobacco and gambling, perhaps. How may the government help? Let us look at farming again, as an example of what government may do.

## Holding stocks

Supply and demand set market price and output. So what can the government do to raise output and to raise the price paid to farmers? It must work through supply and demand, adding its own supply or demand to other market forces.

The countries of the European Economic Community (EEC) join together for this in the Common Agricultural Policy (CAP). This spends most of the money raised by the EEC, partly to improve farming methods and equipment, but mainly to raise farmers' incomes and output. The CAP buys food produced by farmers, so raising market demand. This keeps prices up, and output up, to set levels.

We can show this in terms of supply and demand in figure 1. Let's say that the EEC wants the price of food to be high at level 2. The free market would set its own price much lower, at the equilibrium of level 1. But the CAP buys food to push price up. Ordinary consumers want to buy only 1 890 000 tonnes of food at the higher price, although

How can the government steer markets, so changing output and price? Why may it want to do this? We look at farming as an example.

## Checklist – how can government steer markets?

- it can buy and sell for itself, holding stocks
- it can use taxes or subsidies
- it can use rules and regulations to set price, output, behaviour or the form of products
- it can produce and sell itself, in public enterprise

## THE BUTTER MOUNTAIN

| | 1978 | 1979 | 1980 | 1981 | 1982 | 1983 | 1984 |
|---|---|---|---|---|---|---|---|
| Production | 1960 | 1970 | 1960 | 1895 | 2060 | 2290 | — |
| Consumption | 1670 | 1640 | 1620 | 1595 | 1576 | 1540 | — |
| Exports | 255 | 500 | 596 | 500 | 375 | 350 | — |
| Year End Stocks | 435 | 400 | 260 | 150 | 300 | 860 | 1200* |

*Estimate
Amounts in thousand tonnes

(Source – EEC, 1984)

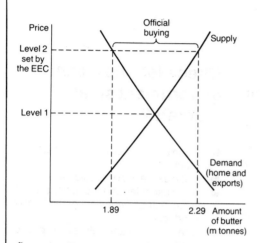

figure 1 – the supply and demand for butter (1983)

## The Butter Mountain

For those of you who are not quite sure what Europe is all about, or indeed quite where it is, here are all the facts you need to know.

**Q. What is Europe?**
A. Europe is a group of countries who have decided to make the regulations for the next war so hard to follow that it will probably never happen.

**Q. What has been the result so far?**
A. A lot of butter and a lot of paper.

**Q. What is the butter for?**
A. It is our main weapon against Russia. If the Soviet Union should ever declare war on us, they know we would drop a million tonnes of butter on them. This would ruin their diet and they would all die agonized, lingering deaths.

**Q. What if Russia doesn't declare war?**
A. We shall have to think of a new use for butter.

**Q. When Greece joined the EEC, did they have any new ideas for butter?**
A. No, but we now have a mount of olives.

**Q. What is the basic idea behind the Treaty of Rome?**
A. The idea, basically, is: when in Brussels, do as the Germans do.

**Q. Why did Britain join the EEC?**
A. To unite the French and Germans against us and make the next war impossible.

**Q. How much paper does the EEC produce every year?**
A. Enough to wrap all the butter in Europe.

**Q. What should I do if I'm passionately pro-Europe?**
A. Go out and buy some butter.

The Times, 14.6.84

## Questions

1 What are 'stocks'? What would be the effect on the price of butter if all stocks were sold in the EEC in 1984? (2)

2 Use the table to show the changes over the years in the EEC's (a) home consumption, (b) production of butter. (2)

3 What are the costs of the butter mountain and who pays them? (2)

4 Suggest 2 ways in which the EEC could end the butter mountain. (4)

farmers plan to sell 2 290 000 tonnes. The CAP must buy up the rest, which is 400 000 tonnes. Otherwise, there would be excess supply, as shown by the gap on the chart.

But where does all this food go? The answer, of course, is that it is kept as 'mountains and lakes' of unwanted stocks. A time may come when there is a shortage, and stocks can be sold to prevent prices from going too high, as happened with butter from 1978 to 1981. If stocks are sold at any other time, however, they will push prices below the set level. So they must be kept in store, or thrown away, or given away, where they can never return to EEC consumers.

If production rises and consumption falls, the mountains of stocks just keep on growing ever faster, as for butter in 1983 and 1984.

## Taxes and subsidies

There has to be some other way, you may think, for the government to help farmers. Perhaps we should use food coupons? These would be tickets given out by the government to all consumers. We could all buy food with them, so there would be extra demand for food. Farmers could sell more, and cash in their coupons with the government to pay the higher price of this extra production.

This is one way that the government could subsidise production. A subsidy is a payment made by the government to help either buyers or sellers. Coupons are given to consumers, and so raise demand at each level of price. Other subsidies could be paid directly to farmers to cut their costs. How would this affect the market for food?

Farmers set a price for each level of their output. A subsidy pays a share of that price, so that they can afford to charge customers less. This is shown in terms of their supply curve in figure 2.

The subsidy to producers cuts the price for each level of supply. You can see the same change in another way, as a rise in supply at each level of price. The supply curve shifts downwards and to the right.

Greater supply should lead to higher sales at lower prices. But for some goods and services the government wants the opposite result. It wants to put people off smoking, say, or buying petrol, or buying imports from other countries. A tax is an extra charge that consumers or producers must pay to the government. Taxes on sales raise the cost of selling each amount, and cut what can be offered for sale at each price. Supply is cut and the supply shifts upwards and to the left – market price rises and output falls, to some extent.

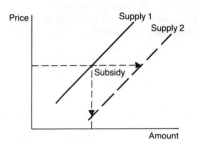

figure 2 – a subsidy to producers

# Ruling the markets

Would it be easier if the government just told farmers what price to sell at? There could be a rule or regulation or law that no one could sell below the set level. This would ignore market forces, however, and would lead to problems.

Suppose price was set above the market price, as in figure 3? More would be offered for sale by farmers and less would be bought by consumers. There would be excess supply, but in this case it would be held by producers. What would farmers do with produce they had grown, but could not find buyers for?

Farmers are strong-minded folk, and do not like losing money. They would try to sell their extra supply. They might find buyers with special offers, or free gifts, or advertising. Or they might break the rules and sell at lower prices, when the government could not stop them. There would be unofficial trade, selling against the law, in a *black market*.

The same is likely to happen whenever price is officially set away from its equilibrium level. Price may be set too low, and buyers may start a black market in order to be able to pay more for the goods they want. This happens when goods like clothes and beer are scarce, in wartime or in controlled economies. It was what made Al Capone his fortune in the years of prohibition in the USA. He knew that it was against the law to sell alcoholic drink, but that buyers would still pay to have it.

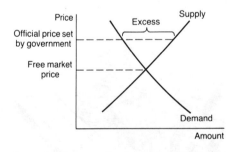

figure 3 – if government sets an official price

# Part 5 Finance

## 5.1 Money

Why is money important? How is it different from loans, and what are the main forms of money in the UK?

Money makes the world go around, or does it? Even without money people make things, want things and exchange things. We saw in Section 1.6 how these actions make up the *real* economy, and how money is clearly different from all this.

People can exchange one product directly for another in what is called *barter*. Farmers may exchange eggs for milk, but they probably call it, as you do, swopping.

*Money* is different from this, for it is anything generally accepted in exchange. You know you have money if you can buy anything you want in shops, or from other people, on the spot. You can use money in exchange, so you start to think about things in terms of money and so does everyone else.

## What can you do with money?

Money is like metres. You can use money to measure spending rather as you use metres to measure distance. You could get along without measuring distances, perhaps, but metres are useful. You can go into a shop and ask for two metres of cloth rather than just 'about that much'. You can measure the size of your wall, cupboard and door, together, in metres, and buy enough paint for the whole job. You can remember your height measured in metres, and compare it with others'.

Money is useful in the same way. You can buy your cloth or paint with money. It is easier to use in everyday exchange than real goods would be. And other people take your money because they know that they can spend it in their turn. Money can be used to pay off a debt that one person owes to another. Money is accepted by everyone, therefore, in a way that real goods, such as eggs, milk, cloth or paint, are not.

Money is important because it is so generally acceptable. This makes the whole process of exchange work more easily. You can buy cloth or paint without having to find some other product that the shop-keepers want in exchange. They are happy to take your money instead. They can buy whatever they want from someone else.

Without money, the world would still go around, but there would be less economic activity. There would be less exchange, less buying and selling, less specialisation. We would all be poorer as a result.

But money is useful in other ways as well. It measures the value of different goods and services added up. You may have bought many different things this week. In real terms, these cannot be added – what do 2 metres of cloth added to 5 litres of paint make? (Other than a soggy mess!) But £5 of cloth and £10 of paint *can* be added together. Your total spending can be measured at £15. In the same way, money is used to measure the total spending and earning of whole firms and countries.

## Checklist – why is money useful?

- it can be spent, and makes exchanges easier than by barter; it also measures the value of different products and work
- it can be held, to store up the value of what you own
- it can be lent, to exchange peoples ability to buy goods and services

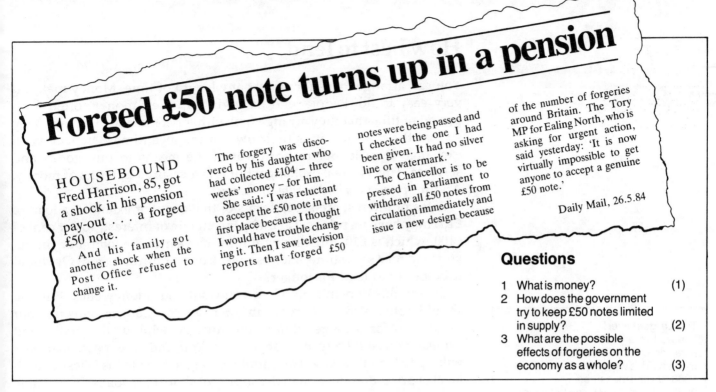

# Forged £50 note turns up in a pension

HOUSEBOUND Fred Harrison, 85, got a shock in his pension pay-out . . . a forged £50 note.

And his family got another shock when the Post Office refused to change it.

The forgery was discovered by his daughter who had collected £104 – three weeks' money – for him.

She said: 'I was reluctant to accept the £50 note in the first place because I thought I would have trouble changing it. Then I saw television reports that forged £50

notes were being passed and I checked the one I had been given. It had no silver line or watermark.'

The Chancellor is to be pressed in Parliament to withdraw all £50 notes from circulation immediately and issue a new design because

of the number of forgeries around Britain. The Tory MP for Ealing North, who is asking for urgent action, said yesterday: 'It is now virtually impossible to get anyone to accept a genuine £50 note.'

Daily Mail, 26.5.84

### Questions

1. What is money? (1)
2. How does the government try to keep £50 notes limited in supply? (2)
3. What are the possible effects of forgeries on the economy as a whole? (3)

Not all money is spent, however. What can you do with it besides spend it?

# Money and loans

How much money do you have on you at the moment? People keep cash in their pockets, their purses, or under the mattress. Shops and offices hold cash in their tills or cash boxes. This is called their *cash balance* of money. Money is often the most useful way you can store up what you have. Bank notes and metal coins are quite easy to look after. But large amounts may be difficult to protect and are better kept in a bank.

Most of people's money is kept in bank accounts of one kind or another. This money can change hands without ever leaving the bank. One person can write a cheque for another. This tells the bank to pay money from one current account to another. It allows people to withdraw their money *on sight*. We look at this, and the other work of banks, in Section 5.4.

But why hold on to money? It has no value in itself, only for things it can buy. And the amount you can buy with money may fall as time goes by. The value of money may fall through inflation. We saw in Section 1.6 how inflation raises the prices of all that is exchanged in the country. You can buy less with the same amount of money. Money is not the best way in which to hold your savings, therefore, especially when there are two much better things to do.

It is better to spend money now rather than later, after inflation. You can buy goods you want and before their price rises. But you may need to borrow in order to do this. You may need to use someone else's money but pay a price for doing so.

And there may be no point in holding on to money that you are not planning to spend. It is better to lend to other people. Your money will be paid a price, so that it is worth more when you do come to spend it.

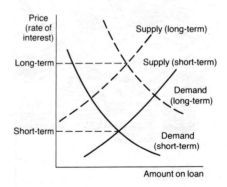

*figure 1 – why do interest rates differ?*

Borrowers prefer long-term loans, but lenders prefer short-term loans, if other things are the same.

# How best to lend?

You can arrange loans for almost any length of time. Money makes it very easy to do. People lend by giving up their money, often for a period of time that they arrange first. Other people borrow that money so that they can use it as their own in the meantime. The *loan* is an exchange from lender to borrower of the means to buy goods and services. This is a real exchange, but it is measured in terms of money. And its price is called a *rate of interest*.

Rates of interest are set in terms of the loan. For example, a loan of £100 may have its price set at a 10 per cent rate of interest. 10 per cent of £100, which is £10, must be paid for each year of the loan. But should you lend for a short time, such as a week or a month at a time? Or would it be better to lend for longer?

Clearly this depends on when you want your money back. But you should notice also a difference in interest rates. Longer loans tie your money up for a longer time. You must go without the goods and services you could buy for a longer time. You, and other people, are less willing to lend this way. The supply of longer-term loans is less at each level of price, therefore, than the supply of short-term loans. In the same way, borrowers can do more with money they can use for a long time. Demand is greater at each price level. Supply and demand together set interest rates, as shown in figure 1.

Interest rates are generally higher for longer-term loans. They are less liquid than short-term loans.

# Liquidity

*Liquidity* measures the ease with which money and loans can be exchanged for real goods and services. It shows your ability to spend. Money is generally acceptable on the spot. It is perfectly liquid. Short-term loans are exchanges of liquidity, but only a little at a time. You can put your money into a bank deposit account, for example, where it is tied up for perhaps a week at a time. You can take your money out without a week's notice, but only by losing the interest normally paid on these loans. Many people and firms know this, and use deposit accounts almost as they use money. Some other short-term loans behave in the same way. Together, these are called *near-money*.

You can lend money in many different ways. We will study these in the sections that follow. Short-term loans are arranged in what is called the money market; long-term loans in the capital market. But all these loans are less liquid than money, and cut what the lender can buy in the way of goods and services.

# What works best as money?

Farmers may use eggs to barter for milk. But what if everyone tried to use eggs in exchange for everything else? How good would eggs be as money? If you tried to take them with you to the shops, you would soon find out. The trouble would start when you climbed on the bus, with your large, heavy basket of eggs. It would be difficult, inconvenient to

**The Largest ever!**
The world's largest note was the 1 Kwan note of the Chinese Ming dynasty. This was issued from 1368–99 and measured 22.8 × 33 cm (larger than this page). The world's largest coin was the 200 Mohur Indian gold coin of 1654. It was 136 mm across (half this page) and weighed 2177 g.

(Source – Guinness Book of Records, 1984)

SUPERMARKET

## Questions

1  What makes large notes and coins *less* useful than smaller money?  (2)

2  What makes large notes and coins *more* useful than smaller money?  (2)

carry. Money needs to be convenient to use.

Then you would pay your fare – 35p please. But how could you pay three and a half eggs? Eggs cannot be split into smaller parts: they are not divisible. Money needs to be divisible.

And when they throw you off the bus, what happens to all your savings? Broken eggs everywhere, so no one will accept them now. Eggs break, go bad or turn into chicks. They are not durable. Money needs to be durable.

Quickly you return home. You rush into the back yard to feed your chickens. Everyone uses their land to 'lay golden eggs', for use as money. There would be more and more eggs to spend. This money would soon lose its value as its supply rose. Money must be limited in supply to keep its value.

Almost everything, it seems, is better than eggs for use as money. Coins such as a 20p or £1 piece last well and are fairly easy to carry. Bank notes such as £5 are easier still to use. These are all made and issued under the control of the government. By the law of the land, they count as *legal tender*. They are limited in supply to a set quantity.

But most money these days is kept in bank accounts. Banks supply most of the money used in the economy to pay for exchanges of goods and services. They make the supply of money rise, as we see in Section 5.4. What if they make it rise too fast? This could make money lose its value, and perhaps even upset the whole process of exchange in the economy. The government must control the supply of money, or it may be left with 'egg on its face'!

# Money in the UK

We see how any number of things can act as money, to pay for exchanges of goods and services. Anything that is used as money is as good as money. The government needs to measure the amount of this money in order to see if it is under control. There are several measures it can use.

Many of the official measures are very detailed, and useful only to economists and bankers who work on matters of high finance. For our purposes, we need only two or three of the measures used officially. These are shown in figure 2. M1 measures money held as cash, and in bank 'sight' deposits. Sterling M3 is larger than this. It measures, as well as M1, the value of bank time-deposits, such as deposit accounts, measured in terms of UK pounds.

The total amount of money was worth around £215 as notes and coins, £773 as M1, and £1814 as £M3, for each person in the UK at the end of 1983.

## Checklist – what can be used as money?

Anything that is
● convenient to use
● easily divisible into parts of different value
● durable, so that it lasts and keeps its value
● limited in supply so that it is scarce

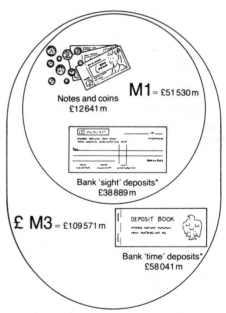

Notes and coins
£12 641 m

M1 = £51 530m

Bank 'sight' deposits*
£38 889 m

£ M3 = £109 571 m

DEPOSIT BOOK

Bank 'time' deposits*
£58 041 m

Reproduced with the permission of the Bank of England
* = Sterling deposits of the UK private sector

*figure 2 – money in the UK*
The UK stock of money, Dec. 12th 1984 (not seasonally adjusted)

Why does inflation matter? What are its effects, and why does it happen?

Inflation is when there is a general rise in prices. But what does this do to you? Prices were four times higher at the end of 1983, for example, than in 1972. So £1 bought only a quarter as much of the same goods and services and the value of money had fallen. With the same number of pounds at each time, you would have become worse off, as in figure 1.

But people do have more pounds. One view of inflation is that it happens only *because* more pounds are made. The rise in prices affects the price of work as well as the prices of goods and services. People earn more pounds with which to pay the higher prices. Inflation on its own makes people neither better nor worse off. So why does it matter?

## Inflation affects people differently

A general rise in prices and pay may not affect everyone equally. You may buy only certain kinds of goods. The prices of these goods may rise faster than others. Your income may be set so that it does not keep up with price rises. People on fixed incomes lose out from inflation.

Why are some incomes fixed? Some are paid at rates set by the government or other organisations. These rates may not be changed as often, or as much as prices in general. Some people are paid pensions or state benefits such as supplementary benefit. These are not prices at all, and are set differently. And many people earn an income from securities. They own government or company bonds that pay a rate of interest. This rate is fixed in advance of the loan, and does not change. Pension funds hold some of their investments in this way.

People on these fixed incomes can buy less with their money as prices rise. Others may keep up with inflation, or even gain. The distribution of national income changes so that some people have more, and others less, simply through inflation.

This has affected lenders and borrowers in particular over the years. People lend and borrow money for their own reasons, at an agreed rate of interest. Most long-term loans have a rate of interest that is fixed, for as long as the loan runs. So inflation cuts the real income of lenders, and also cuts the real cost of borrowing.

The largest borrower in the land is the government. The national debt is still large, but its real cost has been cut by inflation. As a percentage of national income (GDP) it fell from 58 per cent to 42 per cent over the 1970s. Closer to home, the most important loan to many people is the mortgage on their house. But house-buyers have often gained from inflation. Their loan stays fixed, but the house value rises. It is savers with building societies who have lost out.

Savers find that their money is worth less than they had expected. Borrowers find that they gain more from their loan than they had

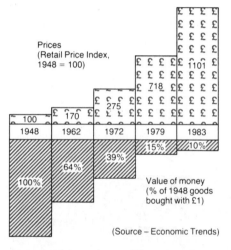

Prices
(Retail Price Index, 1948 = 100)

| 1948 | 1962 | 1972 | 1979 | 1983 |
| --- | --- | --- | --- | --- |
| 100 | 170 | 275 | 718 | 1101 |

Value of money (% of 1948 goods bought with £1)

| 100% | 64% | 39% | 15% | 10% |

(Source – Economic Trends)

*figure 1 – rising prices cut the value of money*

expected. Inflation can put people off saving, therefore, but raise the amount people try to borrow to buy cars, hi-fis, and other consumer goods. This can harm investment in industry, and cut economic growth. Output and jobs suffer, especially if other countries avoid the same problem.

# Inflation can harm the economy

Inflation can make us all worse off. Suppose that the UK has *more* inflation than other countries. UK prices rise faster, and UK firms find it harder to sell their products. Consumers both abroad and at home buy more of the cheaper foreign products and less of the more costly products made in the UK. This can only be bad for business. It is likely to lead to cuts in output and jobs.

But none of this need happen. The UK may be able to match its inflation to that of other countries and keep its prices in line. Do we need to worry about inflation in this case?

There are some economists who say that we do. They believe that inflation, left to itself, always gets worse and never better. Once money begins to lose its value it continues to do so, until it has no value at all. Inflation may lead to *hyper-inflation*, with prices rising at a very great rate. People lose their trust in money, and stop using it in exchange. The whole economy may come to a standstill.

## Checklist – why does inflation matter?

- it makes people on fixed incomes worse off
- it can deter people from saving
- it can make a country's products less competitive, so harming output and jobs
- it can grow out of control until people lose their trust in money

## Inflation turned a life's work into a loss

Harold Stanton started work as a civil servant in 1928. 40 years later, he retired, and right up to 1977 he kept a full record of all his income and spending. How did he make out over the years?

His total income over the 50 years adds up to £155 590, after tax. His total spending comes to £149 285. It seems he gained over £6000 to pass on to his children.

But his income changed greatly over the years. He started work on a salary of £370 a year. He retired on his income from part-time work, pensions and investments. This brought him over £15 000 a year, before tax, in 1975. Inflation makes it difficult to compare these two figures. Prices rose a great deal over the 50 years, and so did money incomes in general.

Most of Mr Stanton's income came from his salary as a civil servant, but also he earned large sums in other ways. His pension as a civil servant was index-linked to the cost of living, and his family savings were invested in securities, as loans to the UK and USA governments.

His spending went on different things at different times. He and his wife spent more on their children when they were young, and more on holidays and cars as the years went by.

Mr Stanton was lucky to have 'private' means. He inherited some £57 000 from his parents, and planned to hand this on to his own children. Sensible investment raised the value of this capital, however, to some £250 000. Half of this has already gone to his children. The rest is kept as investments of £50 000 in government securities, cash worth £15 000, and a house worth £50 000.

His lifetime profit seems at first to add to the value of this capital. But inflation changes this. Mr Stanton's profitable years were towards the end of his working life. Money was less valuable then because it could buy rather less in terms of real goods. Earlier losses, in early and middle age, were suffered when money was more valuable.

Mr Stanton has allowed for inflation by putting each year's figures in terms of what they could buy at the same time, in 1975. (We see how this is done in the next section.) Now real income comes to £388 430 and real spending to £406 890. On balance, Mr Stanton suffered a loss from his lifetime's work, of over £18 000!

(with acknowledgements to The Sunday Times 9.7.78 for information)

## Questions

1 The general level of prices was about 5 times higher in 1975 than in 1928. How well did Mr Stanton's (a) income (b) capital, keep up with inflation? (2)
2 How would you expect inflation to affect Mr Stanton's income from (a) his salary (b) his pension? (2)
3 How would you expect inflation to affect the value of his capital kept as (a) government securities (b) cash (c) a house? (3)

German hyperinflation

This happened in Germany in 1923. By then, there were 400 million, million marks in the country. Prices were more than 750000 times higher than ten years before. People carried their money in wheelbarrows when they went shopping. They tried to spend money as soon as they got it, before it lost any more of its value. They tried not to use money at all and turned to barter. Could this ever happen again, perhaps in the UK?

It took about thirty years, from 1948 to 1975, for the pound to lose three-quarters of its value. It took only twelve years, from 1972 to 1983, for the same thing to happen again. But the government can cut inflation and avoid its ill effects. How should it do so?

# What can be done about inflation?

You or I can do nothing about inflation on our own. The general level of prices is set by general forces in the economy. We study this as part of macro-economics. To correct it we must all act together, and we need the government to lead us – but to do what?

One approach is to try to live with inflation. There are countries in the world, such as Israel and Brazil, that have great changes in prices each year. Some of the worst effects of this inflation can be avoided by *indexation*. This keeps 'fixed' prices and incomes in line with the general level of prices, as measured by the cost of living index.

A different approach is to control inflation with *prices and incomes* policy. The government tries to control payments directly, and so stop them rising. Often this lasts only a short time, however, and controls only some types of payment. There is really only one way to cut inflation fully, and that is to attack its causes.

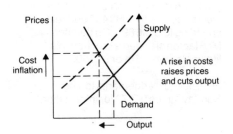

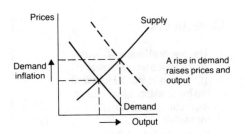

*figure 2 – what causes inflation?*

# What causes inflation?

Why do prices ever rise? We know the general answer from supply and demand. If buyers try to buy more than sellers try to sell, prices rise. In the economy as a whole, there is too much money chasing too few goods. Prices rise to match demand and supply.

But what can cause excess demand in the first place? Perhaps there is a change in supply, caused by a rise in costs throughout the economy. This is called *cost-inflation*. Trade unions may push for higher wages. The strongest unions gain most, and others try to keep in line. Or import prices may rise, due to a fall in the exchange rate of the pound. A jump in world oil prices, such as those of 1973 and 1979, may also raise costs. These changes affect supply as in figure 2. Prices rise but output may fall. Inflation and unemployment may happen together, as *slumpflation*.

Demand may change instead. Consumers or government may spend too much for reasons of their own. Everyone may spend too much because there is too much money in the economy. Again prices rise, as in figure 2. But this *demand-inflation* may come with growth, as firms raise output and create jobs, at least for a time.

| Some possible causes of inflation in the UK: | | Questions |

## Some possible causes of inflation in the UK:

**1976**
the £'s exchange rate drops 14%, so putting up import prices
.......inflation is 16%

**1977**
money supply (M1) rises 22%
.......inflation is 16%

**1979**
wages rise by 14%, so putting up industry's costs
.......inflation is 13%

**1980**
OPEC leads a rise in the world price of oil from $19 to $32 a barrel
.......inflation is 18%

## Questions

1 What does it mean to say that 'inflation is 16%'? (1)
2 Which *one* of the causes shown here is a type of demand-inflation? (1)
3 Which *one* of the causes is most suited to government control by prices and incomes policy? (1)

The government has many ways to control money supply and spending. We study these in Sections 5.6 and 6.4. But it is difficult to be sure how well these control the causes of inflation. Cost and demand causes become tied together. Wage rises lead to price rises, as firms try to cover their extra costs and meet extra spending. Price rises lead to wage rises, as workers try to cover their extra cost of living and gain from firms' extra revenue.

There is a cycle of inflation, as shown in figure 3. People expect inflation to continue and plan price and wage rises in order to keep ahead in the race. Wherever it began, inflation is difficult to stop.

*figure 3 – the cycle of inflation*

# 5.3 Counting the cost of living

How does the Retail Price Index measure inflation? How can we use it, and how good a measure is it?

How much does it cost you to live the way you do? Probably you can work out how much you spend each month, but that changes from time to time. You may have to pay more to live on the same amount of goods and services. But how much more?

We need a measure of the average cost of living. A rise in that measure shows a rise in the general level of prices, which is *inflation*. A fall shows falling prices, which is *deflation*. How could you measure your cost of living?

First you need to keep track of all you buy – bus rides, food, magazines, everything. This tells you which goods and services fill your imaginary shopping basket, and how much you buy of each over a month, say. Perhaps you spend £3 on chocolate but only £2 on soft drinks. Chocolate is the more important to you. A change in its price affects you more than a change in the price of soft drinks.

Now you can measure prices in the shops from time to time. You must take account of how much each price matters to you. This is based on how much of your spending goes on it. Say that the price of chocolate doubles, but the price of soft drinks halves. Prices have risen and fallen, but this price rise affects your spending more than the price cut. On balance, your cost of living has risen. Unless your income also rises, you are worse off.

## What does the cost of living tell us?

We measure the cost of living so that we can compare. You can measure your own cost of living against that of other people at the same time. This may show that it costs more to live in London than in Manchester, or in town rather than the country. Students at London University, for example, are paid higher grants to cover the higher cost of living.

You can measure your cost of living against your income. Many wage claims are set in just this way as people try to raise their incomes to cover a higher cost of living.

But we can also use the cost of living to measure inflation. We can compare one time with another to see how much prices in general have risen. This is made easier by using an *index*. Let us say that your cost of living rises from £5 to £6 a month. We use the first figure as a *base*. We give it a value of 100, and compare all other values to it.

The new cost of living is now put in the same form. If £5 is called 100, £6 is now called 120. In general, we measure the index at each time in this way:

$$\frac{\text{new figure}}{\text{base figure}} \times 100$$

In this example, this gives us $\dfrac{£6}{£5} \times 100 = 120$.

**Movie blockbusters**

Which is the most successful movie of all time? 'E.T. The Extra-Terrestrial' moved ahead of all others when it came out, earning $194.1 million from rentals in North America. 'Gone with the Wind' earned only $76.7 million, but came out 43 years before. Which film earned most, allowing for inflation? We find the answer if we divide by the level of consumer prices in the USA for each year. And the winner is—still 'Gone with the Wind'.

| | North American rentals $m | Order, after allowing for inflation |
|---|---|---|
| E.T. The Extra-Terrestrial 1982 | 194.1 | 5 |
| Star Wars 1977 | 193.5 | 2 |
| Jaws 1975 | 133.4 | 4 |
| The Sound of Music 1965 | 79.7 | 3 |
| Gone with the Wind 1939 | 76.7 | 1 |

(Source—The Economist, 12.2.83)

It may be helpful to think of index numbers as percentages. Your cost of living has risen from 100 per cent to 120 per cent, which is a rise of 20 per cent. But this affects only you. Inflation is a general rise in prices that affects us all. It is measured by the change in the general cost of living of everyone in the country.

# The Retail Price Index

The Retail Price Index (RPI) measures the general cost of living in the way we have seen. It aims to cover all consumers and all the prices they pay, in shops and elsewhere.

About 270 households record their spending each two weeks. They act as a sample for the whole country in this *Family Expenditure Survey*. These results give a basket of goods chosen in January each year, and covering the whole range of spending. They also show the importance of each product, as shown in the factsheet.

Each product in the basket is given a weight to show its importance in consumer spending. Food, for example, is most important and has a weight of almost 250, in total spending of 1000. The price of everything in the basket is measured in the middle of each month. This is done by asking shopkeepers and other retailers throughout the country, on a regular basis. Prices and weights are then put together to work out a *weighted average* of prices for each month.

We saw earlier how you could do this with your spending on chocolate and soft drinks. A simple average of prices is found from their sum, divided by their number. The average of prices 20p and 30p, for example, is

$$\frac{20p + 30p}{2} = 25p.$$

But you spend more on one good than the other. This can be shown by giving different weights to each good, such as 600 and 400.

The weighted average of prices allows for this difference by multiplying each price by its weight. The average is then found from this sum, divided by the total of all weights. In this case, we find (20p × 600) + (30p × 400) = 12000p + 12000p = 24000p, divided by 600 + 400 = 1000. This gives a weighted average price of

$$\frac{24000p}{1000} = 24p.$$

## Factsheet—the Retail Price Index (RPI)

The average household spends different amounts on each type of good. These amounts are shown by 'weights', as shares of a total value of 1000.

## Questions

1 'Bread has a weight of 28, jam a weight of 1.' What does this mean? (2)
2 Suggest how consumption weights might change in a year of low incomes. (2)
3 Suppose that the prices of all food, drink and tobacco rise by 31.25% one year, but no other prices change. What is the rate of inflation? (3)
4 What was the total amount of inflation from Jan 1974 to 1983? (1)

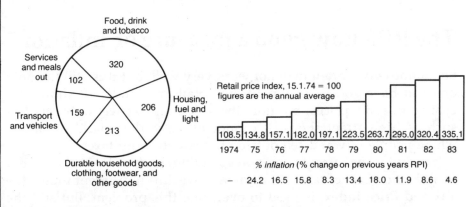

figure 1 - weights (in 1983)          figure 2 - the RPI over the years

## Better or worse off?

In 1928, Mr Stanton earned £370. In 1975 he earned £15 186. Was he better or worse off?
The Retail Price Index rose from a value of 100 in 1928 to around 500 in 1975. Prices were 5 times as high, and £1 bought one-fifth as much in real goods and services.
£370 bought as much in 1928 as £370 × 5 = £1850 in 1975. So at constant 1975 prices, Mr Stanton's income rose from £1850 to £15 186. He was more than 8 times as well off, in real terms.

## Questions

1  How much inflation was there from 1928 to 1975?  (1)
2  What was Mr Stanton's income in 1975 worth in 1928 prices?  (1)

So, more important goods count more towards the general level of prices. In general, the weighted average of prices is found from

$$\frac{(p_1 \times w_1) + (p_2 \times w_2) + \ldots}{w_1 + w_2 + \ldots}$$

where $p_1$ is the price of the first good, and $w_1$ its weight.

Changes in the weighted average of prices are seen more easily from our index. The value of this retail price index is shown in the factsheet, as an average for each year from 1974 to 1983. These figures are compared with the level of prices on 15 January 1974, which is called 100. But they can now be compared to each other as well.

## How to use the RPI

The RPI shows the general price level. Rises in the index show inflation, as the cost of living rises from one time to another. This is shown in figure 2. Prices rose in every year, so there was inflation throughout the period. But how much?

The index rose from 108.5 in 1974 to 134.8 in 1975. It rose by 134.8 − 108.5 = 26.3 after starting at 108.5. This is a rise of

$$\frac{26.3}{108.5} \times 100 = 24.2 \text{ per cent.}$$

Inflation was clearly very high in 1975. By 1983, however, prices were rising more slowly. The index rose by

$$\frac{(335.1 - 320.4)}{320.4} \times 100 = 4.6 \text{ per cent, only.}$$

The RPI helps us to measure inflation, therefore, and to compare it at different times. But why go to so much trouble? This is often because we know how inflation can hide other, more important changes. We must take away the effect of changes in the value of money. Only then can we see the real levels of what money has been used to measure.

Your income may have doubled, but inflation may have doubled your cost of living as well. Changes in the RPI show if this is so. We can use those changes to *deflate* money incomes, so removing the effect of inflation. We are left with a *real* value, measured as if prices had stayed constant.

## Checklist—what is the Retail Price Index (RPI)?

● the RPI is a measure of the general level of prices paid by consumers
● a rise in the RPI shows inflation. We deflate, by allowing for changes in the index, to show real values
● the RPI is quickly measured, but leaves out some prices and some taxes

## The RPI–how good a measure of inflation?

Sometimes your brain may not work very well, but it is still the only one you have got. So it is with the Retail Price Index. It shows the change in some prices, but not others. It aims to cover only retailers such as high street shops. It cannot measure the 'black' economy, where people buy and sell outside the law to avoid taxes.

It includes the effect of taxes on spending, such as VAT. It does not include the effect of taxes on income or wealth. A different index, the Tax and Price index, is used to overcome this problem. But still the RPI is taken by most people to measure the cost of living. It may not be ideal, but it is the best measure they have.

# 5.4 Banking

We all know the banks we see on the High Street – Barclays, Lloyds, Midland and National Westminster. They are the largest of only about ten banks that do business with the general public, in the UK. They are called joint-stock, commercial, or *clearing* banks.

Suppose you have saved £10 or so, and now take it to one of these banks. What do they do with your money?

Banks are firms, run to make profit for their shareholders. Their business is to do with money, and some of them do very specialised work. But the clearing banks offer a range of services to their customers, the general public. One thing they do is to protect your money.

Perhaps you do not feel safe if you carry all your money around with you. Someone else might take it, or you might lose it. You can open an account at a bank to record all you put in and take out. You can ask the bank to look after your money until you want it as cash again. They act rather as Wells Fargo did in the days of the wild west – putting valuables in a safe, and guarding them against loss.

What are banks? How do banks earn their living and what is their importance in the economy?

## Cheques

Wells Fargo bank did more than this. It also ran stage coaches to transfer money from one place to another. This helped customers to make payments to each other. Now clearing banks offer the same sort of service, but with cheques.

Perhaps your father wants to pay you £10, and you have a bank account. He could go to the bank, take out cash and give it to you. But this has no point, if you then take the cash back to the branch and put it in your own account. Better to use a note, telling the bank to transfer money from his account to yours.

A *cheque* is a written order to a bank telling it to make a payment, as in figure 1. This may be for cash if the cheque is 'open', or from one account to another if the cheque is 'crossed'. In every case, this order must be clear, accurate and signed by the person making the payment. Usually it is made out to the one person who is being paid.

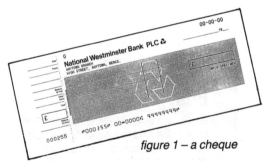

figure 1 – a cheque

## Clearing

It makes little difference if people have accounts at different banks. Orders to pay can still travel from one branch to another, but rather faster these days than on Wells Fargo stage coaches.

What happens to your father's cheque, paying money to you, when you take it to your bank? Your bank uses it to transfer money into your account, but first the cheque must be cleared. We see how in figure 2. The cheque orders your father's bank to pay up. It must be

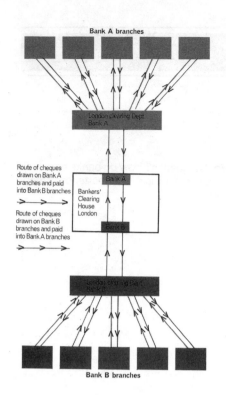

London Clearing Dept
Bank A

Route of cheques
drawn on Bank A
branches and paid
into Bank B branches

Bankers'
Clearing
House
London

Bank A

Bank B

Route of cheques
drawn on Bank B
branches and paid
into Bank A branches

London clearing Dept
Bank B

Bank B branches

*figure 2 – clearing a cheque*

returned to his bank so that they can see it is correctly written and signed. Only then will they send the payment to your bank, to go into your account.

Cheques are sorted each day at the London Clearing House. This happens quickly, but on a huge scale. It may take a few days before accounts are finally adjusted for the payment. But what if there is not enough money in your father's account to pay the cheque? The cheque 'bounces' and the bank does *not* pay up. A *cheque card* stops this, because it shows that the bank guarantees payment. This may cover cheques worth only up to £50, but it means that you would be paid your money by your father's bank, if not by him.

## Liabilities and assets

Let us say that you now have £20 in the bank, in your account. The bank holds deposits from many other customers, from firms and government as well as other people. All these deposits are liable to be taken away from the bank when people make payments. The banks have *liabilities* which are the debts that it owes to other people and organisations.

Some deposits can be withdrawn on the spot, on 'sight'. These are mostly current accounts that people use to make day-to-day payments, by writing cheques and other money orders. But we saw in Section 5.1 how most money is kept in 'time' deposits in banks. Deposit accounts, for example, pay interest because money is lent for a week at a time. Altogether, around £9 in every £10 of money (£M3) is kept in bank accounts of one kind or another.

What do banks do with this money? Banks have borrowed these funds from you and other customers. They have a great deal of money that, at least for a while, they can use as they wish. These are *assets*, owned by banks. Their balance sheets show where banks get their money from as liabilities, and what they do with it as assets. Assets must balance liabilities overall, but can be held in very different ways.

### The bank that 'went bust'

Banks are meant to lend money. But how much and to whom? You would not expect to see loans to just one person to be worth three times the value of the bank. You would not expect that person to be the banker's brother-in-law. But that is what happened to the first bank, set up in Manchester.

It opened at the corner of what is now 'Old Bank Street' in 1771. Its capital of £12000 was raised by three partners, including Williams Bank in London. But William Allen was the partner who ran the bank, and his brother-in-law was one John Liversey.

Liversey was in the local cotton trade, and it was natural that he asked Allen's Bank to finance his business. And business was booming. There was new printing equipment to buy, and competitors to beat. Liversey borrowed in order to cut price and raise output. By 1782 he was borrowing more than £33500.

The usual way to finance business in those days was with Bills of Exchange. Liversey wrote these I.O.U.s and sold them to Allen's bank. But there was little money at that time, as gold, silver or Bank of England notes, that Allen could hand over in return. Instead, the bank made its own 'money'. It paid in notes written by the first class London bank that was its partner. Perhaps this could have gone on for ever. But Liversey's firm tried to print too much cotton, sold at a loss, and

went bust. Allen's bank found it had printed too much credit, could not pay its debts and also went bust. The first Manchester bank failed, and only its London associate remains, as today's Williams and Glynns. And Liversey and Allen – they both went bankrupt.

### Questions

1. Explain the terms (a) bank (b) capital (c) credit. (3)
2. What are a bank's assets and liabilities? What assets and liabilities of the Manchester bank are mentioned above? (4)
3. Explain how the bank should have changed its use of *assets* to avoid going bust. (3)

You are not likely to take all of your £20 out of your bank account straight away. Even if you do, you are likely to pay someone else. The £20 is likely to be paid back into another account. Banks know this, and use it. They find that they need only a part of all their deposits to pay to customers from day to day. The larger and safer they are, the more certain they can be. Perhaps they need only £1 in cash to cover likely withdrawals from every £10 of deposits. But what about the other £9?

# Reserves and loans

You have £20 deposited in the bank. Perhaps only £2 of this is held as cash, or in the bank's own bank accounts. These are kept in *reserve* by the bank, to cover likely withdrawals. If the bank holds too little in reserve it runs a great risk. It may not be able to pay money to customers when they try to draw from their accounts. The bank might go bust.

But it is wrong also to hold too much. Money kept as cash in the bank has an opportunity cost. It has an alternative use. It could be lent out to customers to earn a rate of interest for the bank. The bank makes a profit from the assets it holds as loans rather than reserves.

Some loans are for short periods of time. Clearing banks lend to other types of banks, for example, for a few hours or days at a time. These loans are safe, in that they can be turned into cash quite quickly, to pay customers. But long-term loans earn much more interest. Banks make more profit by lending to their customers for months or years at a time. Banks must strike a balance, therefore, between what is safe and what is profitable. They must use some of their assets as reserves and some as loans.

# Credit creation

This may make you stop and think. You have put £20 in the bank for safe-keeping, but perhaps £18 of your money is lent out to other people. This may earn interest for the bank, and help them to keep your bank charges down. But what happens to your money?

Someone else borrows from the bank, and pays interest. They use the money, perhaps to buy new machines or materials for a firm. They have money and you have money. How much is there altogether – £20, £18 or £38?

Money is anything generally acceptable as payment. Cheques are accepted as payment from one bank account, usually to another. You have £20 you can pay this way, but so too does the person who is lent £18 by the bank. You and the borrower have £38 in money between you.

This is the way that banks *create credit*. Each deposit leads to more loans, although not by as much. New loans lead to new deposits. Bank credit grows by much more than the first deposit. There is a multiplied increase in bank deposits, and a larger money supply as a result. It is no surprise, therefore, that most money is kept as bank deposits rather than as notes and coins.

## Safe or successful?

Banks can use their assets to cover withdrawals, or to make loans, or both in the best possible balance.

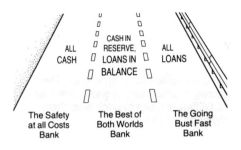

| ALL CASH | CASH IN RESERVE, LOANS IN BALANCE | ALL LOANS |

The Safety at all Costs Bank  The Best of Both Worlds Bank  The Going Bust Fast Bank

## Checklist – what do banks do?

● banks are firms that specialise in selling financial services
● they hold deposits, as liabilities that they owe the general public, for safe-keeping
● they make payments for customers and clear cheques
● they keep some assets in reserve but lend the rest to customers at rates of interest
● banks create credit and so set the supply of money in the economy

# 5.5 Money markets

Where should you go for a loan? The money market deals in short-term loans, but different types of bank work there. What do they all do?

Now that you study economics you may have noticed that people expect you to know some answers. 'Where should I go for a loan?' they may ask. What should your answer be?

We have seen already how loans can be for short or long periods of time. Most banks specialise and deal in certain types of business, and certain lengths of loan. Those lending for several years at a time are part of the capital market, which we will study in Section 5.7. Those lending for only a few months are part of the money market, which we consider here.

Many parts of the market are very difficult to understand. They deal in loans from one specialist bank to another in a way that outsiders do not hear of. But other types of business affect us all, often quite directly. These include the work of commercial banks, finance houses, and discount houses.

## Retail banks

We saw in the last section how the High Street clearing banks raise money from deposits and lend to customers. Their balance sheets show how money is borrowed as liabilities and used as assets. A share of assets is kept in reserve to cover withdrawals from day to day. This may be kept as cash, or as bank accounts in other banks, and especially the Bank of England. It is kept as very short-term loans that can be turned back into cash quite quickly.

These loans are of two main types. Money is lent 'at call and short notice' to discount houses and other banks. And money is lent to firms, banks and the government, by buying what are known as short-term bills. We will study both these loans in the work of discount houses later.

But most of the loans from clearing banks are different from this. They are made for months, even a year or two at a time, to the bank's own customers. This may be an overdraft so customers can draw out more than was deposited in their accounts, or as a fixed term loan. The rate of interest may change from time to time in the first case, or be fixed in the second.

This may be the first way that you should advise people to look for loans. Many people and firms find that this is a convenient and flexible way to borrow. Clearing banks offer a great many different services to their customers and this is just one more.

But not all retail banks are members of the London clearing house.

**Where to go for a loan**

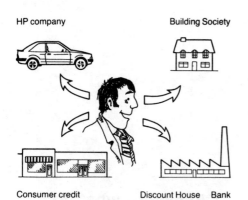

HP company

Building Society

Consumer credit

Discount House    Bank

112

National Giro, for example, is part of the Post Office, and does much that High Street banks do – except lend on overdraft. National Savings is also run by the Post Office, and borrows from the general public but does not lend. The Trustee Savings Banks used to help with personal savings but are now reorganised to act more widely.

And there are commercial banks, such as the Bank of Scotland and UK branches of overseas banks, that work away from the London clearing banks, to some extent.

# Consumer credit

Perhaps you have some friends who want a loan, but who do not want to use a bank. What else could you suggest? If the money is used to buy a household good such as a fridge, TV, clothes or a car, the answer might be consumer credit.

Finance houses are banks that specialise in these types of loans. They raise money mainly on loan from other banks, and lend to

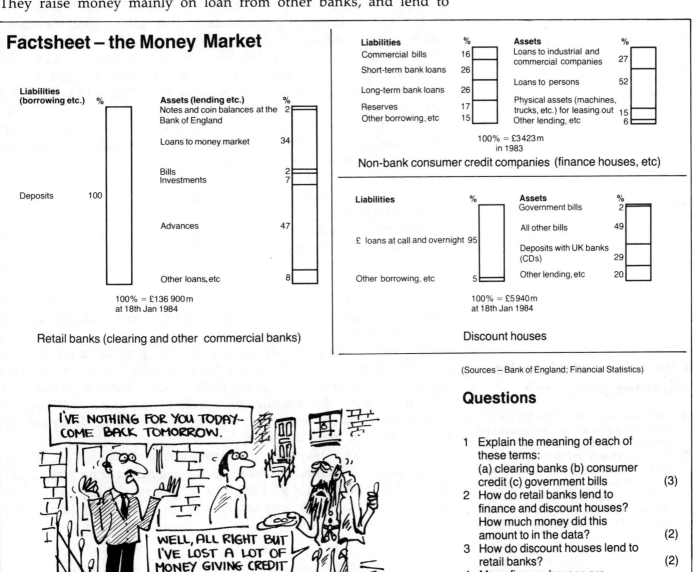

## Factsheet – the Money Market

**Liabilities (borrowing etc.)** %

Deposits 100

**Assets (lending etc.)** %
Notes and coin balances at the Bank of England 2
Loans to money market 34
Bills 2
Investments 7
Advances 47
Other loans, etc 8

100% = £136 900m
at 18th Jan 1984

Retail banks (clearing and other commercial banks)

**Liabilities** %
Commercial bills 16
Short-term bank loans 26
Long-term bank loans 26
Reserves 17
Other borrowing, etc 15

**Assets** %
Loans to industrial and commercial companies 27
Loans to persons 52
Physical assets (machines, trucks, etc.) for leasing out 15
Other lending, etc 6

100% = £3423m
in 1983

Non-bank consumer credit companies (finance houses, etc)

**Liabilities** %
£ loans at call and overnight 95
Other borrowing, etc 5

**Assets** %
Government bills 2
All other bills 49
Deposits with UK banks (CDs) 29
Other lending, etc 20

100% = £5940m
at 18th Jan 1984

Discount houses

(Sources – Bank of England; Financial Statistics)

## Questions

1  Explain the meaning of each of these terms:
   (a) clearing banks (b) consumer credit (c) government bills (3)
2  How do retail banks lend to finance and discount houses? How much money did this amount to in the data? (2)
3  How do discount houses lend to retail banks? (2)
4  Many finance houses are part-owned by commercial banks. Suggest reasons for this. (3)

SPECIMEN BILL OF EXCHANGE (Clients' names are fictitious)

⑧
£8,240

Keighley
11th August, 1982

① ⑥ ⑨
⑦ AT SIGHT OF THIS SOLA OF EXCHANGE PAY TO OUR ORDER THE SUM OF STERLING

POUNDS EIGHT THOUSAND TWO HUNDRED AND FORTY ONLY FOR VALUE RECEIVED

Drawn under Irrevocable Credit of Barclays Bank International PLC Pennine House,

45, Well Street, Bradford No. FDO/2/6769 dated 20th July, 1982

⑤
To: Barclays Bank International PLC
Pennine House,
45, Well Street,
Bradford

②
For and on behalf of
QUALITY WOOLLENS LTD
④

Director

The legal definition of a bill of exchange is:
1. an unconditional order in writing
2. addressed by one person (the drawer)
3. to another (the drawee)
4. signed by the person giving it (the drawer)
5. requiring the person to whom it is addressed (the drawee, who when he signs becomes the acceptor)
6. to pay
7. on demand or at a fixed or determinable future time
8. a sum certain in money
9. to, or to the order of, a specified person or to bearer (the payee).

The phrases are numbered to correspond to the various parts of the bill of exchange shown above. All the information above must be shown on every bill of exchange.

figure 1 – a bill of exchange

consumers buying on credit. Many of the large chains of clothes shops, for example, offer 'credit accounts'. You can buy perhaps £100 worth of clothes now and pay, with interest, over several months. These schemes are usually set up, and paid for, by finance houses.

Cars, furniture and electrical goods can be bought on 'hire purchase'. The finance house buys the product and hires it for a time to the consumer. The consumer pays during that time, with interest. Ford Motor Credit Co. Limited lends to customers in this way, to help them buy Ford cars.

Do your friends have credit cards – Barclaycard, Access or American Express, perhaps? These allow consumers to buy one month and pay the next, or even delay payment for a few months longer. That delay costs a rate of interest, however.

# Bills and discounting

Perhaps you could lend to your friends yourself. They could make out an 'I.O.U.' note in exchange for some of your cash. A good way to do this is with a 'post-dated' cheque. They write a cheque, perhaps for £10, and make it out to you. But they add a date set not for today, but perhaps three months ahead. You give money now, and get it back when the cheque is paid in three months' time. You lend to them for that time.

Bills and certificates of deposit (CDs) work like this. Companies sell commercial bills, or bills of exchange to finance trade in goods and materials. The Bank of England sells Treasury bills to raise loans for the government. Banks sell certificates that show money is held in deposit accounts for a time. All these are very like post-dated cheques. But who buys them?

Discount houses are banks that specialise in lending this way. They borrow often, and for very short periods at a time, from other banks. They pay clearing banks, for example, a low rate of interest for borrowing some of their reserve assets 'at call or short notice'. Discount houses use this money to buy bills and CDs either directly from the government, or at second-hand from firms and banks. And they make their profit by buying at a discount.

What would you give your friends for their post-dated cheque? In three months' time it will be worth £10 to you, but not now. You should pay less than £10, perhaps £9.50 or so, to make something on the loan. This is called discounting. Discount houses buy bills for less than their face value, and so earn interest. Notice that the less they pay for the bills, the more they earn.

But this is still a risky business. Banks might claim back the money lent to discount houses. Discount houses would have no way to pay their debts. They would go bust, but for the special support of The Bank of England. We see why and how the Bank of England offers this help in the next section.

## Checklist – what do the different banks do?

- commercial or retail banks borrow from the general public on deposit and lend credit to consumers
- finance Houses and other consumer credit companies borrow from banks and lend credit to consumers
- discount Houses borrow from banks and lend to firms, bank and government by buying bills or deposits

# 5.6 The Bank of England

Would we miss the Bank of England if it were not there? This is often the case with the most important things, and so it is here. For the Bank of England is the *central bank* in the UK. It is banker to the banks and to the government, and its central work is to bring these two together.

## Banker to all other banks

You can open an account at your bank to keep your money in and to help you make payments. The Bank of England holds accounts in the same way, but from all banks working in the UK. Clearing banks, foreign banks and others must all keep ½ per cent of their total assets on deposit at The Bank of England. They can use these accounts to pay one another. It can use them to pay for its own business.

The Bank of England helps its customers in several ways. Your bank can give you advice and information, and lend to you if you need credit. The Bank of England does this on a larger scale. It collects and publishes information on the money and capital markets, and on other issues that affect banks. It tries to serve their interests and to make the banking system work well.

But accidents happen. Some banks deal in risky business. A bank may go bust, as did the first bank in Manchester. In these cases, the Bank of England steps in to protect investors and the people's trust in banking. It acts as *lender at last resort*, by lending to banks in trouble because they cannot borrow in the usual way.

This happens almost every week in the discount market. Discount houses run special risks in their business, by lending a great deal of money to the government, among others. But the discount houses can always borrow from the Bank of England, at the rate of interest it sets. At one time that rate was known as Bank Rate, then as minimum lending rate. It had a strong effect on money markets. Since 1981, its work is done more quietly as the lending rate is no longer declared officially.

## Issuing notes and coin

Cash is always needed in *circulation* with banks and the general public. But the amount changes as people choose to pay with notes and coins, or with bank accounts instead.

The Bank of England is in charge of issuing notes and coins for the government. It takes in old notes as they wear out, and replaces them with new. It exchanges banks' deposits for notes as the banks wish, in order to meet the demands of the public.

What is the Bank of England? How does it control the amount of money and loans in the economy?

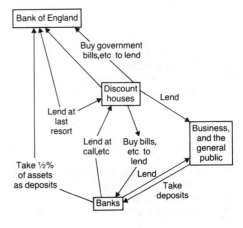

*figure 1 – How does the Bank of England work in the money market?*

## Checklist – what does the Bank of England do?

● issues notes and coins for the government
● acts as banker to the banks, holding deposits, lending at last resort, etc
● acts as banker to the government, holding accounts, arranging loans, holding official reserves and running monetary policy

## 'Bang goes that boom again'

The credit squeeze is back again, and the economic boom looks likely to stop before it even begins. The sharp jump in interest rates could hit every family in the land—dearer mortgages, dearer hire purchase, dearer goods and the chance of higher rates and fewer jobs.

Overdrafts are likely to go up—but not at once. The banks will wait for the money market to settle down before making their moves. But rates and jobs are likely to be hit next year as councils and industry face higher interest charges.

All this started last week when the Bank of England signalled to the markets that interest rate rises were on the way. Then they called in special deposits, and bang went the recovery.

### Questions

1  Explain the following terms:
   (a) interest rates, (b) overdrafts, (c) special deposits (3)
2  Why is it the job of the Bank of England to bring in a credit squeeze? (1)
3  How is the credit squeeze likely to affect Bank of England lending to discount houses? (1)
4  How has the Bank of England caused the credit squeeze? (2)
5  What are the likely effects of the credit squeeze on output, jobs and inflation in the economy? (3)

Once these notes and coins were 'backed' in a real way. The Bank of England held gold and silver to cover the value of at least a share of notes issued. These days, money is supported by little more than people's trust.

But the Issue Department of the Bank does hold something to back the issue of currency. It holds government securities, as claims on the government's income from taxation. This balances its accounts, but does not help you or me. Every bank note 'promises to pay the bearer on demand' a sum of money. But this is one of those government promises that you do well not to test.

## Banker to the government

The Bank of England was first set up in 1694 to raise loans for the government. It was nationalised in 1946 so that the government could take full control of its work. Much of that work is done for its main customer – the government itself.

The Bank holds accounts for the government to cover both income and spending. It acts as an agent for the government to borrow money and manage loans that have been made in the past. It sells government securities, pays back loans that have run their time, and pays out interest as it comes due.

But the Bank also has much to do with government policy to control the economy. It manages the official reserves of international money, such as gold and dollars. This Exchange Equalisation Account can be used to buy and sell UK pounds to affect the exchange rate. We see how and why in Part 7. And it runs the monetary policy of the government.

## Monetary policy

Monetary policy uses money and loans to steer the economy. The Bank of England is best placed to do this because of its close contact with banks. It can change bank lending, interest rates and money supply.

But how can it do this? Where is the wheel, the rope or the handle that the Bank should use? There seem to be two main controls. First the Bank may change bank lending directly. The Bank holds deposits from every bank working in the UK. It can order part of those funds into *special deposits*. Banks cannot use these deposits to pay their debts – the accounts are not liquid. They must cut their loans to put more of their assets into cash and other reserves.

A second control is to work in money markets. The Bank deals in government securities from day to day. It can sell more, so that the public use their bank deposits to buy. This may cut bank reserves and lending. It can buy and sell in a number of ways, to affect the supply of loans, money and interest rates. All these are called *open market operations*.

Rather more closed operations are also possible. The Bank may change the rate at which it lends to discount houses and other banks. It can lead a change in *interest rates*, and so squeeze the amount of credit given in money markets.

Do you want to be a millionaire? The surest way to be one is to start as one. You can put your money to work. You can lend and earn a rate of interest. You can invest in firms that use your money to buy new machines and building. This earns you profit. You can protect your money from inflation and keep its real value. But also you can earn an income. As little as 5 per cent rate of return earns you £50 000 a year!

Long-term loans and investments are arranged in capital markets. Your money is *liquid capital* that can be spent on real goods such as machines, buildings or materials. How would you set about lending it?

How can people invest their money? What are the main parts of the capital market, and how does the Stock Exchange work?

## Long-term lending

Most of us are not millionaires, but we do have savings, and we do lend in parts of the capital market. The Post Office arranges long-term loans from the general public to the government. It sells National Savings Certificates, for example, that pay a rate of interest each year. It sells Premium Bonds that pay prize money to a number of lucky winners each month, in place of interest.

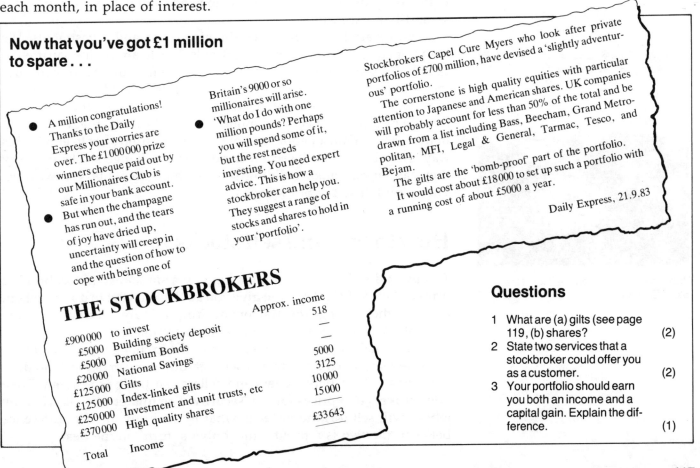

**Now that you've got £1 million to spare . . .**

- A million congratulations! Thanks to the Daily Express your worries are over. The £1 000 000 prize winners cheque paid out by our Millionaires Club is safe in your bank account.
- But when the champagne has run out, and the tears of joy have dried up, uncertainty will creep in and the question of how to cope with being one of

Britain's 9000 or so millionaires will arise. 'What do I do with one million pounds? Perhaps you will spend some of it, but the rest needs investing. You need expert advice. This is how a stockbroker can help you. They suggest a range of stocks and shares to hold in your 'portfolio'.

Stockbrokers Capel Cure Myers who look after private portfolios of £700 million, have devised a 'slightly adventurous' portfolio.

The cornerstone is high quality equities with particular attention to Japanese and American shares. UK companies will probably account for less than 50% of the total and be drawn from a list including Bass, Beecham, Grand Metropolitan, MFI, Legal & General, Tarmac, Tesco, and Bejam.

The gilts are the 'bomb-proof' part of the portfolio.

It would cost about £18 000 to set up such a portfolio with a running cost of about £5000 a year.

*Daily Express, 21.9.83*

## THE STOCKBROKERS

| | | Approx. income |
|---|---|---|
| £900 000 | to invest | 518 |
| £5000 | Building society deposit | — |
| £5000 | Premium Bonds | — |
| £20 000 | National Savings | 5000 |
| £125 000 | Gilts | 3125 |
| £125 000 | Index-linked gilts | 10 000 |
| £250 000 | Investment and unit trusts, etc | 15 000 |
| £370 000 | High quality shares | £33 643 |
| Total | Income | |

### Questions

1. What are (a) gilts (see page 119, (b) shares? (2)
2. State two services that a stockbroker could offer you as a customer. (2)
3. Your portfolio should earn you both an income and a capital gain. Explain the difference. (1)

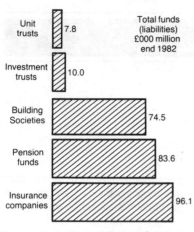

Unit trusts 7.8

Investment trusts 10.0

Building Societies 74.5

Pension funds 83.6

Insurance companies 96.1

Total funds (liabilities) £000 million end 1982

(Source – Bank of England, Financial Statistics)

*figure 1 – most saving is with large institutions*

Brokers and jobbers on the floor of the Stock Exchange

Building societies offer long-term loans to house-buyers. Perhaps you save by paying into a share account at the Abbey National, Halifax, Woolwich or any of the other societies. Your money is lent to people so they can buy houses. The loan may be for twenty years or so, and is a mortgage backed by the value of the house. If the borrower cannot pay back what is owed, the house is sold to clear the debt instead.

Most people save as they work. They put money aside for their old age and for their family in pensions and life assurance. They use these savings as a pension when they retire from work, and as a sum of money for their family when they die or reach a certain age. In the meantime, however, the money must be put to work. Pensions funds and insurance companies have huge sums to invest for long periods of time.

They act as institutional investors – as bodies that protect the value of people's savings for them. (See figure 1.) Investment trusts and unit trusts do the same. They collect funds from a large number of savers, and specialise in the work of investment. They employ experts in the business and they spread their risks by investing in a number of different ways. Savers gain as a result. But what happens to all the money?

## The Stock Exchange

Much of the work of the capital market comes together at the Stock Exchange. This is the building in London with regional branches, that acts as a market for long-term loans and investments. It puts buyers with money in touch with sellers who need capital. It is the market for second-hand securities.

*Securities* are legal certificates showing loans and investments. We know of cheques, for example, and bills. These are both securities in that they secure a claim on a bank account, a firm or government. But the Stock Exchange deals in different securities, called stocks. You can buy stocks as the main way to lend or invest for a long time. You earn interest or profit, and get your money back at the end if that was agreed in the loan. But most people do not hold stocks from start to end in this way. They buy and sell second-hand. They exchange stocks in a way they cannot exchange building society share accounts, for example. They simply use the Stock Exchange.

## How to buy and sell stocks

To buy and sell stocks you must employ a *stockbroker*. Stockbroking firms are specialists. They can give you advice on what to do and when, and then they arrange the deal for you. You and I are not allowed on the floor of the Stock Exchange, where deals are made.

In the usual way, your broker goes to the exchange to meet *jobbers*. These are specialist firms which act as middlemen, or 'shops', holding securities so that both buyers and sellers can trade with them. They offer brokers two prices for any security. The higher price is what the jobber will sell for, the lower is what he will buy at. The difference between the two is a profit – the jobber's 'turn' on the deal.

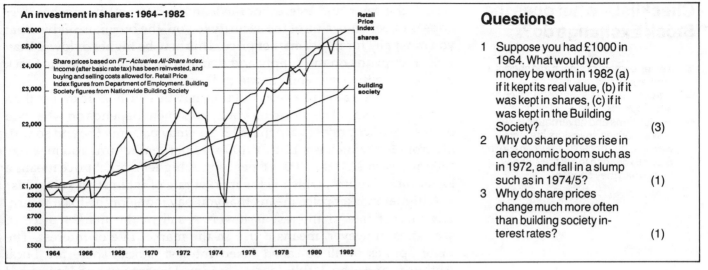

An investment in shares: 1964–1982

Share prices based on *FT–Actuaries All-Share Index*. Income (after basic rate tax) has been reinvested, and buying and selling costs allowed for. Retail Price Index figures from Department of Employment. Building Society figures from Nationwide Building Society

**Questions**

1 Suppose you had £1000 in 1964. What would your money be worth in 1982 (a) if it kept its real value, (b) if it was kept in shares, (c) if it was kept in the Building Society? (3)

2 Why do share prices rise in an economic boom such as in 1972, and fall in a slump such as in 1974/5? (1)

3 Why do share prices change much more often than building society interest rates? (1)

A number of jobbers deal in each type of security. They compete closely with each other for business in the same place. This market is almost perfect, and sets price exactly for each security. That price rises and falls from time to time, as more buyers or more sellers become interested. We saw how demand and supply set price in this way in Section 4.5.

You must pay your broker a 'commission' for arranging a deal for you. This is set at a fixed rate. But changes in 1984 mean that brokers can offer you an extra service. Now they may hold stocks, as jobbers do, on their own. They may buy and sell with you directly, without needing to cover the floor of the Exchange in the usual way.

You use a broker to find the best price around when he or she buys and sells for you. Deals are agreed with jobbers in the Exchange, but 'in good faith' only. Brokers and jobbers keep records, but do not complete their deals until the next settlement day. These come every two weeks or so, and it is only then that cash and securities change hands at the agreed price. Until then, members of the Stock Exchange must trust each other, and hold to their motto: 'My word is my bond'.

# Gilt-edged

What sort of stocks can you buy on the Stock Exchange? Three-quarters of the value of the deals made there are in gilt-edged stock, which are securities sold by the government. These may be short-term if up to five years, medium if up to ten, or long-term if over ten years. These are called gilts because they are almost as safe as gold, but they are known also as British Funds, or Government Bonds. The government can always pay back its debts by taxing the people of the country.

What can you earn by buying gilt-edged stock? You earn a payment of interest each year, and at the end of the loan, you get back its original value. But these payments may be worth more or less to you depending on what *you* paid for the stock.

Suppose you buy a 12 per cent Treasury Stock, 2015. The government first sold this security at an official or nominal value of £100, say. Now it pays 12 per cent of that value in interest each year. This is a fixed level of interest worth £12. In the year 2015, the loan will end, and whoever owns the security will be paid £100. But what is it worth now?

## Checklist – what does the Stock Exchange do?

Both the value and interest of the loan are different from what they appear to be. The value of the security to you, the buyer, is set by what you must pay for it – its market price. This may be higher or lower than £100. It depends on the supply and demand for securities on the Stock Exchange at the time you choose to buy.

The security pays £12 a year, but this may be worth more or less than 12 per cent to you. The return on your investment depends on what you pay as a market price to earn that £12. You may pay only £50 and so earn £12 from £50, which is a $12/50 \times 100 = 24$ per cent return. You may pay £200 and earn $12/200 \times 100 = 6$ per cent. A higher market price means a lower rate of return, which is the market rate of interest on securities.

A higher market price means that you pay more for the fixed return. The market rate of interest is lower. A fall in the market price of securities, however, means a rise in the market rate of interest. The same applies to all so-called 'fixed interest' stock. There are Local Authority and other Public loans. There are Debentures and Unsecured Loan Stocks, issued by companies. These all work in the same way as long term loans. Their rates of interest are fixed to the borrower, but can change, through changes in second-hand market price, to the lender.

## Shares

You can invest in a company by buying its shares. We saw why companies sell shares in Section 3.2, and will ask how good a way this is to raise funds in the next section. But we must see what shares offer an investor. What do you get for your money? (See figure 2.)

You buy a part of the ownership of a company. Often this means that you have a say in what it does and always it means that you earn a share of its profits. There are many different companies, of course, and there are different sorts of shares issued by each. But all these are bought and sold, second-hand in the stock market.

You can make money from shares in two ways. One is to earn a regular income. Preference shares pay a fixed sum if the companies make enough profit to afford it. Ordinary shares, or equities, pay a dividend taken from the profit of the company. As with stocks, your return from shares depends on price and payment. Perhaps you pay a market price of £2 for a share, and earn a dividend of 20p. Your rate of return or yield on the share is $20p/£2 \times 100\% = 10$ per cent.

The other way to make money is by dealing in shares to earn a capital gain. You buy at a low price and sell at a high one so that the value of your money grows. But there are risks. You must predict how buyers and sellers as a whole will change the price of each share. You may guess incorrectly and lose rather than gain on the deal.

Speculators deal in shares like this. The period before each settlement day gives them a special chance. They can sell shares they do not have at a high price and buy at a low price before the period ends. They clear both deals at the same time, and earn a profit on the difference. This is called 'bear' dealing. The opposite is to buy at a low price and sell at a high one. A 'rising market' allows this 'bull' dealing.

You could buy a large number of shares with a million pounds. With wise investment, the value of your money would grow. With bad speculation, it might disappear altogether!

*figure 2 – a share certificate*

# 5.8 Business finance

What happens to all the money people put into banks and the Stock Exchange? Some goes to consumers so that they can buy cars, houses and other things, but most goes into businesses. Firms need money to buy machines, buildings and materials, and to pay for production. They need more capital in order to grow and improve their business.

Firms often look first to their own profits. This can be a good source of funds. The firm can do whatever it likes with money of its own. It does not have to pay interest, or pay it back later. But there is a cost.

The people who own firms expect to be paid. Shareholders expect a dividend, or else they see no point in holding on to shares. They are glad to see some of their firm's profits 'ploughed back' as investment for the future. As the company grows and becomes stronger, their shares become more valuable. Future dividends should be high.

But the firm may retain too much as its share of profits. Shareholders may feel that they want more money distributed so they can lend it at a rate of interest, perhaps. There is an opportunity cost in ploughing profit back into the firm, because that next best alternative is lost. Too many shareholders may sell their shares in protest, and the firm may be taken over by new owners. So, how else can firms raise money?

## Credit

There are many ways to arrange short-term loans, or credit. We met some of them in the work of the money market, in Section 5.5. A firm can sell commercial bills or bills of exchange. These, we saw, act as cheques, but set for a later date. One firm pays another for its goods or services, but only after a wait. Trade credit works in the same way. It allows a shop, say, to pay its supplier for goods *after* it has sold them.

You may have a TV or fridge in your house bought on hire-purchase. Firms borrow from finance houses in much the same way, by leasing. They hire cars or equipment for a few years at a time. The goods are bought and owned by finance houses, but used in production by the firms.

Most important, however, are short-term loans from banks. Firms borrow on overdraft, by borrowing on their current account at a clearing bank. This is easy to set up and easy to change. Or the firm may arrange a special loan for an agreed period of time. But the bank may expect a say in how the firm uses this money, or how it runs its business generally.

How do firms raise money? How can firms use the money market and the capital market, and which is most useful?

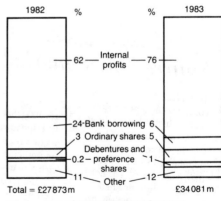

(Source – Bank of England, Financial Statistics)

*figure 1 – how do UK companies raise capital funds?*

## Where did the profit go?

In 1983, BP paid £553 million in interest payments on loan stock, bank loans, etc, and had £1031 million left as profit. This is what they did with it:

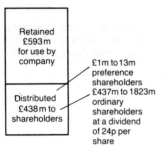

Retained £593m for use by company

Distributed £438m to shareholders

£1m to 13m preference shareholders
£437m to 1823m ordinary shareholders at a dividend of 24p per share

## Questions

1  How much did BP pay to each preference shareholder? (1)
2  In which of the above sums do payments to debenture holders appear? (1)
3  BP's profits were large enough to pay twice as much to shareholders. Why do you think shareholders agree to receive so little? (2)

# Long-term loans

A firm can raise long-term loans in the capital market. We saw how this works in the last section. This can raise working capital for perhaps five years, or much longer, at a time. The firm has free use of the money for all that time, and so can do more with it than with short-term loans. But the rate of interest is likely to be greater, and lenders expect to come top of the list of debts to be repaid, if the firm should go bust.

Perhaps you live in a house bought with a mortgage. This is a long-term loan either at a fixed or a changing rate of interest. The house secures the loan, and is sold if needed to pay it back. Firms borrow in the same way, with mortgages on their property. This can be a good way to raise money for business as a shop, perhaps, or a restaurant. But, of course, firms if they rent rather than own their buildings cannot borrow like this.

But they can still turn to long-term securities such as debentures, or other loan stock. The firm fixes at the start the rate of interest it will pay and the length of time of the loan. But investors can buy and sell these stocks, at second hand. Changes in market price change the rate of return they get for their money.

Firms are free to use investors' money until it has to be paid back. But they can raise money another way so that they never need to pay back. They can sell shares.

# A new issue of shares

A joint stock company sets up in business by selling shares. We saw in Section 3.2 how all large companies raised working capital this way. The firm is a legal body, with authority to sell a certain number of shares. So how can it raise more capital this way if later it needs to grow?

Many firms prepare for this. They keep within what they are authorised to issue. This allows them to raise more capital later on. At first shareholders may have been asked to pay only a part of the value of their shares. Now they would be asked to pay the rest. At first, some shares may have been authorised but never issued. Or others may be authorised by law now. These could be sold in various ways.

The firm can give existing shareholders a chance to buy more

## *Spurred on to market*

Tottenham Hotspur has become the first professional soccer club in Britain to go public after a 1982–83 season in which it was more popular with its supporters than its creditors. The north London club finished up fourth in the English first division and with £4.3m in long-term debts and bank overdrafts. Much of this money was borrowed to pay for a new £5.2m stand completed last year. Hefty transfer fees for players were another big expense.

It was to reduce its interest rate burden of over £600000 that Spurs took the first step towards a full stock exchange listing by announcing a 10-for-one rights issue for £1m and a capital reconstruction. On getting its listing, Spurs planned to raise a further £3m through an offer for sale. The money would be used to pay off its bank debt.

Other clubs, many of them in much rougher financial straits than Spurs, are keen spectators. They have up to now been bankrolled mainly by businessmen keen to be associated with the local team. The recession has made businessmen less willing to play their role, particularly as falling ticket sales are ruining balance sheets.

Spurs, 100 years old last year, saw attendances at its White Hart Lane ground fall by 14% last year and has not paid a dividend since 1979. None the less the club's new chairman reckons it will be paying dividends again soon.

The Economist, 18.6.83

## Questions

1  Explain the terms (a) 'to go public', (b) long-term debts, (c) dividend. (3)
2  Show 2 ways used by Spurs to raise more capital. (2)
3  Why did Spurs want to raise more capital? (1)

shares, in line with what they already own. This is called a 'rights' or 'scrip' issue. The balance of ownership of the firm may not change very much. But it may be better to find more and different investors. Shares can be sold to the general public as a new issue.

For this, the firm needs an issuing house to act as its agent. There are specialist bankers in the City of London, that help firms in a number of ways. Often they are well-respected merchant bankers, such as Rothschilds and Lazard Brothers. They advertise the sale, and arrange guarantees that a certain amount of money will be raised.

# Which shares to sell?

There are many types of shares, but one important difference is between preference and ordinary shares. Firms have a certain amount of profit left after costs, and paying back short and long-term loans. They must use this profit to pay preference shareholders first but only up to a certain, agreed level. This may be perhaps 10 per cent on each £1 share, or $10\% \times £1 = 10p$ a year.

All profit that is left can be paid to ordinary shareholders, as dividends. This may be high in a good year, or nothing at all in a bad year. Ordinary shareholders carry more of the risks of business, but can gain more of the rewards as well. They supply the enterprise behind the firm, and both own it and run its business. But some have more of a say than others.

Ordinary shareholders together choose a board of directors. Directors own shares themselves, but they also run the firm for the shareholders. Some ordinary shares do not let their owners vote on these decisions, but many do. A firm that sells more shares may change its owners, and they may change how it runs. There may be a risk of take-over.

# How to raise more money?

Which is the best way for a firm to raise money: profit, credit, loans or shares? Which is safe, cheap and most available? This must differ from one firm to another, but some things are clear. It is easiest for firms to use their own profits for investment. This is where most of their money comes from, by and large. But small firms need to raise more than they can manage on their own, and so do many large firms.

Firms choose between credit and loans in terms of cost, and their use of the money. Long-term investment, such as building factories or buying land, is suited to long-term loans. Short-term uses such as holding stocks, or paying a high wages bill one month are best served by credit. Large firms may find it much easier than small firms to raise money in these ways. It may be more difficult to choose between loans and share issues. A firm wants control of its work, as it has with loans. But it also wants to be able to use that money for a long time without the cost of paying back, as with shares. Owners of small firms may not want to have others sharing their company at all. Clearly, there must be a balance, so that firms do not become over-stretched with either lending, or shareholders.

## Checklist – what is the best way for a firm to raise capital?

● profit – internal funds are controlled only by the firm, but could be paid out to shareholders
● loans – short-term credit and long-term loans do not change the owners of the firm but must be paid back with interest
● shares – never repaid, but change the ownership of the firm

# Part 6 Steering the economy

## 6.1 Living standards

Are we getting better or worse off? National income may be the best measure of living standards, but how is it worked out?

'You know, things were different when I were a lad.'

'Yes, Dad, but were they better or worse?'

We all want to be well off, but it is sometimes very difficult to tell how we are doing. You may gain by having more only because someone else has less. But what is the change in general living standards? You may gain more one year but less the next. But how have living standards changed over a long period of time?

We can answer these questions using figures for *national income*. This measures the value of all goods and services consumed in a country over a given period of time. We can use this measure to compare things in the 1950s and in the 1980s, for example.

National income in 1955 was worth around £17 000 million. There are different ways to measure this sum, but one common way uses what is known as *Gross Domestic Product* (GDP) at factor cost. By 1983, the same measure had risen to over £250 000 million – a huge rise.

But much of this rise is due to inflation. Inflation raises the prices of all the goods and services which are counted in national income. There may be no more around, but they may appear more valuable in terms of money. It is the value of money which has fallen, not the value of income which has risen.

## Money and real income

We must talk of money and real income. *Money income* measures the value of goods and services in terms of their prices at the time. These current prices are the only way we have to measure that value. But *real income* measures the amount of goods and services, with the effect of price changes taken away. This shows the volume of income at constant prices.

How can we make this change? We must measure changes in the general level of prices. We saw how the Retail Price Index does this, in Section 5.3. We use the index to deflate money figures, to allow for changes in the cost of living. So how has real national income changed?

Prices in 1955 were only about one-eighth of their 1983 value. In 1983 prices, therefore, the real value of 1955's national income was some £17 000m × 8 = £136 000m. This compares with a 1983 value of over £250 000m. In real terms, therefore, national income had almost doubled. The country is better off. Your parents' share may have risen in line with this, to make them twice as well off. But would this be a fair share or not?

**Living standards in the '50s and the '80s – spot the difference!**

| | Then – 1950s | Now – 1980s |
|---|---|---|
| Real income per head | £2720 | £4570 |
| Life expectancy – male/female | 59/64 years | 71/77 years |
| Housing – average number per dwelling | 3.8 | 2.6 |
| Cars – average number of people per private vehicle | 21 | 3.5 |
| Phone calls – average number of calls per person a year | 66 | 385 |

(Source – Social Trends)

## Questions

1 Explain the term 'real income per head'. (1)
2 Why do only *new* houses and cars count as part of each year's national income? (1)
3 What do the pictures show you about the change in living standards over 30 years? (2)

# Better or worse?

Perhaps there are more goods and services for everyone to have, but are there more people looking for a share as well? This depends on how the population has changed. In the mid-1950s there were around 50 million people in the UK. By 1983, there were about 6 million more.

How did an average share of income change over the time? We can show this by measuring real income *per head* of population. Each person's average share was worth about £136000m ÷ 50 million = £2720 in 1955, and £250000 ÷ 56 million = £4570 in 1983.

But we are not all average, and some people actually get much more than others. Your parents have more income now than when they were children, just as you should gain more in future.

'Real incomes are double what they were in your day, dad.'

'I don't know about that. All I know is that we had a good time then. We could have a pint of best, go to the cinema, ride home on the bus and buy a packet of Woodbines, and still have change from a pound.'

Changing incomes bring a change in your way of life. More families own their own houses, and housing is much better. There are bathrooms, fridges, telephones and central heating now. People do not go to the cinema so much, or take bus rides, because they can enjoy watching TV at home and can drive in their own cars. Such things were owned by only a few in the early 1950s.

So far, so good, but what of the quality of life? Were things really so much better then? Perhaps things were less crowded, and more goods were hand-made. Perhaps more people lived in the countryside and had more open space to enjoy. There were fewer divorces, and perhaps less violent crime.

## Checklist – how to compare living standards

- measure national income, in terms of real goods and services
- measure the average share, per head of population
- consider the quality of goods and services and of people's way of life

# Penny pinchers
## Parents forced to cut pocket money

HARD-UP parents are saving on the pennies – by slashing their children's pocket money.

Britain's 10 million children between five and 16 have suffered a 14 per cent pay cut this year.

A survey by Wall's ice cream company shows today that boys have come off worst, and girls are now better off than the boys for only the third time in a decade.

Last year's bonanza when pocket money ROSE by 29 per cent has been shortlived as parents feel the pinch of rising prices and unemployment, says the survey.

The youngsters now have less money in their pockets than the year before last, when their "salaries" failed to keep pace with inflation for the first time.

Children in the Midlands and Wales have been hit hardest this year, with their "pay" being cut by a fifth.

Even in the North of England and Scotland, where parents are traditionally more generous, children have had a cut.

Curiously, children in London and the South of England, the most prosperous parts of Britain, do less well than those in other parts of the country.

Those who rely on help from friends and relatives have fared even worse. The average fall in weekly income from this source slumped by a third.

The report says: "The only age group to have any cause for celebration is the 14 to 16-year-olds, whose average weekly pocket money has risen – a five per cent increase in line with inflation."

These children who also have Saturday jobs, paper rounds and other odd jobs have done better. Their weekly earnings have shot up by 57% per cent.

Daily Express, 12.3.84

## Questions

1 How have the real incomes of children on average, changed (a) 'this year', (b) 'last year', (c) 'the year before last'? (3)
2 Which groups of children have done best in terms of real income 'this year'? (2)
3 Suggest a reason why children's earnings from part-time jobs have risen more than pocket money. (1)

But in most ways, the standard of life is now much better. More children have a chance to learn fully through the education system. People are more healthy, less than half as many young children die each year, and fewer people smoke tobacco. These points are difficult to sum up in any one measure. And the quality of goods and services is even more difficult to compare. There may be more TV programmes to watch these days, but are they better?

'And the beer tasted better then.' There is really no answer to that!

## Income and output

Where has all this extra income come from? Goods and services must be made before they can be consumed. It is the level of output that sets the level of income in the country. National income is the same as national output.

Output has clearly risen since the 1950s. Each person in work is producing more real goods and services from each hour of work. Productivity is greater. We will look at the reasons for this in Section 6.3. And extra output must go somewhere in the economy. There are more cars and houses; more machines and roads; more teaching and health care. Consumers gain from all this production, either now or in the future.

## How to count the national income

The national income is made up of all the real goods and services produced by a country from its resources. This can be counted in different ways.

As income, it can be counted from the earnings of people in the country. They earn from their own work, or by putting their money and property to work for them. They earn from work at home and overseas. A second way to count the same value is by measuring output. This is counted as the value of all goods and services made by firms in the economy. A third way is to count the money that people spend on goods and services made in the economy. This covers the value of both consumer and capital products.

The danger, in all three methods, is of counting the wrong payments. People may be paid money *without* earning it from work. Payments are simply transferred from one person's pocket to another – as a gift, or pocket money, or government benefits. Or one firm may pay for production by another when it buys imports for its own work. We must not count the value of one piece of production twice. We must count only the value added to inputs by a firm, at its own stage of production.

These and other pitfalls make it difficult to count national income exactly. Methods of counting may need to change as years go by, or may be different in different countries. But this is unlikely to change our main result. Incomes have risen since the 1950s. In most ways, things are better now than then – whatever Dad may say.

High output is good for jobs and for living standards. But output does not always stay high – there is often a trade cycle of good years followed by bad. How can we explain these changes in national output?

Firms make goods and services to sell to their customers. If customers spend more, then firms start to produce more. If customers spend less, then firms produce less. It is spending which determines the general level of output.

This may not happen right away. A rise in spending means that firms sell more, but they may sell from their stocks. Records, for example, are kept in shops and warehouses and at the factory, where they are made. As stocks run low the firm will decide to make extra records and employ more materials and labour in order to do so.

Notice that spending causes more spending. The record company pays more to its workers and to its suppliers. It gives other people income they can spend in turn. People earn more as producers, and spend more as consumers, to boost the circular flow of income.

We saw in Section 1.2 how income leads to spending, and spending leads to income, in the economy as a whole. Now we know that income is measured in terms of the production of goods and services. Spending sets that level of output to be either high or low.

Our real income is set by the economy's output of goods and services. Why does this change from time to time? The answer lies in spending, on consumer and capital products.

## Bread today or jam tomorrow?

You can spend your money in very different ways. One is to spend on things like food, films and bus-rides. You benefit from what you buy, but not for long. You can gain for longer if you buy a radio or clothes, but these also are for your own benefit. These are all *consumer goods* that give a benefit to the buyer but are not used to produce any other goods or services.

Another way to spend is by putting your money to work. You could lend to a firm, and the firm could buy production or *capital goods*. It invests in machines, materials or buildings, and uses these to produce more goods and services.

You can consume more of your income today and enjoy benefits from doing so. Or you can invest more of your income in capital goods that raise output in the future. The country is the same, and must split its spending between consumer and capital goods. It must choose to have more bread today or more jam tomorrow.

## Capital goods

What sets the level of spending on capital goods? Firms *invest* in new machines such as trucks, cranes or ships, because they expect to gain

| Consumer goods | Capital goods | |
|---|---|---|

 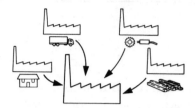

**Questions**

- bought to give benefits to the consumer, now.

- some are perishable, and their benefits do not last – grapes, bus-rides, soft drinks . . .

- some are durable and give benefits over a long time – radios, clothes, cars . . .

- more consumption spending helps industries such as food, electrical 'white' goods and distribution. They may invest more as a result.

- bought by firms to produce goods and services in future.

- some are fixed as capital equipment – buildings, machines, trucks, roads, etc.

- some are bought as materials like wood, copper, or parts for cars, to be made into finished products.

- more capital spending helps industries such as steel, chemicals and construction. And it leads to more output of goods and services in future.

1 State whether each of the following are consumer goods or capital goods: (a) toys (b) beds (c) cement mixers (d) ambulances (e) daffodils (f) office blocks.　(2)
2 A planned economy decides to use its resources to make more capital goods and less consumer goods.
(a) Suggest a reason for this.
(b) How will this affect producers and consumers?　(2)
3 Explain how *paper* can be used either as a perishable consumer good, durable consumer good, or capital good.　(1)

by doing so. They compare the cost of investing with the returns they hope to get back. The main cost is often the rate of interest paid to borrow money, and returns are often counted from extra sales of output made by the machine.

So when will spending on new capital equipment be high? Sometimes this will be when interest rates are low and borrowing is cheap and easy. But mainly it is when firms expect to sell more output.

Not all investment is in fixed equipment, however. Firms also spend on stocks of material to use as inputs, and on products they have made but not yet sold as output. They spend more on these stocks if they wish to be ready for an expected rise in sales.

## Checklist – what makes up total spending in the economy?

- consumption spending is on products bought for personal benefits, now
This comes from private consumers, and government, and foreign buying of exports
- capital spending is on goods and services used by firms in production. It comes as investment in buildings, machinery, or stocks of materials and products

# Consumption

Your spending on magazines, drinks and cassette tapes, for example, counts as part of total private consumption in the economy. But there are two other types of spending on the same types of products. These are government spending and the spending by foreigners on UK exports. What are the reasons why all this consumption spending may rise or fall?

You can choose to spend or save. Consumers as a whole behave in the same way, and if they decide to save more, they have less left to spend. But they may be stopped from spending in another way, for the government taxes income and taxes spending, to raise money. Finally, they may spend, but not on goods and services made in the economy. They may buy imports instead of home production.

There are often changes in saving habits, in tax rates, and in the way people choose between imported and home products. These cause spending on consumer goods made in the economy to rise or fall.

# Leakages and injections

Changes in spending bring changes in the level of output. More or less is left in the circular flow of income. We can see this another way, in terms of leakages and injections.

*Leakages* measure the value of all income that is not spent on the output of the economy, at least for a time. This we have seen can be for three reasons – because of savings, or taxation, or imports.

*Injections* measure the value of any spending on the output of the economy, that does not come from income at the same time. This follows from investment of one kind or another, or government spending, or foreigners' spending on exports.

If injections are greater than leakages, then there is extra spending and output rises. If leakages are greater than injections, there is too little spending and output falls. It is the balance between injections and leakages that sets the level of spending, and so the level of national output.

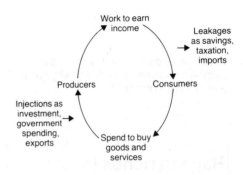

*figure 1 – the circular flow of income*

---

## UK Recovery 1982–83

Demand for UK GDP

|  | % share of GDP in 1983 | % growth 1983 |
|---|---|---|
| **Capital spending** | | |
| Fixed investment | 17 | 5 |
| Stocks | 1 | 1 |
| **Consumption spending** | | |
| Consumers spending | 61 | 4 |
| Government consumption | 21 | 3 |
| Exports | 27 | 1 |
| *less* Imports | 25 | 5 |

(Source – Financial Statement and Budget Report, 1984–85).

Output rose in the UK by about 2% in 1982 and 3% in 1983, after several years of slump. What explains this recovery?

Consumers spending led the way. This is worth nearly two-thirds of all spending, and it was kept high by a low rate of saving. The Budget also played its part by cutting income tax; and bank lending to the personal sector rose as public sector borrowing fell.

Government spending on consumption goods and services also rose to help the recovery. The main cuts in public spending fell on capital projects such as roads and council housing. But private investment recovered, with a strong revival in house-building thanks to lower interest rates.

Payments for imports rose faster than earnings on exports, so cutting the growth of GDP. But the years of de-stocking seemed to be ending, as firms began a slight build-up of stocks.

### Questions

Use the information given to answer the following questions:

1  What share of GDP is taken by
   (a) consumer goods and services?
   (b) capital goods and services?   (1)
2  Suggest a reason for the rise in investment in stocks.   (1)
3  What were the main causes of recovery? Would you expect these to be a sound basis for continued growth of the economy?   (3)

What is economic growth and is it good or bad? What causes growth and why has it been so low in the UK?

What do you want most in all the world – a personal stereo or a home computer, perhaps? Thirty years ago such things were unknown, and other goods that are now very common were then a dream for all but a few. Real output has doubled and brought telephones, TVs, washing machines and cars within the reach of most people. There has been economic growth.

*Economic growth* is the rise in real output of goods and services produced by an economy. This can come as consumption or capital goods, to one group of people or to us all. It may happen more or less from one year to another. There are, in other words, different forms of growth.

## Rags to riches to . . . what?

Shiva Naipaul visited Iran before the Ayotollahs' revolution. These are excerpts from what he wrote in *Among the believers – Islamic Journey* (Deutsch, 1981).

Tehran is rife with rags-to-riches stories – tales of street-corner hawkers who have become millionaires, of building contractors who have become multi-millionaires, of chauffeurs who have become property tycoons.

The money is new. Very new. Nearly all of it has been conjured up within the last 10 years, the 10 glorious years of OPEC. It is these new rich who give Tehran its flashy glamour, whose buying power, whose taste, is reflected in the shops crammed with costly foreign goods; whose cars flood the broad avenues and make a journey at any time of the day a torment.

Tehran's boom town atmosphere is oppressive. Fifteen years ago the city had a population of about three million. Today, it is approaching five million. As in all boom towns, little attention is paid to engineering properties. For Tehran, this negligence spells future catastrophe. The city is in a high-risk earthquake zone. On the fateful day of its destruction, it will be a death-trap.

The factories are devoted to the assembly of consumer goods. They cannot satisfy the hunger for their products.

The showpiece worker I met at the Paykan factory was a true child of the White Revolution. He had come to Tehran from Isfahan where, traditionally, his family had traded in brass. The new world of the assembly line excited and fascinated him. 'I *like* working in factory,' he said.

He took me to see his new apartment on the company's nearby housing estate. We were welcomed by the man's plump wife who, obviously, was well-prepared for the visit. They piloted me into the kitchen.

'Look,' he said, 're-frigerator.'

'Look,' he said, 'gas cooker. With automatic timer.'

'Look,' he said, 'Hoover vacuum cleaner.'

Agriculture has suffered because the farmers cannot always compete with the wages offered in the factories and on the building sites. Some land has actually gone out of use. Many of the villages round and about Tehran are half-deserted. Neglected orchards line the roadsides. It is a rare sight to see anyone actually at work in the fields. One of the consequences is that Iran has to import more and more of its food.

A businessman I met told me 'An oil-less Iran is going to be worse off than Bangladesh. At least they still know how to grow food for themselves.'

The White Revolution is founded on affluence and consumption. A kept workforce profits from a kept 'industrial' revolution. The normal process of development – sacrifice now, satisfaction later – has been thrown aside. 'We're running before we have learned how to walk,' a pessimistic economist conceded. 'The balloon's bound to burst. What a bang that's going to be!'

## Questions

1 What is economic growth? What caused the growth described above? (2)
2 Why do you think workers might 'like working in factory' rather than in traditional crafts and farming? (2)
3 What is wrong with growth mainly in the production of manufactured consumer goods? What other forms of growth are there? (3)
4 What do you understand by 'the normal process of development – sacrifice now, satisfaction later'? (3)

## The effects of growth

What is good about growth? Mainly it means there are more goods and services around that can be consumed. People can achieve more of their wants and live on higher real incomes. The economy goes further towards meeting the basic problem of scarcity.

This extra output can be used in different ways. It can help the poor so that no one goes short of food, clothes, or housing. It can raise the standard of health and education. It can be invested in new factories and machines so that output continues to rise, faster and faster, in future. A growing economy is often a changing, successful economy. It adapts to new methods of work, new attitudes, and new products.

But can you also lose out because of growth? This may happen because of changes to the quality of life. There may be more goods and services, but of a different kind from the ones that went before. People buy consumer goods for the house, for town life and for themselves. They may become cut off from other people or from their old way of life. Firms may make products which sell well instead of products which last. They may replace old forms of work with well paid but boring new work. And growth may only come if the rich gain more income and invest it for the future. The poor may lose out.

# What causes growth?

Real incomes doubled in the UK over thirty years or so. But incomes doubled in some other countries in about half the time. Countries such as Japan and Turkey seem to grow almost four times faster than the UK, and most countries grow faster to some extent. (See figure 1.) What causes this growth, and why does the UK do so badly?

A country produces goods and services by using its resources – labour, capital, land and enterprise. Output grows when the country gets extra resources to use, or makes better use of what it already has.

There may be gains in labour. Developing countries like Kenya have growing populations that add to the size of the workforce. Countries like the UK improve their workforce through education and training. But most gains come in terms of capital. Firms can produce capital goods such as machines and buildings. These can be used as resources to make output grow. Investment leads to growth.

How can a country make best use of its resources? It can specialise in what it makes best and trade with other countries. It can put resources to work in larger firms or in certain areas. Economies of scale raise the output gained from the same amount of resources. And a country can adjust to new methods of work and new forms of products. It can use technical progress to improve production.

The UK has not taken all these opportunities. There has been too little investment, with too much in private housing perhaps and not enough in manufacturing industry. Resources are still used in old industries. They have not moved fast enough into new areas that gain most from economies of scale and technical progress.

# Making the best of a bad job

Perhaps you have less to offer than some other people, but you can still do your best. It would be a waste to do otherwise. But that is what countries do. They raise output through investment and technical progress. But they waste some of their resources, through unemployment.

There is only so much that an economy can produce. This is its *potential* output that would be made if all resources were in work, in the best possible way. A country may come close to this level in the boom years of its trade cycle, when most workers are employed and growth is high. But slump, or recession, cuts growth and the employment of people and machines together. Spending is too low to keep all the country's resources in work.

Spending may fall because private consumers choose to save or firms choose not to invest. But it is also set by government. Why should the government change its spending, and the spending of others, from time to time? This is the question we turn to in the following sections.

## Checklist – what are the effects of growth?

- more output means that a country can satisfy more of its consumers wants
- it may become easier to change the distribution of income, one way or another
- it may become easier to change methods of work and products to continue growth in future
- but growth may make people want and expect more possessions, and care less about the quality of life

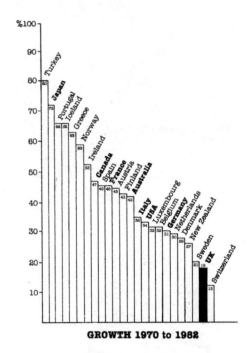

**GROWTH 1970 to 1982**

*figure 1 – how well does the UK grow?*

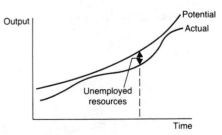

Actual output can fall below potential because of wasted resources, and can grow faster or slower

*figure 2 – two types of growth*

# 6.4 Control of the economy – the government's aims

What should the government aim for if it is to control the economy? Why can it never really win?

'I think the government has done really well to get the economy growing again. It means we're all better off.'

'But the unemployed aren't better off. And there are too many of them.'

'That's because of the battle against inflation. We've got to keep inflation down in order to make our way in the world.'

'But the country is *not* making its way. The balance of payments is in the red again, and we're buying too many imports. What's the government going to do about it?'

No government can expect to please all the people all of the time. But when it comes to steering the economy, the government cannot please them *any* of the time. It can never win.

## What to aim for?

The problems start because the government must aim for a number of different targets. Suppose you must decide how to use your time this weekend. If you only need to please yourself, this might be possible. But what if you need to please your teachers, family and friends as well? Should you do homework, visit relatives or have a party? It is difficult to keep everyone happy.

It is the same for government. The main aim of steering the economy is to make it grow. Growth raises living standards by making extra output. This can be used to help the poor, or those with 'get-up-and-go'. It can be used for consumption now, or investment for the future. Either way the country should gain.

But there are other targets as well. Unemployment wastes resources and brings hardship to those without jobs. The government aims to keep unemployment low. And there is inflation. Inflation cuts the value of money and harms people on fixed incomes. It can cut growth and might even harm the basis of the whole economy if people lose trust in money.

All these targets – growth, jobs and low inflation – measure the *internal* performance of the economy. But there are also targets for how the economy performs in its dealings with other countries. We study these in Part 7, and see that the balance of payments measures how well the country is paying its way. This shows the *external* balance of the economy. It is tied quite closely to the value of the pound in exchange for other countries' money and the exchange rate.

The government faces four main aims, therefore, in trying to steer the economy. It wants growth, high employment, low inflation and a balance of payments with other countries. Why should it be so difficult to win on all four counts together?

# Trade-offs

Suppose that you have now decided how to spend your weekend. You are going to have a good time, listen to music in your room and have friends over for a party. You please yourself and your friends, but what of the others? You do not please your teachers, because you miss their homework, or your family, because you do not go visiting with them.

But it is worse than that. The more you please yourself and your friends, the less you please teachers and family. You win and you lose. You *trade-off* pleasing one group for pleasing another, because more of one aim is possible only at the cost of less of the other.

Government targets are often linked in the same sort of way, through spending. More spending leads to more output, and growth, at least for a time. More spending leads firms to employ more resources in order to raise output, which often means more jobs. So growth and employment are linked together by spending.

But low spending is low demand for goods and services, which cuts prices or the rise in prices. This is the main way to control inflation. And low spending also cuts demand for imported goods and services, but does not affect foreign demand for exports. So the balance of payments for exports less imports improves. The control of inflation and of a weak balance of payments are also linked together by spending.

More spending helps growth and jobs, but less spending helps control inflation and the balance of payments. Other influences are likely to affect all four aims as well. But still there is a trade-off between one set of targets and the other. Government must often choose to aim one way or the other: growth *or* the balance of payments; inflation *or* unemployment.

## Checklist – what are the government's targets?

- a good rate of growth, to raise living standards
- low unemployment, to make full use of the country's resources
- low inflation, to keep the value of money under control
- a sound balance of payments for exports and imports

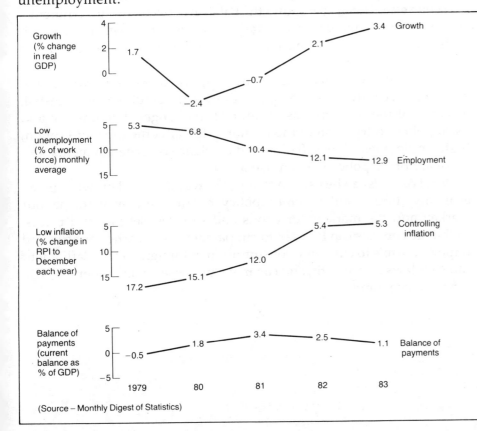

(Source – Monthly Digest of Statistics)

## Factsheet – how well does the government steer the economy?

### Questions

1. Why does the government want to keep down (a) unemployment, (b) inflation? (2)
2. Use the data to show how the government succeeded or failed from 1980 to 1983 to achieve the 4 aims of controlling the economy. (4)
3. Use the data to suggest an explanation of (a) the strong balance of payments in 1981, (b) the low wage-inflation of 1982 and 1983. (2)
4. Suppose the government had tried to keep the economy growing in 1980 and 1981 at all costs. How would this have affected its other aims? (2)

How can the government steer the economy? Why is there so much disagreement over the right form of control?

Imagine a ball game like pin-ball. You have two handles you can use to hit and steer the ball. You have four targets to aim for: two on one side and two on the other. You must try to hit the targets with the ball to gain as good a score as you can. But you have only two handles to use, and sometimes they do not serve you all that well!

The government faces some of the same problems. It has different targets to aim for, as it tries to steer the economy on course. It has different controls it can use, but often with mixed success. The two most important tools are called monetary and fiscal policy.

## What can the government do?

Government policy shows how it tries to control the economy in order to achieve its aims. *Monetary controls* change the amount of money and levels of interest rates. We saw how the Bank of England works at this for the government in Section 5.6.

*Fiscal controls* change the payments made in the economy to and from the government itself. The government sets the level and form of its own spending. It sets rates of taxation to affect the spending of everyone else. The *Budget* shows the balance between the government's spending and its income from taxation. This is mainly set out in March each year, when the Chancellor of the Exchequer makes his Budget speech to Parliament.

These two are perhaps the most important ways in which the government controls the economy. They are its handles on the pin-ball machine of the economy, as in figure 1. It changes its monetary and fiscal policy to try to steer the economy towards the aims of growth, high employment, low inflation and a balance of trade payments. But there are other policies it can use as well.

*Direct controls* can be used to change the way that markets work in the economy. Prices and incomes policy controls the way the labour market, and the markets for goods and services, set pay and prices. Exchange controls can be used to cut payments out of the country, and import controls to cut home consumption of foreign goods. Parliament can pass laws as it sees fit, and can make up these, or any other ways, to steer the economy.

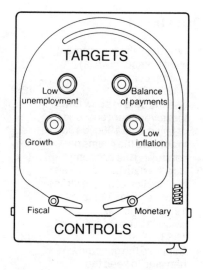

*figure 1 – a pin-ball economy*

# What to aim for?

How should the government use all these controls? Clearly, this depends on what it aims for out of its different targets. It needs an order of priority to know which comes first, second and so on, from growth or the balance of payments, unemployment or inflation. How can we tell what it decides?

Suppose the government *reflates* the economy. How will that change things? Spending will be greater, and so output and employment rise. But this may also raise prices faster and bring in more imports. The government may achieve economic growth and may cut unemployment, but at the cost of more inflation and a weaker balance of payments.

*Deflation* has the opposite effect. This cuts spending and so cuts growth and employment. But its point is to cut inflation and to make the balance of payments improve. These aims take a higher priority.

# How to control spending

Does the government have the right tools for the job? It wants to raise spending to reflate the economy, or cut spending to deflate the economy. This can be done with monetary and fiscal policy.

Suppose the Bank of England raises interest rates and makes it more difficult for banks to lend money. We saw in Section 5.6 how it can do this. The result is likely to be a fall in investment as firms cut their plans to buy extra machines or stocks. There may be a fall in consumption as people put off buying cars or hi-fis, for example, rather than pay more for credit. Spending drops, leading to a fall in inflation and imports.

Fiscal policy works in a different way. The government may cut its spending on consumer or capital goods. Perhaps it employs less people as civil servants, or puts off its plans to build new roads. Or it may raise its rates of tax and so cut the amount that people can spend for themselves. Perhaps it raises the standard rate of income tax or VAT. We will see how all this works in the sections that follow. The result, again, is a fall in spending, and deflation.

# How much of a change?

The government can use monetary and fiscal policy, therefore, to deflate the economy. This helps it reach the aim of less inflation and a stronger balance of payments. But the opposite policies lead to reflation. Monetary reflation brings lower interest rates and more bank lending. Fiscal reflation brings more government spending or lower rates of tax. This should result in more growth and more jobs.

In all cases, the government can take the lead and steer the economy the way it wishes. It may not need to change spending by very much. More spending leads to more income and so to even more spending. The first effect of a change in spending is usually made larger, because of the circular flow of income. There is a *multiplier* effect on the economy.

## Checklist – how can government control the economy?

● monetary policy changes bank lending, interest rates and the amount of money
● fiscal policy changes government spending, taxes, and the budget balance
● direct controls can work on imports, prices and incomes, and so on

135

## How well do economists think the government does?

There was a national survey
of economists
in the USA banks in 1982 to find out.

Bank economists predict that the gross national product – total U.S. output of goods and services – will rise by 3.75 per cent in real terms next year, well above this year's pace but modest as recoveries from recession go.

Economic growth, the survey shows, is expected to be restrained by an unemployment rate which isn't likely to fall to lower than 9 per cent by the end of next year.

In fact, most bankers and economists give the central bank high marks for trying to curb inflation by putting a lid on growth of the money supply. Two thirds of the economists called upon the government to hold to its tight-money course. Yet, a significant number of money experts fear that it may have clamped down too hard and too long, and are urging the central bank to ease up.

Some economists argue that we can afford to let the money supply expand faster. The reason: Business demand for credit is so weak that there is little danger that the government budget deficit – projected to be 150 billion dollars next year – will overheat the credit markets in the near future.

However, bankers are worried that once the recovery is under way and businesses increase their appetite for funds, government red ink of 150 billion dollars or more will send interest rates and consumer prices skyward again.

US News & World Report, 1.11.82

### Questions

1  How well is the USA economy expected to do 'next year' in terms of the government's internal aims? (3)
2  Explain the term 'tight money'. How does this affect growth, employment and inflation in the USA economy? (4)
3  What is a 'budget deficit'? How does it affect the economy (a) when business spending is low, (b) when business spending recovers to a high level? (3)

Once people see that first change in spending, they may choose to change their own consumption or investment. The government may lead them to expect deflation or reflation. Perhaps it only needs to get things started, to 'prime the pump'. Then spending will continue to change, for these other reasons.

This raises a problem. How much should the government try to change spending? It is difficult to tell how monetary and fiscal policy will affect spending in the first place. This depends on how investors respond to interest rates, say, or how people use the money gained by tax cuts.

But there are added changes in spending that follow this first effect. The government may cause too much reflation or deflation without meaning to. It may cause inflation when it tries to solve unemployment. It may cause balance of payments problems when it tries to raise growth. Perhaps the economy needs less government control rather than more?

# Less control or more?

Spending sets output, but it is not all that matters. We saw in Section 6.3 how growth may be short- or long-term. There must be investment and technical progress if output is to continue to grow in future. In the same way, there are causes of unemployment, inflation or balance of payments problems, other than the level of spending. Government policy must cover these.

Unemployment is of different types. Demand may be generally too low if spending falls. But also there may be structural changes, or frictional causes, that give rise to unemployment. We saw how this could happen in Section 2.5. What does it mean for government policy?

Clearly there are policies that can help these other types of unemployment. The government can support industry, for example, to help the switch from old jobs to new. But changes in spending as a whole cannot help. There are a number of economists who feel they make things worse. The more government tries to cut unemployment, the more it leads workers to expect support. Trade unions push for higher wages. The end result may be inflation *instead* of employment.

And what of inflation? We saw in Section 5.2 how monetarist economists believe there is only one real cause of inflation: a rise in the supply of money. Too much money causes too much spending, and leads in the end to inflation. So the government can control inflation only one way – by cutting the amount of money lent by banks. Other policies, such as fiscal policy, are helpful only in support of this.

Some economists come to a clear conclusion. They see that government policy upsets the work of free markets. In the end it causes more problems than it solves. But others feel the opposite. They want more control, to steer the economy on course. It is difficult for these two to agree.

# 6.6 Government spending

The government spent around £2300 for each person in the UK in the year up to April 1984. What did you get for your money and was it worthwhile?

Most public spending is on matters such as social benefits, defence, industry and so on. This money is spent by the central departments of government, such as the Ministry of Defence, and their branches.

Much of the rest is spent by local authorities such as Cornwall County Council or the London Borough of Brent. These spend on council housing, schools, the police, and so on.

There is one other part of government, the public corporations. These are owned by the state for us all, but are run separately from government departments. The nationalised industries, such as British Rail, charge customers for their work and are expected to cover most of their costs on their own. Other public corporations, such as the BBC, do not pay for themselves in this way, and count as part of general government spending.

So how is each £1 used?

## A reward or a gift?

Perhaps you will get a job working for the government or with a firm which sells to the government. Perhaps you will not get any job at all but be paid 'dole' or social benefits instead. Either way, you are paid out of public spending. But the spending is different in each case. It is either for goods and services, or as transfers.

About half of all spending is on real goods and services. The government hires staff, called civil servants, to run its central and local offices. It pays bills for phones, electricity, rent, window-cleaning and so on. These payments are all made in return for people's work. They are paid as rewards, in exchange for real goods and services.

Most other spending is as transfers to people or firms that the government wishes to help. This uses money taken from one group of people to give to others. Over 25p in every £1 of spending is on social security payments, such as supplementary benefit. Retired people are paid pensions; mothers are paid child benefits. People out of work are paid unemployment benefit, at least for a time. All these payments are transfers of income. The government acts as Robin Hood and makes gifts to those in need.

How does the government choose to spend the money it has? What does this do to the economy?

**The forms of public spending**

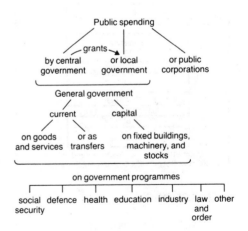

137

## Factsheet – government spending

**General government spending** was £138 000 m in 1983–84, or about 54% of national output.

A quarter of this spending was by local authorities, although half their money came as grants from central departments for education, law and order, etc.

**What form of spending?**

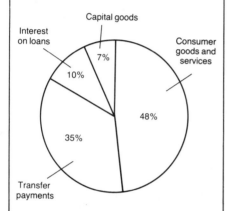

Interest on loans
Capital goods
Consumer goods and services
Transfer payments

7%
10%
48%
35%

**How much on each programme?**

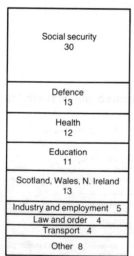

| Social security 30 |
| Defence 13 |
| Health 12 |
| Education 11 |
| Scotland, Wales, N. Ireland 13 |
| Industry and employment 5 |
| Law and order 4 |
| Transport 4 |
| Other 8 |

(Sources – Financial Statement and Budget Report 1984/5; Economic Trends)

## Questions

1  Explain the terms (a) general government, (b) transfer payments, (c) social security.  (3)
2  Suggest ways in which spending on education could be on (a) consumer goods, (b) capital goods.  (2)

# For this or that?

The government must choose between different types of goods, services and transfers. Should it hire more soldiers or doctors, or give more as child benefits or as pensions? Clearly, these choices affect us all. That is why people vote for a government to do what they want.

When you spend a pound, you buy a range of different things. It is the same for the government when it spends on social security, housing, defence or education. How is each £1 spent, on average?

Most is spent on social security – around 30p in the £1. This covers pensions and personal benefits. Next largest is defence, with 13p. But nearly as much is spent on health and personal social services with 12p, and education with 11p. The remaining 35p is spent on industry, trade and employment, roads and transport, housing and the environment, law and order and many other programmes. As much as 8p in £1 is spent just as interest on money borrowed by the government.

# Current and capital spending

Should the government spend on things it wants now, or on things that will last? Should it spend more on goods and services for current consumption or for capital investment?

Current spending helps people now and keeps their living standard higher. It means more jobs for nurses or teachers, for example, or better standards of work by dustmen or the police. But capital spending builds roads and bridges, schools, housing and hospitals. This sets up buildings or equipment to help provide a better public service in future. We met the two terms consumption and capital spending in Section 6.2, and saw there how they form the country's spending. But what of the government?

Most government spending is current. This is on goods and services for current consumption, and as transfers of income to people in need. Less than 10p in every £1 is spent on capital projects that act as investments for the future. And capital spending has risen much more slowly than current spending in recent years.

# Why have public spending?

You spend your own money on the things you choose. But the government taxes you to spend on the things it chooses. Why should the government think that it knows better how to spend people's money for them?

Clearly the government hopes to change the economy. It changes the pattern of spending so that some people have more and others less, and so that more is spent on some goods and less on others. It may also change the level of spending, to make it higher at one time and lower at another than would happen without government. Public spending means that the government can steer the economy the way it chooses. So how does it choose?

It transfers income between groups of people. It takes more from the rich with taxation, as they earn or spend their money. It gives more out

# Harry Hawkins goes on the dole

On the first day he was out of work, Harry Hawkins went to the unemployment benefit office to get unemployment benefit. He claimed extra benefit for his wife, who doesn't go out to work, and his 2 children aged 8 and 11.

When his benefit came through, Harry found that he got £41.05 a week, which includes the extra benefit for his wife and children.

As well as this Harry Hawkins can get supplementary benefit if his resources fall below his requirements (according to the official definitions).

His only savings are £200 in a building society, so he's below the £2500 limit which would disqualify him from supplementary benefit. Using the figures for November 82, Harry works out that his requirements are approximately as follows:

- £4.83 a week rates and water rates
- £6.75 a week mortgage interest payments
- £63.60 living allowance for himself, wife and children.

Total requirements, therefore, work out at £75.20. Harry's resources when he is first unemployed are his unemployment benefit (£41.05 a week) and child benefit (£11.70 a week altogether) – a total of £52.75. He can get supplementary benefit of £75.20 – £52.75 = £22.45.

Harry had, of course, registered for work at his local job centre after claiming unemployment benefit. There seemed to be no suitable jobs in the area, but Harry did not expect to be unemployed for long. However, the months ticked by, and still no suitable job came along.

When Harry had been unemployed for a year, his unemployment benefit ran out. He now had to depend entirely on supplementary benefit – and his fast-dwindling savings.

(Source – The Which? Book of Money, The Consumers Association, 1982)

## Questions

1 Under what form, and programme, of government spending are these benefits counted? (2)
2 Show 3 ways in which these benefits were set to take account of Harry Hawkins' need for support. (3)

to the poor with social benefits, pensions and other transfers. It supports weak industries and poor areas of the country.

The Welfare State aims to help people in need by spending in these ways. Everyone gains something as a result, even if they are well off themselves. They know that the poor are being helped. They know that they are protected themselves from the worst hardships that poverty can bring. People in society are safe and secure from so much hardship. Social security changes the distribution of income, making it more even between people.

# Social goods and services

But public spending does much more besides. It allows the government to provide all sorts of things that would not otherwise be made. Without government there would probably be no armed forces or police, and the country would not be protected. Without government there might be too little education, housing or health services. Why should this be so?

In one way, the government really does know best. You choose what to buy for your own reasons. You cannot know how your spending may affect everyone else. Only the government is in a position to see all points of view and to allow for all 'external' effects. It can look to see if some people's wants are missed or if some resources are wasted. It can allow for social goods and services.

Firms cannot sell services like those of the army or the police. These are called *public goods* and services. We all gain from their production even if we pay nothing for them. Only a government can make us pay, with taxation. Firms cannot sell enough health or education if customers do not know what is best for them. Would you pay £50 to a dentist *before* you had any toothache? A government can help to raise consumption of these and other *merit* goods and services.

There are good reasons, therefore, to explain much of government spending. They go some way towards explaining the great rise in public spending over the years. Government has taken on more and more work in trying to steer the economy well. But many people now feel that government has grown too large and its spending should be cut. The problem is to choose how.

## Checklist – why have public spending?

- to change the distribution of income
- to provide the right amount of public, merit and other social goods and services
- to steer the economy towards the government's targets

# 6.7 Taxes

Why have taxes? What are the main types of taxes in the UK and how do they affect us?

Are you a tax-payer? Perhaps you think that people who pay taxes must earn wages, fill in a tax-form and be well off. But we all pay taxes, for example, when we buy things and pay VAT or other taxes. There are often only two ways not to pay taxes: to break the law, and to do nothing at all.

The government has no money of its own, and yet it spends a vast amount each year. It raises this money from the people of the country and spends it for them. Parliament must pass laws each year to let the government take people's money from them, in taxes.

## Raising money

There are many different kinds of taxes. Some we hear about quite often, and especially at Budget time in March each year. This is when the government states its plans for tax rates and sets out the laws on taxing and spending that it wants Parliament to pass.

How much do we all pay in taxes? The government raised about £2500 from each person in the UK in the year up to April 1984. Some of this came as income, earned by the work of public corporations and other parts of government. But around nine-tenths was raised by taxes and contributions of one kind and another.

*Income tax* brings in more than any other tax and raises around 23 p in every £1 of government revenue. This tax is set, or *levied*, on personal incomes. You pay tax on income earned by working for someone else, or by earning interest, rent or profit from your money or your business. Your employer usually pays the tax on your pay before even paying you, under the Pay As You Earn (PAYE) system. Otherwise you must pay each year and save enough from your earnings to do so.

*Value Added Tax* (VAT) is the next largest money raiser. It collects 11 p in each £1 of revenue. It is levied on the work done by all producers. So most shops charge you VAT on what they sell, because selling is their work. But other firms also charge VAT when they sell the parts and materials that they produce. The tax is charged at each stage of production, but only on the work done at that stage. This covers only the value added by the firm to its inputs of parts and materials. The firm must take the cost of inputs away from the money gained by selling its output. It pays VAT on the difference.

The Budget always seems to put up the taxes on petrol, tobacco and alcoholic drinks such as beer and wine. These are called *excise duties*, and together they raise over 10 p in each £1 of money. They are set as 'lump-sums', of so many pence, or pounds, for each amount sold. The shop that sells beer or cigarettes, say, must charge the tax to its customers and pay it to the government. The amount of tax is raised often to keep up with price rises in inflation.

---

## Factsheet – taxes

General government raised £138 600 million in 1983–84 to pay for its spending.

**How was each £1 raised?**

| | | |
|---|---|---|
| Borrowing, etc.- | 8p | |
| National Insurance contributions | 15p | |
| Earnings from rent, interest, and profit | 9p | |
| Taxes on expenditure | 36p | 9p Local authority rates |
| | | 10p Excise duties – petrol, drink, tobacco |
| | | 11p Value Added Tax |
| | | 7p Other |
| | | 4p Petroleum Revenue Tax |
| | | 4p Corporation Tax, on company profits |
| Taxes on income (and capital) | 32p | 23p Income Tax |

(Source – Financial Statement and Budget Report 1984/5, HM Treasury)

## Questions

1  What share of total government income was directly related to people's incomes? (1)
2  Find two taxes from those shown above that are paid by most businesses. (2)

140

These taxes raise a lot of money. But there are many others as well, that do not raise as much. The more important ones are shown in the factsheet.

# Direct or indirect

You pay income tax when you earn money by working. This taxes your income *directly*. Other direct taxes do the same on other forms of income. Corporation tax takes a share of a firm's profits. Capital gains tax takes a share of people's income from selling property at a higher price than when they bought it. Direct taxes are collected by the Inland Revenue.

You pay VAT and excise duties when you buy certain goods or services from shops. These taxes take another share of your money, but only when you decide to spend it. They fall on your income *indirectly*. Other indirect taxes also fall on spending, such as the special tax on sales of new cars. These are all collected by HM Customs and Excise.

No one likes paying tax. The only good tax to a tax-payer is the one that taxes everyone else. But try to see things from the tax-collector's point of view. What are the different effects of direct and indirect taxes?

People may not like direct taxes such as income tax, but what can they do to avoid them? The surest way is to earn less income.

# The effects of taxes

Direct taxes put people off earning more income to some extent. You may choose to work eight hours a day and not nine if the tax rate feels too high. Perhaps you could earn £10 in the extra hour, but pay £5 of it in tax and contributions to the government. Tax can act as an incentive not to work harder. It can be a *disincentive* to effort.

The tax-collector does not want this to happen. It is bad for you, bad for the country, and bad for the government's income from tax. But every tax is a disincentive on what it taxes. So what can be done?

Indirect taxes fall on spending and mean that you need more money to buy as many goods and services. This is a disincentive to spend. But it also encourages you to earn more money, perhaps by working nine hours instead of eight each day. This way you can still buy the goods and services you want.

The government can use direct and indirect taxes together. The effects of one can be set against the effects of the other. A balanced tax system keeps people keen to work and keen to spend. The government may try to change tax rates from time to time, in order to keep this balance. In 1980, for example, the government cut the standard rate of income tax from 33 per cent to 30 per cent and raised VAT from 8 per cent to 15 per cent.

With some taxes, of course, the government hopes that people *will* be put off spending or earning. High rates of tax on smoking, drinking and betting are meant to cut the amount that people do these things – up to a point. There are costs to society that the government can help people to avoid.

## How to buy cheap take-aways

### Questions

1  What is VAT? (1)
2  Why do you think there is no VAT on food? (1)

## What is oil worth in taxes?

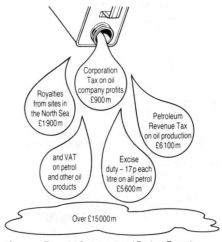

(Source – Financial Statement and Budget Report, 1984–5 HM Treasury [1983–84 figures])

### Questions

1  Find two examples from the above of (a) direct (b) indirect taxes. (2)
2  Total government spending was almost £140 000 m. What share was paid for by oil? (1)

## Checklist – what are the effects of taxes?

- taxes raise revenue, but by different amounts
- direct taxes fall on income, and indirect taxes fall on spending
- taxes are disincentives to either work or spend
- progressive taxes take a larger share from higher incomes and
- regressive taxes take a larger share from lower incomes

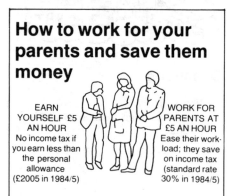

## How to work for your parents and save them money

EARN YOURSELF £5 AN HOUR
No income tax if you earn less than the personal allowance (£2005 in 1984/5)

WORK FOR PARENTS AT £5 AN HOUR
Ease their work-load; they save on income tax (standard rate 30% in 1984/5)

You earn £5 – BUT – you cost them only £3.50

### Question

1 Suggest a reason why the tax system sets (a) personal allowances against tax, (b) a standard rate of tax to cover most incomes. (2)

**3 friends, on 3 incomes, pay 3 taxes –**

|  | | | |
|---|---|---|---|
| their incomes before tax | £505 | £5005 | £50005 |
| Tax A a lump sum of £500 from everyone – leaves | £5 | £4505 | £49505 |
| | | | REGRESSIVE |
| or Tax B a flat-rate, 20% from everyone – leaves | £404 | £4004 | £40004 |
| | | | PROPORTIONAL |
| or Tax C a personal allowance, standard rate, and higher rates as in 1984–5 leaves | £505 | £4105 | £28245 |
| | | | PROGRESSIVE |

142

# Fair play

What would you see as a fair tax? You want the tax to fall on other people and not just on you. It is wrong if people can get money without paying tax, simply by luck, or because they know something you do not.

The 'black economy' is made up of people who earn without paying direct taxes, and spend without paying indirect taxes. They break the law and risk being caught. But other people avoid taxes in a better way. They find gaps in the way the tax laws were written, or employ accountants to do so for them. They use those gaps to keep their tax bill low.

So you want taxes to catch everyone, but also you want taxes that are easy to pay. They should catch you at a time when you have the money to pay. Income tax does this through PAYE, for example. And taxes should leave you free to earn and to spend on the essentials of modern life. Everyone has allowances that are free of income tax, for example. You can earn a sum each year as your personal allowance. House-buyers can pay interest on mortgages with income that is free from tax. And VAT is not charged on essential shopping, like children's clothes or food.

# Rich and poor

More important than all this is how taxes fall on the rich and the poor. We all agree that the rich should pay more, but how much more? Some people say that taxes should rise as an equal share of income. These taxes are *proportional* to income. Someone with twice your income pays twice as much tax as you.

But why not just treat all tax-payers the same? A poll (or head) tax would charge each person the same sum of money, whatever their income. Rich and poor alike would pay the same – perhaps £3000 each a year. Would this be fair?

Most people say not. They see that £3000 is only a small share of a rich person's income, but it may be all that a poor person has. This tax would take a smaller share of higher incomes. It would be *regressive* because the tax rate is less than proportional to income. A single rate of VAT on all spending would be regressive. Poor people spend a larger share of their income, and would pay a larger share in tax. The excise duties on cigarettes and beer are like this.

So how can taxes be *progressive*? This means they take a larger share of higher incomes. The rich pay a higher rate of tax than the poor, as with income tax, for example. Here there are allowances so that the very poor pay no tax. Then there is a standard rate of tax that most people pay. Then there are higher rates of tax that people pay on the extra income they earn over a certain sum.

At one stage, in 1967, it was possible for the very rich to pay a tax rate of 136 per cent on their income from investments. Each extra £1 they earned from shares, say, meant that they must pay £1.36 in tax! Clearly, this went too far – not only was it unfair, but it put people off investing. Now the top rate of tax is around half that level, and most people pay very much less.

# 6.8 Public borrowing

In 1975 the UK government borrowed around 10p from every £1 earned by the country. It spent more than it had coming in, as taxes, contributions and so on, and borrowed to make up the difference. Public borrowing has been cut since then, but the government is still the largest borrower in the country.

It has borrowed for hundreds of years, and many of its loans are for a long time. The *national debt* measures the total value of all loans to the government that are still running, and is worth around half of each year's national income. We would have to cut all our incomes in half one year to pay back the national debt.

But that will never happen. Instead, the government adds new debts each year. Mostly it is central government that borrows but local councils and public corporations do so as well. The Public Sector Borrowing Requirement (PSBR) measures the value of new loans to all these parts of general government each year. From 1984 to 1985 its value was planned to be £7.2(000m). This is worth about £130 for each person in the UK. How does government raise all this money?

The government borrows more than anyone in the country. Why is this, and how does it affect us?

## How does government borrow?

We saw in Section 5.8 how firms raise money in different ways. They borrow from banks or sell stocks and shares in the capital market. The government does the same.

Most public borrowing is done through selling securities. These are like certificates, setting the length of loan, its value, and the sum payed as interest. Stock can be short-, medium- or long-term, running for perhaps five years, or perhaps for ever. Treasury bills and other public sector bills are sold for three months or so at a time, at a discount. But some borrowing is also arranged as bank loans, or as trade credit, as well.

Who buys government securities? This can be most important, for different answers lead to very different results on the economy. Most public borrowing is from the private sector, made up of you and me, the general public, and the pension funds, assurance companies, and other institutions that work in the capital market. Most of people's savings are invested by these bodies, and a large part of that is put into government stocks.

But banks also hold securities. Discount houses, for example, buy treasury bills, and commercial banks buy public sector bills and stocks second-hand. Usually these loans have only a short time left to run, and count as part of a bank's liquid reserves. And a number of securities are bought by foreigners, by people living abroad, or by foreign banks and institutions working in the UK.

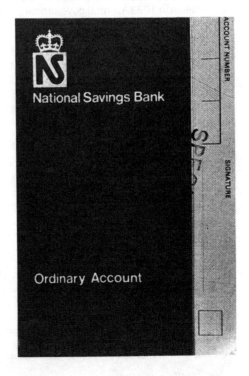

National Savings Bank

Ordinary Account

# Why not just balance the books?

Would it be better for the government to balance its books? It could cut spending, raise taxation, and match the two. There would be no need to borrow.

This is very difficult to do. Public spending goes on throughout the year, to pay the wages of civil servants and the rents of offices, for example. But some important taxes are only paid from time to time – perhaps at the end of the tax year, in March. In the meantime the government must borrow, and then pay back loans when taxes come in.

But spending and taxes may be difficult to plan. Growth raises incomes and the amount paid in income tax, as well as spending and the amount paid in indirect taxes. It may also cut unemployment and the amounts paid out in dole and other social benefits. So growth cuts the amount of government borrowing, and in the same way slump raises it. These are automatic changes in public finance caused by changes in the level of economic activity.

Inflation can change spending and taxes as well. Old debts are mostly fixed in money terms – they do not rise with inflation. So the *real* value of the national debt is cut by inflation, and so is the real level of public spending on interest payments. In this way the government gains from inflation, and people who have lent to it in the past lose out.

In other ways, however, the government can try to cover against inflation. It sets *cash limits* on spending. These set the money value of spending, even if that buys less goods and services because of rising prices. Roads may not be built on time, perhaps, but spending stays on plan. And fixed-sum taxes can be raised in each Budget to keep in line with prices. Otherwise taxes like excise duties become worth less, as do personal allowances against income tax.

## Factsheet – public borrowing in the UK

**How big is the national debt?**
Public sector borrowing has fallen, as a share of national income

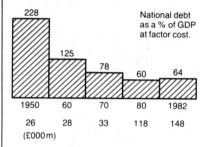

**but rises as the government borrows more each year:**

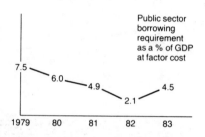

Public sector borrowing was £11 536 million in 1983. Central government alone borrowed a quarter more than that, but local authorities and public corporations balanced that by repaying old loans.

**Where does the money come from?**
Most is borrowed from private savings, held by assurance companies, pension funds or individuals.
Some comes from overseas and the government can also borrow more or less from banks.

**How was the PSBR financed in 1983?**

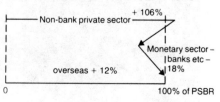

The government borrows by selling securities, but must also pay back old loans as they come due – for example, in 1982–83 (£m)

|  | New borrowing | Repayments |
|---|---|---|
| Marketable securities | 10 705 | 6266 |
| National Savings certificates | 2078 | 1332 |
| National Savings Bank deposits | 1414 | 874 |

(Sources – Annual Abstract and Monthly Digest, 1984)

## Questions

1  What is the national debt? What was its value for each of the 56 million people in the UK in 1982? Suggest a reason why it was so high just after the second world war. (3)

2  What is the PSBR? In which of the years shown did the government appear to come closest to balancing its budget? What was the state of the budget balance in all years? (3)

3  Suppose the government decided to end the national debt. How would it set about doing this? What would happen to the PSBR? What would happen to the economy? (4)

# The point of borrowing

Suppose the government builds a new bridge to the USA! This costs a fortune, but helps everyone in the country and lasts for hundreds of years. How would you want to pay your share of its cost?

Would you want to pay now, in high taxes this year? It would be difficult to find all the money as fast as this, and it would not be fair. You would pay for the bridge before using it. Other people who use it in future pay nothing at all. You would do better to pay a little in extra taxes each year, and for others to do the same in future. This spreads the cost over the time and amongst the people who gain. But how can government pay for the bridge now?

The answer, of course, is by borrowing. Government should borrow to pay for the capital investment, and use taxes to pay back the loan and its interest over the years ahead. It makes sense for government to borrow in this way for roads, swimming pools, hospitals and other long-term investments in the public sector.

But there is another aim for public borrowing, that covers both capital and current spending together. It helps government to steer the economy. The government can spend more than it taxes and borrows the difference from the country's savings. This raises spending and can cause output and employment to grow. The government uses fiscal policy and runs a *budget deficit* as it is called. Public borrowing reflates the economy. We saw how in Section 6.5.

But perhaps inflation is the main problem, or the balance of payments? Then the government can cut spending or raise taxes. It can take in more than it gives out and run a *budget surplus*. It stops borrowing and starts to pay back the balance of its old debts. This cuts spending in the economy and brings deflation. These changes are planned in advance and made on purpose. The changes in public spending, taxes and borrowing are *discretionary* changes in fiscal policy.

# Too much of a good thing

The government can use its borrowing to raise the level of spending and reflate the economy. This can help raise growth and create more jobs. But it can do more besides.

Perhaps the government takes money away from other people when it borrows? If it took less then firms in the private sector could use more. Some people feel that this happens and that government *crowds out* private investment. Firms invest less in machines, buildings and new products because the government spends too much and borrows to pay for it.

But the government may borrow in order to invest in industry itself. Or there may be too little spending on investment in the first place. Where is the harm in public borrowing then?

There need be none at all. But this may depend on how money is raised. Borrowing from banks may raise bank lending and the money supply. Monetarists believe that this causes inflation after a while. Public borrowing may raise output and jobs for a year or two, but then comes the inflation instead.

**Should government borrow?**

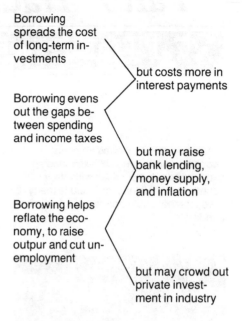

Borrowing spreads the cost of long-term investments — but costs more in interest payments

Borrowing evens out the gaps between spending and income taxes — but may raise bank lending, money supply, and inflation

Borrowing helps reflate the economy, to raise output and cut unemployment — but may crowd out private investment in industry

Borrowing can help the government to pay for long-term investments.

**The government's budget**

| | | |
|---|---|---|
| spending (£m) | 100 000 | 101 000 |
| income from taxes, etc (£m) | 101 000 | 100 000 |
| budget balance | + 1000 Surplus | − 1000 Deficit |

145

# Part 7 Trade

## 7.1 Trade – what's the deal?

What is trade? Why does an open economy such as the UK exchange so many goods and services with other countries? Why does this include many products that could be made perfectly well at home?

Would you like a pocket calculator, some oranges or a holiday in the sun? If the answer to any of these is 'yes', you almost certainly will buy from abroad. All these products are bought and paid for in the UK but come from another country. We *trade*, exchanging products between countries, in order to get them.

The goods and services brought into a country are called its *imports*. Most UK imports are '*visible*' – goods such as oranges or calculators. Other imports are services, such as holidays, and are call '*invisibles*'. People in the UK spend about 30 p in every £1 on imported goods and services. How do they pay for them all?

The answer, of course, is with *exports* that are sold by the UK to buyers in other countries. The UK exports oil, chemicals and machinery. These goods are all visible exports. But the UK is noted also for services such as banking and insurance. These are invisible exports.

Visible exports are worth twice as much as invisibles to the UK and yet more people work to provide services at home, in the tertiary sector of production (see Section 1.3). Why do these people not trade more of what they produce?

## Long-distance car wash

Say that you work washing cars. Would you expect to do much work for people living in other countries? Obviously not. You need to deal directly with your customer so either she must bring her car to you, or you must travel to her. This might give you more customers, but there would be few economies of scale. Altogether your costs would be too high. There would be other car-washers based abroad who could sell much more cheaply than you.

The same is true in similar types of work. The gains from trade apply to visible goods more than to most personal services. Long-distance car sales make more sense than long-distance car washing.

## What's the deal?

Much trade is like that between stamp or record collectors. Two people exchange quite different things in order to add to their collections. The only way to get the items they want is by trading with someone else. But the two people must want different things, and own different things, to make the trade worthwhile.

So it is for a country. The UK can buy oranges and sell apples, buy motorbikes and sell tanks, buy one type of oil and sell another. This pattern of trade was shown most clearly a number of years ago. Then, the UK traded most with the countries of the old British Empire. The UK sold manufactures to, and bought food, materials and fuel from, countries like Nigeria.

Some of this pattern remains today. UK imports of food, drinks, tobacco and minerals are still worth twice as much as exports. But in other ways the old pattern has changed. Most UK trade is now in manufactured goods, both as exports and imports. And the UK relies upon exports of North Sea oil to pay for imports both of fuel and other materials. (See factsheet.)

Invisible trade remains as an area of strength for the UK. Of course, we are an island and trade greatly with the outside world. Invisible trade in shipping, air travel and tourism is accordingly high. But so too are British exports of financial and other professional services. And North Sea oil has made UK firms particularly skilled in looking for, and tapping, oil.

The new pattern of trade is largely in manufactured goods. Naturally, this trade is with other countries that also make and consume more of these goods. The industrial countries of the world, therefore, tend to trade mostly with each other. As with all trade, this tends to follow political ties. Thus, the UK now trades more with the EEC than with any other group of countries. The USA and Japan are also important partners. India, Singapore and Hong Kong are growing in importance as their industries develop.

But much of this trade involves products that all countries could make for themselves – cars, TVs and calculators. Why do industrial countries such as Britain choose to import goods they could make themselves? The answer is one of the most important in economics, and is based on the simple idea of specialisation.

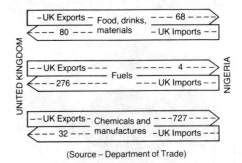

(Source – Department of Trade)

*figure 1 – UK trade with Nigeria (£m, 1983)*

---

# Factsheet – UK Trade

### Which products?
The UK exports almost a third of the goods and services it produces, and imports almost a third of what it consumes. About half of all this trade is in manufactured goods:

export + import payments as a share of all goods and services traded (%, 1982)

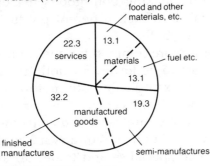

Total 1982  £73.1 for exports
£67.1 for imports (000) m

### What changes?
Trade has grown faster than national income as a whole, and much more in goods than services. North Sea oil accounted for one-seventh of all exports, even by 1982.
Manufactured imports grew 3 times faster than exports in the 10 years up to then.
Most UK trade is with Europe, and this is growing faster than trade with most other parts of the world.

## Questions

1  How much UK trade is in goods? Why is this more than in services? (2)
2  Suggest 2 reasons why so much UK trade is with Europe. (2)

Where to?

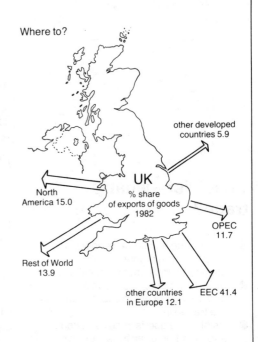

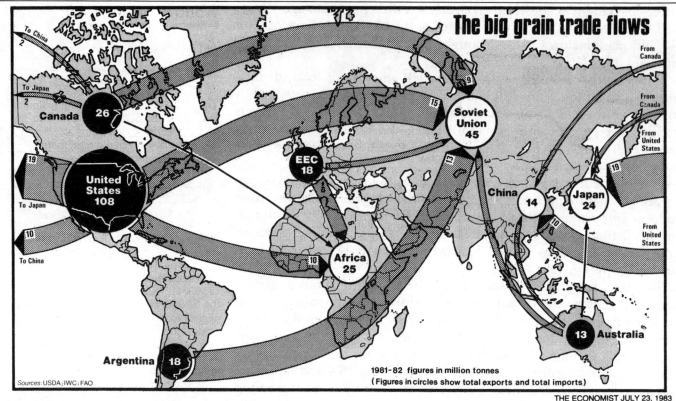

**The big grain trade flows**

To China 2

To Japan 2

Canada 26

To Japan 19

United States 108

To Japan

To China 10

Argentina 18

*Sources:*USDA;IWC;FAO

Soviet Union 45

EEC 18

Africa 25

China 14

Japan 24

Australia 13

From Canada

From Canada

From United States

From United States

1981-82 figures in million tonnes
(Figures in circles show total exports and total imports)

THE ECONOMIST JULY 23, 1983

## Questions

1 Which country was the world's largest (a) exporter, (b) importer of grain? **(1)**
2 Which is the largest single trade flow in grain? Suggest 2 reasons for this trade. **(3)**
3 What might be the effects on the world economy if the USA stopped exports of grain? **(2)**

## Checklist – what is trade?

● trade is the exchange of goods and services from producers in one country to consumers in another
● exports are products made at home and traded out of the country; imports are traded in
● visibles are goods such as materials and manufactures: invisibles are mainly services such as banking and travel

# Specialisation

You and your friends know that if you each do the homework you are best at, and then share, you can get it done more quickly. In economics this is an example of specialisation. Producers can raise their total output in the same way. They need to use their resources to make what they do best, in comparison with each other. But how does this explain trade?

The case is most clear for only two countries, making the same two goods. We know how many resources are needed for each country to produce each good. This sets their *comparative costs* of production. Let us say that each country is clearly better at producing a different good – as, for example, with Japan at motorbikes and the UK at rock music. The total amount each could produce of each good, if they wanted to, is clearly different. They each have an absolute advantage in production. It would be a waste to try making both goods in both countries. Clearly they should specialise in their different products, and trade. This way they get more of both.

But things are not often so clear. It is more common for one country to be better than another, and its costs to be lower, for both goods. This is so for Japan against the UK, for example, in both motorbikes and cars. But how much better? If the advantages are the same for both goods, there is no point in trade. Each country should go its own way, providing entirely for its own wants. But if one country has more of an advantage in one good, it should specialise and trade. Britain should allow Japan to make all the motorbikes, and produce instead what it does best – which is cars. This makes use of each country's *comparative advantage*.

# The gains from trade

Each country produces more of what it does well. It no longer produces so much of what it does less well. On the whole production rises and there are gains from trade.

In practice this works because of prices. Traders export goods to make a profit by doing so. Consumers gain by buying more at lower prices. But this can be upset if prices do not match cost differences. Countries may not be willing or able to change their use of resources if resources are immobile within the country. Traders may pay more to transport goods between countries – as with long-distance car washing – than they can gain in price differences.

Gains from trade are greater if there are economies of scale. UK car firms may learn how to make better products, and cut costs by producing and selling in bulk. This explains much of UK trade in manufactures, and the way it has grown.

But comparative costs of production can change as new techniques and resources are found. Countries such as Hong Kong and India develop their industries and produce at lower cost than firms in the UK. Hence firms must change their line of business, and specialise in high technology, good quality products instead. Otherwise there will be decline and unemployment. People will begin to think that the UK should be protected from cheap imports.

## Checklist – what causes trade?

- tastes – countries may want to consume different products
- scarcity – countries may not be able to produce the goods they wish to consume
- comparative costs – countries specialise in what they produce well, relative to other countries
- politics – trade often follows political or other ties between countries

# 7.2 Protection

Cheap imports cost jobs, but can offer better value for money to consumers. How can we protect home industries against trade, and is it worth the cost?

If you could buy a stereo, would you buy British or foreign? Most of the audio equipment – radios, tape players, record decks – bought in Britain now is made in other countries. Buyers must think they get a better deal this way. Either the equipment is of better quality or it costs less money.

If you had the choice would you want to work making stereo equipment in Britain? The number of imports could put your job at risk. Your earnings might not be very high, and in the end there might be no jobs left at all. Your industry might go the way of the motorbike industry and disappear under competition from imports.

Cheaper and better imports help consumers but cost jobs. Should we protect our firms against this competition? How can it be done?

## Ways to protect

How could you stick to a diet and protect yourself from eating too much? You could ban certain goods – chocolate or biscuits – from the house. You could count calories and eat only a certain amount each day. You could charge yourself more for over-eating, perhaps with a 'sin box' to pay into. You could give yourself treats – new clothes or records when you manage to lose weight.

The government's problem is very different, but its approach is almost the same. It can use regulations, quotas, tariffs and subsidies.

*Regulations* control the types of products that can be traded in a country. The EEC, for example, controls the quality of food in the Common Market. It bans eggs that are too small, or wine that is too weak, from shop shelves. Britain controls the safety of electric fittings sold in the country – imports from other countries may not be approved. Japan controls the exhaust content of cars, and it is difficult for other countries to change their cars so that they can sell in Japan.

*Quotas* control the amount of a certain product that can be imported. Japanese car firms agreed to limit the number of cars they sold in Britain. Zimbabwe limits the amount of money that people can take out of the country with them to spend on holiday.

*Tariffs* are taxes on imports of certain products, and are very common in world trade. The EEC sets a common external tariff of around 5 per cent to protect its members from the rest of the world.

*Subsidies* are when the government offers money to support home producers. This can come directly, as with British support for the steel industry, for shipbuilding and textiles. It can be indirect, and general, as with government support for fuel, power and transport. French industry, for example, pays less for its electricity than industry in Britain.

### Checklist – how to protect?

- regulations – to ban or restrict forms of trade
- quotas – to limit the amount of trade
- tariffs – to tax imports with customs duties
- subsidies – to support home industry against foreign competition

# The effect on consumers

Your diet is your business, but what if everyone joined you? This would cut sales of food and affect shopkeepers and food firms. The same happens when firms are protected against foreign trade. One group of people is helped at the expense of others. Your work in the electrics industry may be saved, but consumers have to do without their cheap, better quality stereos. Protection changes the distribution of income inside the country. Is this worthwhile?

Imports compete with British products on home markets, and consumers choose between the two on the basis of price and quality. Tariffs, for example, make it harder for imports to sell. In one way or another, either it cuts the number on sale, or it raises their price, or it cuts the profit that importers can earn. The supply curve of imported goods is changed. Less can be supplied at each price level, as shown in figure 1. Buyers must either pay a higher price or to go without.

So far protection has cut imports, but it has not yet helped home producers. How does it do so? The answer lies with those disappointed buyers who go without the imports. Home firms must attract them to their own products. Buyers must think that a British stereo is nearly as good as an imported one. Then they will *substitute* from one to the other. The demand for British goods will rise as the demand for import falls. This is shown in figure 1 as a shift of the demand curve for home-made goods. Buyers plan to buy more at each price level.

Now your job is safe. But for how long? This depends on how your firm and producers as a whole make use of their advantage.

# The effect on producers

How will producers respond? The best that can happen is that industry will invest, grow and gain new strength. A secure home market allows firms to invest for the future. Higher levels of output bring economies of scale that cut costs and prices. Not only will your job be safe, but new work will be created. The industry may grow up from being an 'infant', too small to compete in world trade. After some years, the industry would no longer need protection. Economies of scale give it a comparative advantage. It could sell not only at home, but in world markets too. Consumers throughout the world could gain from cheaper and better products.

The worst that could happen is that industry will take to the easy life. Firms will raise their prices to match those of imports. High profits will line the pockets of shareholders or be spent on union wage claims. There will be too little investment and the firm's products will compete less well against foreign imports. The industry will need stronger and stronger protection if it is to survive.

In the end, consumers may call 'enough'. They must pay for protection one way or another. Perhaps they pay more for imports, perhaps they buy more costly or lower-quality goods made at home. Perhaps they go without altogether, or pay higher taxes so that the government can subsidise industry. They have to pay the cost of protection while it remains in force.

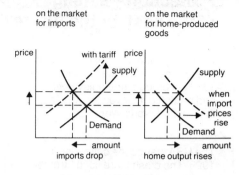

figure 1 – the effect of a tariff

In the early 1800s the British government put taxes on imports of corn and other grains. The Liberal Party was in power, and represented land-owners. The Conservative party opposed the Corn Laws, and represented merchants. The fight against the Corn Laws became more and more bitter, until free trade was bought in around 1846. This poster was one of many used in that struggle.

## Questions

1  Which groups gained and which lost out as a result of the Corn Laws? (2)
2  What form of protection were the Corn Laws? What other methods could the government have used towards the same end? (2)

151

## Protection – a thing of the past, or the future?

We all hope that the world will never see another slump like that of the 1930s. It brought unemployment and hardship. It paved the way for the Second World War.

The USA started the ball rolling in 1929. The crash there soon hit other countries in the same ways. What else could happen? The USA brought over a fifth of all world imports. But its spending overseas fell by two thirds between 1929 and 1932.

The crash hit lending, prices and trade. Trade dropped 11% in food, 18% in materials, and a massive 40% in manufactures. Countries were shocked, and governments looked for ways to avoid their share of the slump and the unemployment.

Nearly all turned to trade barriers. This was the way, they thought to keep out cheap imports. Money spent at home would keep home industries in business and workers in work. Tariffs rose on average to around 30% on manufactures by 1931. This was double the level of 20 years earlier. Tariffs on food and agricultural materials went even higher, to an average of over 60%. Quotas and exchange controls were also brought in, with the aim to cut competition from imports.

But one country's imports are another country's exports. Countries tried to beggar their neighbours, but ended up being poor in return. World trade fell much more than world production, and high-trading countries suffered most. The slump got deeper still.

We hope we have learnt the lessons of that time. Tariffs these days are mostly under 10%. But again, we hear complaints about cheap imports, and again there is pressure to protect jobs at home. Surely protection is a thing of the past – or is it?

### Questions

1 What is (a) a tariff, (b) a quota? (1)
2 How would a tariff affect imports of a good in (a) elastic, (b) inelastic demand? (c) Use this to explain the higher tariffs on food and materials in the 1930s. (3)
3 What would be the effect on the world if all countries now returned to the tariff levels of the 1930s? (2)

## Checklist – world trading blocks

- EEC – the world's biggest; a third of all world exports. Half of member countries' trade is with each other.
- USA – has 12% of world exports, but 92% of U.S. output is bought within the country itself, as the richest country in the world.
- Comecon – includes the USSR and its partners in the East of Europe. – 9% of world exports. Much internal trade, but 'planned' rather than free.
- OPEC – a group of major oil exporting countries – responsible for 14% of world exports, and for setting agreed, high, prices, for their oil.

# Free trade

But they may see some point in this. You, as a consumer, may be willing to pay more for your food, for example. You may see this as a fair price to pay for keeping EEC farmers in business. You may wish to see other industries such as coal and steel kept alive, so that the country is stronger in times of war or other difficulties. There again, you may want tariffs on British imports to set against other countries' protection in return. This can be a way for a country to capture more of the world's gains from trade. It can allow a country to *bargain* in trade. The EEC is just such a bargain – Britain cuts away all its restrictions on imports from the EEC countries, as they do from her.

Certainly this is one way to gain more from free trade. Protection cuts trade, and costs countries the chance of gains. The advantages of specialisation that we saw in the last section are too easily lost. But countries can join together in trading blocs to cut the barriers to trade between them. The EEC countries form a customs union to do just this, as we will see in Section 7.8. They have seen great growth – of trade, specialisation and incomes – as a result.

There is another way to increase free trade in the world as a whole. The General Agreement in Tariffs and Trade (GATT) was set up to protect the world from protection! All member countries agree to common rules of fair trade and meet to find ways to cut existing tariffs. This offers hope that the world will never again return to the full, widespread protection that came in the slump of the 1930s.

# 7.3 Capital movements

What would be the best way to invest £100 if you had it? Should you lend to a match factory in India or buy a share in a hotel in Britain? Would your money be safer at home or abroad?

Many of the payments from one country to another are made in exchange for goods and services traded. These are called *current* payments, for they affect the current income of the country at that time. Overseas investment is very different, for here the payment is not in exchange for anything. Instead there is a payment of money, called *capital*, made as a loan or to buy ownership of other countries' resources.

Some of the capital that moves between countries is owned by government. Most is owned privately, and moves as either *short-term* loans or *long-term* investment. But why does capital move at all – why might you want to invest your £100 in India instead of Britain?

## Speculation

Speculators use their money for short-term gain rather than long-term investment. They buy bills, make bank deposits or give trade credit. You can change these forms of loan quickly if you find a better way to make money. But where is the profit?

All loans earn a rate of interest. But short-term loans generally earn less than long-term. Their advantage is their flexibility, as lenders can change quickly from one loan to another, one country to another or, say, from pounds to dollars. This is worthwhile when interest rates, exchange rates or inflation change in each country.

Suppose interest rates are set at 10 per cent in the USA, but they rise and fall in the UK. A rise in the UK interest rates attracts capital into the country. The supply of short-term loans rises. The opposite happens if UK rates fall below those in the USA. Capital moves out of the UK. The same level of interest rates in the UK as in the USA should keep those capital movements in balance – if other things are equal.

But speculators can gain in two other ways also. They may want to lend in pounds because they expect the pound's value to rise. This could be due to the exchange rate, as we shall see in Section 7.4. It could be due instead to inflation, which cuts the real value of money. Inflation might be less in the UK than in the USA.

Firms that trade with other countries deal in foreign money all the time. They must speculate to protect the value of their money. But you may have only £100, and feel that this is not worth the bother. You may be interested more in long-term investment.

Why do people and firms move their money from one country to another? What are the effects of capital movement?

Why take capital out of the UK?

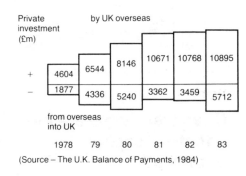

(Source – The U.K. Balance of Payments, 1984)

*figure 1 – private investment into and out of the UK*

## Questions

1 What was the *balance* of private investment in and out of the UK in (a) 1980, (b) 1981? (1)
2 Suggest two possible reasons for this change. (2)

153

## Brits out, Mexicans in

Ford will spend $500m on a new plant in Hermosillo, in northern Mexico, to build 100000 small cars a year mostly for sale in the United States. Japan's Toyo Kogyo, makers of Mazda and 25% owned by Ford, will design the car. It will also supply the main components. Some 2000–3000 Mexican workers, paid hourly rates around an eighth of their American counterparts', will put them together.

Ford will be hiring in Mexico, but may be firing in Britain. Workers at Ford's Dagenham plant near London fear the company is planning to close its foundry there. This would mean the immediate loss of 2000 jobs.

The foundry casts almost all the cylinder blocks, cylinder heads and crank-shafts Ford puts into the car engines it builds in Britain for vehicles made throughout Europe.

But the car industry is looking for lighter metals, like aluminium, to substitute for iron in some engine parts. Because of exchange-rate changes, Dagenham's products have become too expensive for Ford's continental European subsidiaries. These newer operations do not have their own foundries: with modern casting techniques, economies of scale usually outweigh the economies of vertical integration.

The Economist, 14.1.84

### Questions

1 What capital movements by Ford are described (a) to Mexico (b) to Japan? (1)
2 Why is Ford investing in Mexico rather than in Britain? (2)
3 What will be the effects of Ford's capital investment on the Mexican economy? (2)
4 Why has Ford's demand for its Dagenham foundry fallen? (2)

## Checklist – what are the effects of capital outflows?

- less investment may mean less output and employment
- lower growth in the long term
- the outward movement of money now should lead to inward payments of the returns on investment in future
- investors can expect higher incomes from more profitable use of their capital

# Investment

All investors expect a return. You buy shares, or start a business, to earn an income from your capital. The £100 you invest in an Indian factory today should earn you *interest, profit or dividends* over the years ahead – perhaps £10 a year from now on. Why should this return be any better than if you had invested in Britain?

Different businesses grow at different rates. Some make more profit than others, both in India and Britain. A gold-rush in Australia attracts capital as British investors buy mines there. Oil discoveries in the North Sea attract capital into Britain, from the USA and elsewhere. So capital moves both in and out of a country, depending on the state of its industries.

But movements do not always balance. Private investment flooded out of the UK between 1978 and 1983, as shown in figure 1. Outward investment was greater than inward investment by almost £28000 million. UK investors put £1 in every £5 of their capital to use in other countries. What caused this?

There was a greater supply of capital for use overseas. The UK is an advanced, industrial country, with high incomes and high savings. There are close ties with many other countries, and a long record of overseas trade and investment. North Sea oil has added to the income that can be invested. The government encouraged overseas investment by freeing capital movements from *exchange controls* in 1979. Before this, the Bank of England limited people's access to the country's reserves of foreign exchange. All this explains the shift of supply of capital.

But demand also changed. Investment opportunities seemed brighter overseas. Faster growing and more successful economies offer better returns on capital. Taxation on profits is lower in many other countries. The demand for UK capital overseas also rose at each level of interest rates.

# The importance of overseas investment

How will it affect the economy if you send your £100 overseas rather than invest it at home? Clearly, your money is a drop in the ocean of UK investment, but all capital is important.

Investment raises spending, growth and employment. It makes industries more productive and raises living standards. Overseas investment may develop new industries. UK imports of New Zealand lamb, Canadian wood and Argentinian beef were helped this way. But so too were other industries that have now replaced British production. Indian cotton and Hong Kong toys are just two examples.

British investors gain from these new industries. Overseas investments earn higher returns and bring greater incomes into the UK as interest, profit and dividends. This is valuable now, but will be even more important when North Sea oil runs out. But UK industry may invest too little and become uncompetitive. British producers lose out.

# 7.4 Pounds for sale – foreign exchange

Question – when is a pound not a £?

Answer – when it is used in Cyprus, or Gibraltar or The Falklands, because these countries have pounds of their own, different from UK pounds.

A Cyprus pound was worth about £1.25 (UK) in mid-1984. £1 (UK sterling) was worth about .85 of a £ Cyprus. People moving between the UK and Cyprus can exchange their money one way or the other at the going *rate of exchange*. This measures the price of one country's money in terms of the other's.

But you may never go to Cyprus, so why should the exchange rate matter? One reason is to do with the balance of payments. Your money might travel much more than you. Perhaps you buy grapes grown in Cyprus, or perhaps you work for a firm selling there. Your savings may be invested there by a pension or insurance company. Any of these payments causes an exchange of money one way or the other, at the going rate of exchange.

In the same way, there are payments made between the UK and any number of other countries. Pounds are bought and sold for all these countries' currencies. The UK has any number of rates of exchange – for francs, marks or lire. Perhaps the most important of these is between the pound and the dollar. This rate of exchange is shown in figure 1. Clearly it changes from time to time. A rise, as in 1980, is called a *revaluation* or *appreciation* of the pound. A fall, as in 1983, is called a *devaluation* or *depreciation*. These changes can be sudden and large. But why do they happen?

## The market for foreign exchange

The exchange rate is a price set by market forces. Buyers and sellers meet in a foreign exchange market to make their deals. You can join this market at a local bank or a tourists' exchange centre. This is where you would go to buy your francs, for example, for a holiday in France.

But all the major deals involve banks and companies buying or selling large sums at a time. These deals are arranged in the City of London or other financial centres. Sellers find buyers quickly, perhaps by phone, perhaps in different countries. The market is complex and world-wide. A seller knows that he can always find a buyer by working through a specialist bank, providing the price is right.

So many different exchange rates make it difficult to measure the pound's value. It may become worth more in francs but less in dollars. We need a general measure that takes all the different rates into account. The effective exchange rate is just such a measure. It is a weighted average of prices given as an index. It works very like the

What is the exchange rate of the £? How is it set in the foreign exchange market, and why is it so important?

## Holiday money

## Checklist – what sets the exchange rate?

- payments for exports and imports – more exports usually raises the exchange rate and more imports lowers the exchange rate
- all other payments, of capital, etc. A fall in interest rates, or business confidence, usually lowers the exchange rate, and a rise helps it
- government policy can change all these payments, and it can buy and sell from the official reserves to help fix the rate

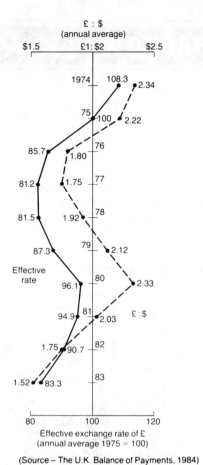

$£ : \$$
(annual average)

| $1.5 | £1:$2 | $2.5 |

1974  108.3  • 2.34
75  100  2.22
85.7  1.80  76
81.2  1.75  77
81.5  1.92  78
87.3  79  • 2.12
Effective rate
96.1  80  • 2.33
94.9  81  2.03  $£ : \$$
1.75  90.7  82
1.52  • 83.3  83

80        100        120

Effective exchange rate of £
(annual average 1975 = 100)

(Source – The U.K. Balance of Payments, 1984)

*figure 1 – the £'s exchange rate*

## Questions

1  Over what period did the £
   'appreciate'?                                    (1)
2  By how much did the £ fall from
   1980 to 1983?                                    (1)
3  Suggest a reason why its $ value
   fell by more than against all other
   currencies.                                      (1)

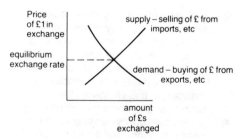

Price of £1 in exchange

supply – selling of £ from imports, etc

equilibrium exchange rate

demand – buying of £ from exports, etc

amount of £s exchanged

*figure 2 – supply and demand set the
exchange rate*

Retail Price Index, as we saw in Section 5.3. Currencies are weighted according to their importance in UK trade. A rise in the index shows that the pound has become more valuable. Changes for the UK are shown in figure 1.

## Who buys, who sells?

We see how foreign exchange deals follow directly from payments made between countries. Let us say that you do buy grapes from Cyprus. Your money goes to the shop and you pay in pounds. The shop pays a grapes firm in pounds. But somewhere along the chain of distribution those grapes were bought from Cyprus. British pounds were sold in exchange for Cyprus money in order to buy the grapes. It is the same with all payments between countries.

Payments into the UK lead to people buying pounds. Payments out lead to selling. A payments deficit means that less is paid in than out, and that fewer pounds are bought than sold. In the same way a payments surplus means more buying than selling of pounds.

We saw in the last section how trade and capital movements set the flow of payments. The same forces explain the buying and selling of pounds. Suppose incomes drop in the UK, for example. This cuts imports, cuts payments out of the country, and cuts selling of pounds.

Suppose, instead, that speculators expect a rise in the value of the pound. Capital moves into the UK in the form of short-term bank deposits. More inward payments cause more buying of pounds. Some deals may be arranged straight away – in the 'spot' market; others will be set for some later date – in the 'forward' market. But will the speculators gain the right result – will the exchange rate rise? To a large extent, this depends on the government.

## Floating or fixed?

Suppose the government steps aside and leaves the foreign exchange market to set the value of the £. Buyers meet sellers and agree a price for each deal. More buying than selling causes the price to rise; more selling than buying causes price to fall. Market price *floats* towards equilibrium to match demand and supply in the usual way. This sets the exchange rate as in figure 2.

So a strong balance of payments leads to a rise in the exchange rate; a weaker balance of payments leads to a fall. But this change in the value of the £ itself brings demand and supply together as in the figure. A change in the £ affects incomes, the way products compete in trade, and short-term capital movements. So the equilibrium exchange rate in figure 2 is the one that matches payments into and out of the country.

But a change in exchange rates may have other effects as well. It changes the value of all payments made from one country's money into another's. It affects prices set for imports and exports. A fall in the exchange rate makes it easier for home firms to compete with those in other countries. This can bring greater sales, more jobs and higher living standards in the future. Or it may turn instead into extra inflation as prices and wages rise faster than output.

What can the government do about this? There must be any number of things, for any change to payments for trade or as capital will affect the exchange rate. We will look at some of these changes, and how the government can make them happen, in Section 7.7. But, also there is a more direct approach. The government can take control and *fix* the value of the exchange rate. It does this by buying or selling in the foreign exchange market for its own reasons.

What happens if the government sells pounds, and buys other currencies, in the foreign exchange market? This keeps the exchange rate down at a chosen level, as shown in figure 3 at point P. Pounds are sold in exchange for other currencies, so what does the government do with the dollars, francs and other money that it has now bought? The answer is that it puts them away in the official reserves. The reserves rise by the amount of extra selling of pounds.

The government can keep the pound's value high in the same way. It may print and issue pounds at home, but to keep the exchange rate up, it must do more. It must buy pounds in the foreign exchange market and sell from the official reserves to do so.

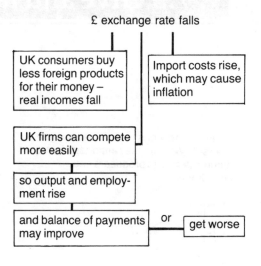

## The effects of a fall in the £

# Bank of England supports sterling

Sterling was heavily supported by the Bank of England on the foreign exchanges yesterday.

Some estimates of the amount spent by the Bank yesterday ranged as high as £250m.

The official purchases helped to boost sterling against the weaker dollar. The pound closed half a cent higher than on Friday.

In effective, trade-weighted terms the pound finished the day at the same level as on Friday. This is the lowest it has touched since August last year.

There has been a steady

build-up of pressure on sterling over the last four weeks. The pound has fallen by more than 5 per cent against a basket of currencies and by 3½ per cent against the dollar.

Market worries about the prospects for Britain's trade balance have been one reason for the weakness. Another has been speculation that the Government would be quite happy to see the rate drop.

Officials believe that much of the selling of the past few days has been speculative and could easily be reversed. For this reason they used some of Britain's reserves to prop up the

pound and counteract the speculation.

The March reserves total, to be published today, will not be affected by the most recent official intervention. However, it is likely that it will show a fall in the reserves from their level at the end of February.

The Government's attitude to the pound's recent weakness is not clear. On the one hand it does not want a sterling fall to threaten its inflation target. On the other hand a lower pound helps British industry to compete internationally.

The Times, 4.4.78

## Questions

1 Explain the terms (a) foreign exchanges, (b) speculation. (2)
2 Explain the fall in the value of the £ described here. (1)
3 Show 2 ways in which the government supported the £. (2)
4 Why should the government be glad to see the value of the £ both (a) higher, (b) lower? (2)

Before 1973 all governments did this a great deal. Since then, there has been less government action, and mostly to help the markets work in an orderly way. Official buying and selling keeps the exchange rate from changing, as a result of too much speculation, from day to day.

Many governments want to do much more than this. They want a return to a system of fixed exchange rates. This would keep rates steady to perhaps within one per cent each side of an agreed level. Traders and investors can be more sure about the values of their deals with other countries. This encourages growth.

The International Monetary Fund was set up in 1944 to run the so-called Bretton Woods system of fixed rates. It still holds international reserves that countries may borrow, on conditions, when they wish to make their exchange rates stronger. And the European Monetary System, since 1979, has given EEC countries the same sort of help. European countries, but not the UK, keep their rates fairly well fixed with each other, to encourage trade and growth.

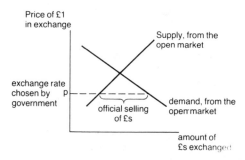

figure 3 – official selling keeps the exchange rate down

# 7.5 Give and take – the terms of trade

What are the terms of trade and how are they set? Why are they important, in such different ways, to producers and consumers?

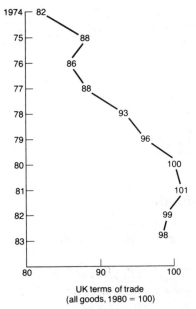

UK terms of trade
(all goods, 1980 = 100)

(Source – The UK Balance of Payments 1984)

*figure 1 – the UK terms of trade*

## Questions

1  If import prices stayed the same, what was the change in export prices from 1980 to 1981? (1)
2  The terms of trade rose before, and fell after 1981. What difference would this have made to (a) consumers (b) producers? (2)
3  Suggest 2 possible reasons for the change. (2)

Trade is a matter of give and take. It allows us to specialise and so produce more. But how are these gains shared out? It depends on the terms of trade.

The terms of trade show how much a country must give up of its own goods to get more of other countries' goods. It measures prices in trade, and is found from the price of exports divided by the price of imports. The official measure uses weighted averages of prices, usually just for visible goods, and puts this as an index of 100.

Its value changes from time to time, as export prices change relative to imports. Figure 1 shows the value of the UK's terms of trade. Why does it rise and fall like this?

Suppose the UK terms of trade rise. This means that export prices have risen compared to import prices. Perhaps the country has changed its pattern of trade and is exporting higher priced goods. But it is more likely that UK prices have risen compared to prices in other countries. There are several possible reasons for this.

One is a change in the exchange rate. A rise in the value of the pound means that every price set in pounds is worth more in terms of other currencies. Take a Spanish holiday costing 50000 pesetas. When £1 is worth 250 pesetas, the holiday sells for (50000 ÷ 250) = £200. When £1 is worth only 200 pesetas, the holiday costs £250. A fall in the exchange rate causes a fall in the terms of trade.

Inflation is also important. Inflation raises prices, probably in all countries together. But the UK may have more inflation than other countries. Export prices rise faster than import prices. Extra inflation raises the terms of trade.

Lastly, there are relative costs of production. Other countries may find ways to save resources, and so cut costs of production more than the UK. Labour productivity may rise faster in other countries, and be used to cut prices. Import prices may fall faster than export prices, and again cause the UK terms of trade to rise.

The same change may be caused not by technical progress, but by government policy instead. Governments can use taxes and subsidies to change relative prices, and turn the terms of trade their way. But why should they want to?

## High life for consumers, high risk for producers

How could you take more of the gains from trade – say on your Spanish holiday? Clearly you want to pay less for all you buy, and make your own British money go further. As a consumer, you want the terms of trade to be high.

The same idea works at home. Here consumers buy foreign imports as well as British products. They get more for their money if the terms of trade rises. They can buy more imported goods with money earned from the same amount of work. Their real income is raised.

But will there be the same amount of work to be done? A rise in the terms of trade means that home-produced goods cost more compared to those made in other countries. British producers find it more difficult to compete. They must either improve the quality of their products to justify the higher price, or they must expect to sell less. Either way, a rise in the terms of trade is bad for business.

Low output soon leads to low employment. Firms that fail to compete have to close down factories and sack workers. A rise in the terms of trade can lead, after a time, to slump and unemployment at home. Those who keep their jobs can enjoy being rich consumers; those who lose their jobs cannot.

## Checklist – what changes the terms of trade?

- a change in the exchange rate – a fall cuts the terms of trade
- different rates of inflation – less inflation cuts the terms of trade
- changes in relative costs of production – lower costs can cut the terms of trade
- government policy, perhaps using taxes or subsidies
- a change in the types of products traded, and their prices

## Falling pound may bring tourists in

Britain's tourist industry is preparing for a record level of United States visitors this year, as the pound reaches new low levels against the dollar.

The dollar's fortunes have made this a bumper year – with 2 275 000 trans-Atlantic travellers visiting Britain in the first nine months of the year, compared with 2 136 000 in the whole of last year encouraged by an exchange rate that had dropped.

As a result, travel firms in the United States are persuading Americans that now is the time for a foreign holiday: "We have to teach our clients that they can save money now."

British Airways feels it will need the trade to compensate for a possible decline in Britons travelling in the other direction. The British invasion of Florida, at its height three years ago, has waned.

The Times, 11.1.84

### Questions

1 Explain how the dollar's rise changed the UK terms of trade. (1)
2 Explain how this affected holiday-makers in the USA and Britain. (2)
3 Who has gained and who has lost in the USA as a result of this change? (2)

## Bread today or jam tomorrow?

Would you choose bread today or jam tomorrow? A high terms of trade is good for consumers and for living standards now. But a low terms of trade is good for producers and for future growth and jobs. How is a country to know the right path?

It all depends on competition. We know that a rise in prices, for one country compared to others, makes it more difficult to compete. But this effect might be either strong or weak. Sales might fall by more than the rise in price, so cutting the total amount of money paid by customers. In other words, demand for the country's products might be elastic. The opposite is also possible; sales might fall by less than the rise in price, so raising sales revenue, if demand is inelastic.

The balance of payments, therefore, may be made either better or worse. A fall in the terms of trade makes it easier for a country's producers to compete. This improves the balance of payments, but only if the demand for imports and exports is elastic. This effect may take a year or two to show through. For the same reason, the effect on output and jobs may be either large or small, and quick or slow.

For many producers, it is not prices that matter so much in competition anyway. Most trade is in manufactured goods, and these sell for their quality as well as their price. A country that specialises in high-quality goods, such as aircraft, machinery or Rolls Royce cars, would expect a high terms of trade. Improvements in quality mean that the terms of trade can rise, and still allow firms to compete well.

## How far for your money?

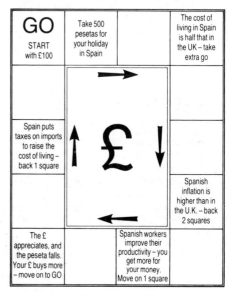

159

How is the balance of payments made up? What does it tell us, and why does it matter to the country?

How do we know if a country breaks even in its trade? Money comes into the country as *credits* and moves out as *debits*. But this can be as payments for trade in goods and services, or as movements of capital. The overall flow of payments always balances, one way or another. Each form of payments may not, however.

A *surplus* shows more paid in than out. You have a surplus in your bank account if you have paid more in than you have taken out. Your account is 'in the black'. But a *deficit* shows the opposite: that you have paid more out than in, made a money loss, and put your account 'in the red'.

How can we tell if a country is 'breaking even or breaking down' with each type of payment? We must turn to the official accounts.

## Current account

The *current account* measures all payments that affect the current income of the country. Mostly, this covers trade in goods and services. Visible trade in goods is the largest part of the account, and its balance is often called the *balance of trade*. Invisibles cover trade in services, added to two other payments of income between countries. One is the interest, profit and dividends earned on property held in other countries. The other is the transfers paid by government, say, to the EEC, and by people, for example, to their families.

Exports earn payments into the country, and are shown as positive credits in the account. Imports lead to payments out of the country, and are shown as negative values, or debits. We take the value of imports away from the value of exports to find (the largest part of) the current balance. We must remember to see it as the difference between two large figures. This is similar to a difference of a few metres between the flying heights of two aeroplanes. A small change in one or the other causes the balance to change sharply from, say, surplus to deficit.

## Why does the balance matter?

Does it matter if you pay out more or less money than you have coming in? For a time, of course, it does not. You may expect to spend above your means for this month because you will live more carefully next month. It is much the same for a country: only a lasting deficit, or lasting surplus, gives cause for concern.

What does a trade deficit mean? It shows that the country is paying more out than is being paid in. We are living too well, and buying more foreign goods and services than we can really afford. Either our income

## Payments in or out of £s?

| CREDITS | DEBITS |
|---|---|

U.K. selling North Sea oil to Europe.

U.K. buys Japanese cars.

U.K. earning profit from overseas rubber plantation.

U.K. buys pineapples.

U.K. earnings from U.S. tourists.

U.S. airman sends his earnings in £s home.

Speculator putting foreign cash into U.K. banks, as £s.

U.K. investors buy factory in Hong Kong.

## Question

1 Find 2 examples from those above that would be counted in the UK balance of payments as (a) visible trade, (b) invisible payments, (c) capital movements. (3)

is too high, and is being spent on too many imports, or we are making products that do not sell well enough. Our producers are not competing with the rest of the world as well as they might.

A surplus in trade shows the opposite. It shows that the country is living within its current means, at a lower level of income than it could really afford. But it is trading well, so its firms are probably producing competitively. This may not hold for all industries, however. A large gain in one area such as trade in North Sea oil, for example, may overcome a loss in other trade such as in manufactured goods.

The official accounts show us how the current balance matters in another way. They show how it is matched by other types of payments.

# Capital payments

How could you afford to go on living beyond your current means? Suppose you spend £50 each month and have only £40 coming in. Probably you would borrow to cover the balance, but you might also have to sell off your possessions. First some of your records, then your watch, then the shirt from your back!

We know that countries exchange capital in these ways – as loans of money, and as possessions of stocks, shares, bills and so on. A deficit on current account must be paid for by a surplus from these capital movements. A current surplus is paid for by a capital account deficit. But there are different ways in which this can work, depending on the exchange rate and the government.

Capital movements are shown in the accounts as *investment and other capital flows*. We saw in Section 7.3 what causes these payments. The accounts divide private from public sector loans, and long-term investment from short-term bank or trade credit. The size of these payments is great, and changes sharply from year to year. Short-term speculation alone can change one year's surplus into next year's deficit.

Suppose the government leaves the exchange rate to be set by free market forces. It floats freely in the way shown in Section 7.4, and matches payments in and out of £s. Current and capital payments change with the exchange rate until they balance. The government can affect these payments by steering the economy, with high interest rates or a low budget deficit, for example. But it can also act directly, using its reserves.

# Official reserves

The *official reserves* are dollars, francs, other currencies and gold, held for the nation by the Bank of England. These are part of what the country owns, rather like your records, or the shirt on your back. The Bank of England can choose to sell reserves to help pay for a deficit, or buy when there is a surplus, on all other payments. But why should it choose to?

We already know the answer. The government can use the reserves to ma̶ the exchange rate, and set it higher or lower than it would ̶e. It sells reserves to buy £s, to keep the £'s value up. This ̶icit on current and other capital payments. The govern-

## Checklist – why does the current balance matter?

● a deficit shows the country is not paying its way in trade – living too well, or not competing well enough
● a surplus shows the country could afford a better standard of living
● the current account must be balanced on capital account – by loans, by selling property, or by official financing.

The country paid out more for imports than it earned from exports. The figures each month for the 'balance of trade' cover visible trade in goods, only.

161

# Factsheet – the UK balance of payments

The current balance changes from year to year, but is now helped greatly by oil:

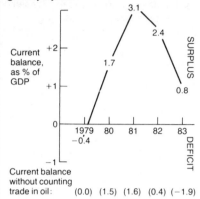

Current balance, as % of GDP

SURPLUS

3.1
2.4
1.7
0.8
1979  80  81  82  83
−0.4
DEFICIT

Current balance without counting trade in oil:     (0.0)  (1.5)  (1.6)  (0.4)  (−1.9)

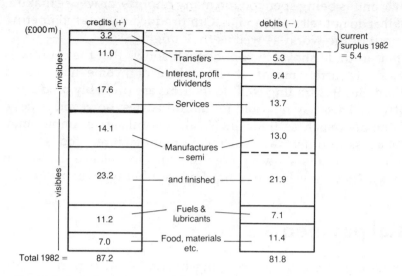

| | credits (+) | debits (−) | |
|---|---|---|---|
| invisibles | 3.2 | | current surplus 1982 = 5.4 |
| | 11.0 | Transfers | 5.3 |
| | 17.6 | Interest, profit dividends | 9.4 |
| | | Services | 13.7 |
| visibles | 14.1 | Manufactures – semi | 13.0 |
| | 23.2 | and finished | 21.9 |
| | 11.2 | Fuels & lubricants | 7.1 |
| | 7.0 | Food, materials etc. | 11.4 |
| Total 1982 = | 87.2 | | 81.8 |

But this is the balance between 2 large values for credits as payments come in, and debits as payments go out:

And current account payments must be added to capital movements to show the overall balance of payments:

*UK Balance of Payments 1983*

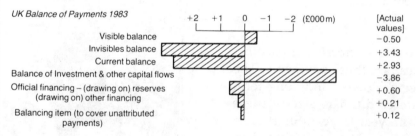

+2  +1  0  −1  −2  (£000m)

| | [Actual values] |
|---|---|
| Visible balance | −0.50 |
| Invisibles balance | +3.43 |
| Current balance | +2.93 |
| Balance of Investment & other capital flows | −3.86 |
| Official financing – (drawing on) reserves (drawing on) other financing | +0.60 |
| | +0.21 |
| Balancing item (to cover unattributed payments) | +0.12 |

(Sources – UK Balance of Payments, 1983; Economic Trends, March 1984)

## Questions

1  Explain the terms (a) invisibles, (b) current balance, (c) official financing. **(3)**
2  What was the overall balance of UK payments in 1983 that was met by official financing? Explain your answer. **(2)**
3  Find the main points of strength and weakness in the UK's trade balances for different goods and services in 1982. **(2)**

## Checklist – how are the accounts laid out?

● current account covers visible trade in goods, and invisible payments for services, property income, and transfers
● investment and other capital flows covers short and long-term, private and public movements of capital
● official financing covers changes in the reserves, etc, made to balance all other payments

ment buys reserves by selling £s to keep the exchange rate down, when there is a surplus on all other payments.

These changes are shown in the part of the accounts called *official financing*. It takes in changes in the official reserves, as well as similar deals in international money. These are mostly loans to and from central banks in other countries or the International Monetary Fund. The form of the accounts puts the official financing in 'reverse' as a surplus, say, to balance a payments deficit. A positive change in reserves, therefore, shows a fall in the Bank of England's funds.

Since 1973, the government has used the reserves less, as it only manages the exchange rate to balance payments in an orderly way from day to day. But before then there was much more dealing to fix the exchange rate of the £. The government could return to a similar sort of system if, for example, the UK joined the European Monetary System.

How can you get out of debt? Say that your living expenses have grown too large for your income. You borrow to cover the gap, but in the end something will have to give.

Should you cut down on the things you do? This would cut your spending and save money. Or perhaps, you could work harder to earn more income.

The same sort of problems apply to a country in debt. Exports do not earn enough to pay for imports, and there is a current account deficit in the balance of payments. More spending leaves the country than enters it – this cuts national income. So should the government leave the problem to solve itself? If all other payments balance, this will happen through a change in exchange rate. A deficit leads to a fall in the value of the pound. This helps UK firms to compete, and so improves their performance in trade. The current account returns to balance, as in figure 1.

There may be costs in this, however. The exchange rate affects more than just the balance of payments. A fall in the £ cuts the terms of trade, and the real income of consumers. It helps firms to raise their output and employment, but leads to inflation. Higher import prices and higher profits may soon lead to higher wages at home. The government may object to some of these effects, and they may not trust the exchange rate to solve the trade problem anyway.

The exchange rate is set by the flow of all payments together, and can appear higher or lower than it should, based on trading performance alone. A change in the exchange rate may take some time to improve trade. It may even make things worse before it makes them better.

## Borrowing

For one reason or another, the government may want a different way to deal with its payments problem. At least for a time, it may help the country to borrow. But for how long?

Borrowing can go on as long as people abroad are willing to lend. But it is costly. Interest must be paid on capital and the outward flow of interest payments puts an extra strain on the current balance. The government can use *monetary policy* to attract loans. It keeps bank lending down at home, and interest rates up. This may not attract long-term investors, but it should keep up the flow of short-term deposits in from other countries.

The government can also choose to finance a deficit officially. It can spend from its reserves of foreign currency to buy pounds and pay for a deficit. This can go on as long as the reserves last out. Or it can go on even longer with help from the International Monetary Fund (IMF).

Why does the balance of payments matter to the government? What can be done to improve it, and at what cost?

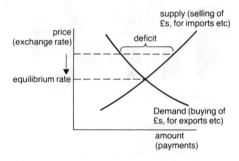

*figure 1 – the exchange rate balances payments*

163

# IMF

MORE GOOD NEWS — HONOURABLE BRITISH ARE PLANNING TO BOOST INDUSTRY IN THEIR BUDGET."

## Questions

1 Suggest 2 ways in which the government could 'boost industry in their Budget'. (1)
2 Why is that good news for Japanese exporters? (1)

Imagine a box, into which you and your friends put in a little of what you have each year. If you run short of money you can borrow from the box while you sort out your problems. The IMF works in the same sort of way, but for countries, and in international money.

All the major trading countries in the world are members of the Fund. They pay in a small share of their national incomes so that rich countries like the USA pay most. The Fund collects all sorts of currencies, but two in particular. These are the forms of money most acceptable in payments around the world: gold and US dollars. The dollar is most widely used, and is the main *international currency*. For many years it was trusted, partly because the USA government agreed to exchange it into gold: it was *convertible* currency. Since 1971 this has no longer been so, and the exchange value of the dollar is less certain. But its importance as international currency is not.

The IMF is responsible for managing the system of world money. It collects information, gives advice, and creates its own form of money, called special drawing rights. But its importance is much less now that governments no longer hold to a system of fixed exchange rates. For now they need to borrow reserves much less.

Member countries can borrow international money from the IMF. Perhaps they have a payments deficit that has gone on for some time. Many developing countries are in this position, because they need to import machinery for their growing industries. Extra reserves buy time in which to improve the payments position. Often the IMF gives help only on condition that such improvement will come. What must governments do?

# Trade figures fire a warning shot

The October trade figures are hardly a cause for panic, but certainly show a reversal to a monthly current deficit of £269m, the worst since May.

A year ago monthly imports and exports of goods other than oil were balanced at £3.9 billion apiece. By October, imports had climbed to £5 billion while exports were stuck at a little above £4 billion. Some of this was to be expected because Britain's recovery started before those in Europe, North America and elsewhere. But that story is beginning to wear a little thin.

The export boom to the United States is starting to

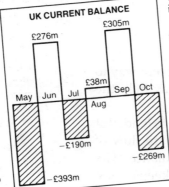

UK CURRENT BALANCE

tail off and the EEC balance is not going well.

This all adds to the argument that the consumer boom, even if it does continue, will prove unhealthy.

If the Chancellor is to achieve his forecast 3 per cent growth rate next year, he must rely heavily on a switch to invesment and/or a crucial contribution from recovering overseas demand for British exports.

Otherwise, there are bound to be inflationary pressures, whether exerted through trade and the exchange rate or elsewhere. This message had not yet got through to policy-makers.

The Times, 25.11.83

## Questions

1 In which of the six months shown above was there a current account surplus? (1)
2 What was the balance in October (a) in goods other than oil (b) in oil? (1)
3 What was the current account balance in the 3 months 'August to October'? (1)
4 Explain why a 'consumer boom' for UK imports may be 'unhealthy' for (a) the exchange rate, (b) inflation. (2)
5 Suggest 3 ways in which the government could improve the current balance. (3)

# Spend less

One sure way for you to get out of debt is to spend less. A government can approach this same end in different ways. One is cut spending by the country in general, by deflation.

The government can use fiscal policy to raise tax rates and cut public sector spending. It can use monetary policy to cut bank lending and raise interest rates, so reducing investment. In either case, general deflation cuts national income and the demand for imports. Exports should not change, since these follow from spending of other countries' incomes. The balance of payments should improve, but how much? The UK spends around 30p in every £1 of income on imports. Incomes may have to fall by more than £3 to cut the imports bill by £1. The other £2 falls on home production and employment, and this may be a heavy cost to pay.

There is another way to cut imports. *Import controls* directly limit the payments made for foreign goods and services. They may take the form of tariffs that tax certain imported goods, or quotas that limit the amounts brought in each year. Both aim to switch spending away from foreign goods and towards those produced at home.

There is still a cost to be paid, however. Controls cause shortages and raise prices. There is likely to be more inflation as a result. Controls protect home firms, even those that are inefficient. In this way, they cost the country the full gains from specialisation and trade. They could give no more than a breathing space while UK industry moves to new methods and products. They affect other countries who may respond with controls of their own on UK exports.

# Earn more

It might be better for the government to try to raise exports rather than cut imports. This could come with a rise in UK output and employment. Exporting firms would do well, and help the economy as a whole. But is this possible?

The government can try to cut the rate of inflation to below that in other countries. And government may be able to help firms to improve work practices and capital investment. The UK government may be able to use the gains from North Sea oil to help the economy in future.

It is clear that the government can help the country to overcome a payments deficit. It can work in the opposite way to end a surplus. But in doing so, it must consider that problem alongside others. The exchange rate, deflation and import controls, may all change the balance of payments. But they have very different effects on the country's income, employment and inflation, and in each case, there is some cost to pay. You may succeed in getting out of debt, but you are not likely to enjoy doing so.

## The UK payments problem

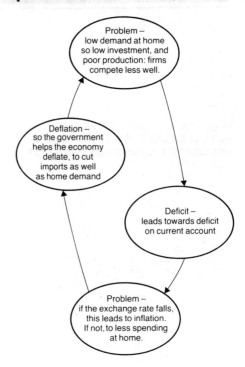

## Checklist – how to improve the balance of payments

- the exchange rate can change to match payments in and out of £s
- government can use monetary policy to change interest rates, and capital movements
- government can deflate to cut spending on imports or reflate if there is a surplus
- government can control imports directly with tariffs or quotas, or support exports directly with subsidies

# 7.8 The Common Market

What is the European Economic Community (EEC)? What does it do, and how does the UK gain or lose from being a member?

The European Economic Community was set up in 1957 and the UK joined in 1973. Perhaps the main reason for joining was political – to become fully a part of Europe, and to have more to do with countries such as France and Germany. But clearly the EEC affects the UK economy as well, in a number of ways.

The EEC is a common market of over 270 million people. The ten countries which make up the EEC (in 1984) agree to its rules, and its ways of doing business. They must aim for free trade with each other, and apply standard regulations to their markets. UK firms should find it almost as easy to sell in Italy as in Britain. The only problems the EEC does not aim to remove are transport costs and speaking the right language!

How does it make its markets common to all countries? Mainly, it works as a *customs union*. There are no tariffs between member countries, but there is a common external tariff. This is set at the same level between all member countries and the outside world.

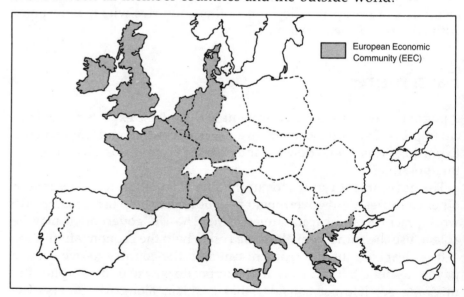

European Economic Community (EEC)

## Checklist – why join a customs union?

- new trade begins because there are no tariffs or other barriers inside the union
- there can be extra gains because of economies of scale in production
- but old trade and old gains from specialisation may be lost because of the common external tariffs of the union

The organisations of the EEC are set up to control its markets, and make them equal in all countries. Member countries agree to common economic policies. These cover agriculture and fishing, as we saw in Section 4.8. There are also policies on competition and monopoly, on aid to industry and poor regions, and on social issues. Separate organisations help to support coal and steel and nuclear power. And the European Monetary System helps member countries support their exchange rates in a relatively fixed system.

All this is meant to lead to more trade, and other contacts, between members of the EEC. This should bring growth and improve the living standard of all. But has this happened for the UK?

# Trading for better and worse

Half of all UK trade is with the EEC and it has grown twice as fast as other trade. Clearly there are great gains to be made from selling to the largest market in the world. The EEC offers a total market four times the size of the UK alone. And it is not only the better UK producers who gain from this trade. Consumers gain also form imports of better or cheaper products.

But some of these gains would come even if the UK left the EEC. Most trade, and most trade growth, is in manufactured goods. It follows, therefore, that the UK must trade more with other advanced countries, including those in Europe. These are the countries that make most and buy most of the products the UK trades in. Similar gains would come in a different trading group, if the UK joined the European Free Trading Association (EFTA). These countries are not as rich as those in the EEC, but their organisation is less complicated. Members trade freely with each other, but have their own external tariffs and do not join up in other economic policies.

A greater loss perhaps is the trading and other links with the Commonwealth countries. Many of these countries are very different from the UK in structure. They gave more room for specialisation and gains from trade. Now the UK must import its food and materials from the EEC. This replaces the cheap, efficient production of, say, New Zealand lamb or Canadian wheat. The customs union protects British and European producers, but it protects inefficiency as well. Resources are wasted as a result.

# Counting the cost

Most of what the UK gains from the EEC is difficult to measure. Growth and living standards may be higher than would otherwise have been the case, but we cannot be sure. But some of the costs are clear for all to see. The government's share of the EEC budget is one such case.

Governments pay into the EEC budget all tariff payments plus a share of what is raised by VAT. They receive back as the EEC spends on its different policies. Most of this spending is on agriculture, from which British farmers happen to get only a little. They produce the 'wrong' products, and produce them too well. As a result, the UK pays in much more to the budget than it gets back – its net contribution is high. This is shown for example in figure 1.

Another cost is seen in the UK's balance of payments with the EEC. This was in deficit throughout the first ten years of membership, and by almost £10 000m in 1982. Clearly, British consumers were doing well by buying from Europe and British investors were doing well lending to Europe. But British firms were not doing nearly as well in earning export payments from sales to Europe. Perhaps they have not yet made the most of selling to the largest free market in the world.

## Join the Club of Europe

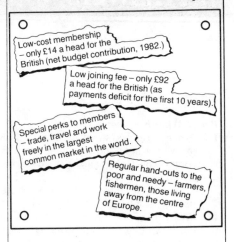

Low-cost membership – only £14 a head for the British (net budget contribution, 1982.)

Low joining fee – only £92 a head for the British (as payments deficit for the first 10 years).

Special perks to members – trade, travel and work freely in the largest common market in the world.

Regular hand-outs to the poor and needy – farmers, fishermen, those living away from the centre of Europe.

| From the EEC | |
|---|---|
| Agriculture | 1060 |
| Social | 122 |
| Regional | 130 |
| Budget refunds | 807 |
| Other | 52 |
| Total | 2171 |
| To the EEC | −2998 |
| Net contribution: | −827 |

(Source – Economic Trends, 1984)

*figure 1 – UK government contribution to the EEC budget (£m, 1983)*

## Questions

1. What is the EEC? (1)
2. How is the UK contribution to the EEC budget raised? (2)
3. How does the EEC help UK industry (a) through its budget, (b) in other ways? (2)
4. Suppose all other payments in and out of the UK are in balance. How would you expect the net contribution shown above to affect the balance of payments and value of the £? (2)
5. What other reasons are there for the UK to belong to the EEC, despite its net contribution to the budget? (3)

# Answers

## Part 1 What is economics about?

**1.1** *Africa* 1. (a) Too many in towns and industry, not farms (2); (b) want wheat and rice, not millet, etc (1); (c) low prices, poor roads and finance (2); (d) more imports, less home-grown (1)
2. Next best alternative forgone. Natural scarcity (2)
*Bus* 1. (a) 60p (1); (b) 0p (1)

**1.2** *Beef* 1. (a) 23.9 (b) 6 (2) 2. Loaf, milk, bacon (2)
*Bottles* 1. Eggs, geese, water; croupier etc, nurse, etc (2)
2. Pump, purifier, tap, bottles, etc (2) 3. Spending on products for satisfaction; to earn income, plant trees, etc (2)

**1.3** *High Street* 1. Distribution (1) 2. (a) Clothes, toys, etc (b) bank, café, etc. (2)
*Jobs* 1. Growing vegetables; Rolls-Royce engines, etc; waiters and services (2) 2. For fast and reliable production, with lower labour costs; using new, high technology (3) 3. 27 lost jobs in 30, for 27% of 21m = about 5 million (2)

**1.4** *Factsheet* 1. (a) About 74% (b) about 17% (2) 2. (a) Buy new products, (b) enjoy having property (2)
*Directors* 1. Skilled labour (1) 2. Salaries, profits (2) 3. Some do more or better work (1)
*Palace* 1. Own land that gives oil (1) 2. Helicopter pad, hospital, armed defence, etc (1)

**1.5** *Painting* 1. Unique product, specialist buyers (2) 2. Backed by spending; can afford to pay more, and want paintings more (2) 3. Amount offered for sale to all buyers; wants painting to keep (2)
*Petrol* 1. Lower price than competitors; excess demand (2) 2. (a) rise; (b) fall (2)

**1.6** *Motoring* 1. (a) up × 20; (b) down × 20. (2) 2. (a) £171 to £4460, more; (b) 7.9p to £1.49, less (2) 3. As products not prices; (a) more (b) less (3) 4. (a) Better quality; (b) faster, easier but more crowded; both real changes (3)

**1.7** *Scots* 1. (a) Spending by government, (b) social security (1) 2. (a) Agriculture and industry = £78; (b) education = £28 (2) 3. less private industry may mean less growth; less independence? (2)
*Smoking* 1. To cut costs of deaths and disease (1) 2. Taxes, end to TV adverts, etc (1) 3. (a) Cut health services costs; (b) lose tax revenue (2)

**1.8** *Which country?* 1. (a) China, Russia; (b) W. Germany, Britain etc; (c) Japan, Singapore, etc (3) 2. Better conditions of work and of life (1)
*Cambodia* 1. Less income, small range of output, fewer consumer durable goods and poorer health, etc (3) 2. Large number of very young people, low trade, making products where output cannot grow fast, etc (3)

## Part 2 Working

**2.1** *Pets* 1. Labour, more skilled. (2) 2. (a) Own effort, (b) money from mother and government, (c) car (4) 3. Mother, government, and Graham (4)

**2.2** *Secretaries* 1. Between jobs, or areas (a) More skilful use of computers (b) almost anywhere – even at home (4) 2. To write on word processors, and calculate using computers, 'literate', 'foreign language', etc. . . (3) 3. (a) less work; (b) more, (c) less (3)

**2.3** *Factsheet* 1. (a) 1951 (b) 1991 (c) 1961 (d) 1981 (e) 1951 (f) 1981 (3) 2. Children born to the 'baby-boom generation' of around 1961 (2)
*Future* 1. More births and young people. Possible fall in death rate (2) 2. Europe = quite stable, but Africa – many more people, may be hard to provide for, but a large work force in future.

**2.4** *16s* 1. 61%; for satisfaction, as training for work, because jobs so difficult to find instead (3)
*Factsheet* 1. (a) 21.5m (b) 26.4m (2) 2. More males before, more females after 65 (1)
*Time bomb* 1. (a) more people to have families – so more births, and family-products; (b) more people reach retirement age, and want different products again (4)

**2.5** *Diary* 1. Doing nothing, messing about with bike, cupboard, etc (1)
*Factsheet* 1. Numbers looking for work at Job Centres; jobs offered by firms at same; as many people as jobs – so perhaps only frictional (2) 2. About 1m. Different skills, areas, attitudes, etc (2) 3. SE, SW, E Anglia – all in south, with less heavy, old industry, etc (2)
*Young* 1. (a) Offer fewer qualifications, skills, experience; (b) similar; (c) less motivation to take the first jobs offered (3)

**2.6** *Software* 1. Natural ability, limited university training etc (2) 2. Less supply so pay rises (2) 3. They make a valuable product for which demand is rising (1)
*Dentists* 1. More, and bigger fillings, better anaesthetic (3) 2. Less work to do, less demand, so less pay (2)

**2.7** *Closed shop* 1. All workers join union. Clearer bargaining, higher pay for members, but costly and inflexible production, etc (3)
*Miners* 1. Overtime ban; strike (1) 2. (a) Job cuts, less than 5% pay rise, pit closures; (b) the opposite (2)
*Factsheet* 1. (a) Workers join together to support each other on pay, etc; (b) workers refuse to work, but without full support of union (2) 2. Economies of scale — large unions can offer more benefits, more protection to members (1) 3. Workers fear losing jobs – so do not strike (1)

**2.8** *Soccer* 1. Despite the cost of training, they may not be good enough (1) 2. To cut the costs of unemployment, etc (2)
*Pay* 1. Less skilled, less productive (1) 2. Less productive workers can now pay for their costs to firms. Unions want higher pay for members, even if by cutting jobs. (2) 3. (a) Body to protect low-paid workers in certain industries; (b) rates below which firms cannot pay, by law (2) 4. Replace more costly workers; help firms stay in business and employ more people (2)

## Part 3 Business

**3.1** *Factsheet* 1. (a) 13% (b) 59% (2) 2. Materials from farms, processed by food firms, sold in shops (2)
*M & S* 1. (a) Riverside Pork Farms; (b) BOC Transhield (1) 2. 6, to cover the whole country (2) 3. Take over their own farms, manufacturers and delivery operation. Specialisation (2)
*McDonalds* 1. (a) 1 (b) 8304 (c) 50 billion (1)

**3.2** *Reuters* 1 (a) On board of control; (b) running the firm from day to day; (c) part-ownership of a business (3) 2. (a) till 1915; (b) from 1916 to 1984; (c) from 1984 (3) 3. (a) To limit the risks of its owners; (b) to raise much more capital for growth (4)

**3.3** *State firms* 1. A publicly-owned business is the only seller. They want choice, range and freedom for this most important of goods (2) 2. Less efficient; offer social as well as commercial services (2)
*BR* 1. It is owned by the government for the country as a whole (1) 2. Cut unprofitable lines; raise fares for London commuters (2) 3. To passengers – transport from place to place. To taxpayers – social services, less congestion, way of life in outer areas, etc (3)

**3.4** *Oil* 1. Rig, men, materials, boat (1) 2. Probably over £43 000 (2)
*Costs* 1. £280 (1) 2. (a) £50 (b) £140 (1) 3. (a) £150 (b) £80 (1) 4. (a) £50 (b) £60 (1)
*Plants* 1. 93% (1) 2. Static prices, rising costs, leads to loss (2)

**3.5** *Scale* 1. (a) Small, local market; (b) national market, many branches (1)
*Morris* 1. (a) Internal; (b) horizontal; (c) vertical (3)
*Bouquets* 1. (a) Growth of output and scale; (b) new products in different industries (2) 2. (a) Close controls and interest; (b) personal contact (2) 3. Economies of scale in production; spreading risks (2)

**3.6** *Dairy* 1. More of all inputs cuts production costs per unit of output (a) Large tanks – technical; (b) research and development; (c) continuous production line – technical (3) 2. risk of faults – in tankers, tanks, computer control, etc. Unable to change for new products and methods, etc (3)
*Shops* 1. Marketing, financial, managerial (2) 2. Large scale of shopping – storage, cash, transport, etc (2)

**3.7** *Heathrow* 1. Gravel extracted from land; convenient and specialised area for metal manufactures (2) 2. Main market for air travel, with access to main routes west, north etc, large flat site (2)
*Commodore* 1. Growing UK market, 'free trade' (2) 2. For research, specialised staff, access to London and markets, etc; but Corby is for manufacture, using different forms of labour, and much capital, with good access again, and government aid (2) 3. Growth, more income, and extra service business (2)

**3.8** *Regions* 1. Low incomes, high unemployment, declining industries, people leave, etc (3)
*Mean street* 1. (a) Access to main roads, southern markets, EEC, etc; growing fast (4) 2. Government grants and support to industry and people in poor, depressed areas. Capital grants and tax cuts. (3)

## Part 4 Buying and selling

**4.1** *Factsheet* 1. (a) 1 shop or many shops; (b) owned by customers or shareholders (2) 2. More of all inputs cuts production costs of each unit of output. More output per worker – suggests economics in marketing, finance, management, etc (3)
*Supermarket* 1. Large shop selling food, household goods etc. For economies in buying, selling, advertising, management, etc (2) 2. 'Unplanned, impulse' buying, influenced by where products put, how presented, . . . so lack of knowledge, etc (2) 3. 'Bar-codes', twice as big (1)

**4.2** *Coal* 1. (a) NCB, (b) CEGB (2) 2. Shows amounts that would be bought at each price level, other things the same. (a) shift left, (b) move along and to the right, (c) shift right, (d) shift left (5) 3. Less natural gas, less oil, not replaced by nuclear (3)

**4.3** *Turkeys* 1. 1.5m to 28m. Constant temperatures, selective breeding (3) 2. More or less supplied at each price level. Higher cost, shifts supply to left, so less offered at each price level. (4) 3. Lower costs of production as food, than the alternatives, so more profitable (3)

**4.4** *Banks* 1. How much changes in price, say, affect demand or supply. Not elastic – 19% cut to 14% but 'no difference' to borrowing. Other issues still more important (5)
*Water* 1. How much changes in price affect supply. Elastic – easy to change, etc (5)

**4.5** *Tea* 1. (a) fall; (b) fall (2) 2. Matches supply and demand. 'Shortfall made up', 'price remained steady'. (2)
*Gold* 1. Prices cut bulk-buying etc; buying large amounts for economies of scale (2) 2. (a) £1; (b) £3

**4.6** *Cola* 1. Many sellers, in a perfect market. Only two firms make most cola, much advertising, so not very close to 'perfect'. (2) 2. Price, taste, advertising, etc (2)
*Groceries* 1. Low prices, low profits, good choice (3) 2. Different levels of competition for different shops (1) 3. Less choice, less competition, so prices may rise (2)

**4.7** *Patents* 1. Only the inventor can produce the patented good – by law. So a single seller, with no competition (2)
*OPEC* 1. Price-fixing agreement, to keep prices up, cut competition, to raise profits and avoid risks (3) 2. Have more to sell, need money now rather than later, etc (1) 3. (a) Greater supply – so lower price (figure 1, reversed.) (b) less supply – so higher price (figure 1)

**4.8** *Butter* 1. Production held, but not sold. Greater supply so price falls. (2) 2. (a) Falls every year; (b) fairly steady till 1982, then rises. (2) 3. Cost of buying and storing and perhaps selling butter – paid by EEC, from taxes on people, and by consumers in higher prices. (2) 4. Cut price, export more, subsidise farmers directly, use regulations, etc (4)

## Part 5 Finance

**5.1** *Forgery* 1. Anything generally accepted in exchange (1) 2. 'Silver line', 'water mark', special design (2) 3. Less trust in money – people do not accept, or exchange it (3)
*Notes* 1. Heavy, inconvenient, indivisible, etc (2) 2. Less likely to lose, convenient for large values (2)

**5.2** *Inflation* 1. Prices are 16p in £1 higher than 1 year ago, in general (1) 2. Money (1) 3. Wages (1)
*Mr Stanton* 1. (a) Income kept ahead – up from £2000 to £15000; (b) capital not kept up – about £285000 down to £250000 (at 1975 prices). (2) 2. (a) Goes up in pay rises, (b) index-linked, so matches inflation (2) 3. (a) Fixed interest – may lose out; (b) money loses value; (c) house prices may match inflation (3)

**5.3** *Factsheet* 1. Consumers spend £28 on bread to every £1 on jam (2) 2. More on basics, less on services, household goods, etc (2) 3. 10% (3) 4. 235.1% (1)
*Better off?* 1. 400% (1) 2. £3037 (1)

**5.4** *Bank* 1. (a) Firm specialises in dealing in money and loans; (b) Money put in by owners of the business; (c) lending out the ability to pay (3) 2. What it owns; and what it owes to others. Capital, bills of exchange; bank notes. (4) 3. Bought fewer bills from Liversay, kept more in reserve, as cash, to cover debts (3)

**5.5** *Factsheet* 1. (a) 'High Street' banks, doing general cheque-book business; (b) lending to people to buy TVs, cars, etc; (c) short-term, post-dated, cheques written by the government to borrow money (3) 2. 'Loans to money market'; about £47000m (2) 3. Deposits with UK banks (2) 4. Diversification into specialised consumer-credit business; etc (3)

**5.6** *Bang* 1. (a) Price of loans; (b) flexible loans by banks to sight-account customers; (c) illiquid accounts of banks set up by the Bank of England (3)   2. Banker for government (1)   3. Raise it, at first (1)   4. Higher interest rates; extra, special deposits (2)   5. All down (3)

**5.7** *Million* 1. (a) Government stock; (b) part-ownership of limited companies (2)   2. Advice; buying or selling your shares (2)   3. Payments of interest and profit each year; sell for more than you bought (1)
*Shares* 1. (a) £6000 (b) £5500 (c) £3000 (3)   2. Profits high or low, so demand for shares changes (1)   3. Free market supply and demand; set by a few large firms, etc (1)

**5.8** *BP* 1. About 8p (1)   2. £553 in interest payments (1)   3. For future growth and profit and capital gain (2)
*Spurs* 1. (a) Sell shares to the general public, not a private company; (b) debentures, mortgages, etc; (c) profit paid to shareholders (3)   2. Bank overdraft, rights issue, offer shares for sale (2)   3. To pay off debts on new stand and players (1)


## Part 6 Steering the Economy

**6.1** *Living* 1. Goods and services produced for each person (1)   2. Measures only current production, not wealth saved from the past (1)   3. Better range and quality, etc (2)
*Money* 1. (a) Down (14%); (b) up (29%); (c) down (3)   2. 14 to 16s; those with part-time jobs (2)   3. Greater demand or less supply for their work (1)

**6.2** *Goods* 1. Consumer (a), (b) (e); Capital (c), (d), (f) (2)   2. (a) For long-term growth; (b) different types of products; less personal consumption (2)   3. As a letter, or a painting, or for keeping as an official file (1)
*Recovery* 1. (a) 82% (b) 18% (1)   2. Expecting a rise in consumer spending (1)   3. More private and public consumption, and house-building. Investment needed for long-term growth of capacity (3)

**6.3** *Iran* 1. Rise in national output. Oil revenue spent on consumer goods (2)   2. More pay, or prestige (2)   3. It may raise imports and cut investment in 'basic' industries. Growth from exports or investment (3)   3. Investment in factories, etc, to produce consumer goods later (3)

**6.4** *Factsheet* 1. (a) Wastes resources, social cost; (b) changes distribution of income and harms trust in money (2)   2. Improved growth, and inflation, worse unemployment, better then worse balance of current payments (4)   3. (a) Low output, so few imports; (b) high unemployment (2)   4. Better on unemployment, (but perhaps only at first) worse on inflation and current payments (2)

**6.5** *How well?* 1. Better growth, bad unemployment, improved inflation (3)   2. High interest rates, low growth of money supply. Deflates, so cuts all 3 (4)   3. Government spending is greater than its income from taxes, so it borrows. (a) reflates – so raises growth and jobs; (b) may 'overheat' – so raises inflation (3)

**6.6** *Factsheet* 1. (a) Central and local; (b) 'gifts' from one income to another, for no work done; (c) welfare benefits such as 'dole' (3)   2. (a) Recreation facilities; (b) buildings and equipment (2)
*Dole* 1. Transfers; social security (2)   2. Extra for family, for low savings, for 'requirements' (3)

**6.7** *Factsheet* 1. 32% (1)   2. Corporation tax; rates (2)
*Take-away* 1. Value added tax on all production (1)   2. An essential, basic good (1)
*Oil* 1. (a) Corporation, PR Tax; (b) VAT, excise duty (2)   2. About 11% (1)
*Work* 1. (a) Individual 'needs' – for fairness; (b) simple, and even, to make the system clear and easier to work (2)

**6.8** *Factsheet* 1. Total amount owed by government. Over £2600. Borrowing to pay for war-time expenses. (3)   2. New borrowing by government and public corporations each year. 1982. Budget deficit (3)   3. Paying back old loans, Negative PSBR – budget surplus. Extra taxes, less spending, so deflation. Low output, jobs, inflation, imports (4)


## Part 7 Trade

**7.1** *Factsheet* 1. 78%. Goods are more transportable, better suited to mass production and economies of scale, etc (2)   2. Close, large market for manufactured goods, etc (2)
*Grain* 1. (a) USA (b) Soviet Union (1)   2. USA to Japan. High supply in USA due to production advantage, high demand in Japan due to incomes, tastes, etc (3)   3. Other countries import more of other foods, produce more themselves, etc (2)

**7.2** *Laws* 1. Farmers; consumers and merchants (2)   2. Tariffs, quotas, regulations, subsidies (2)
*Protection* 1. (a) Tax on imports; (b) a limit to the amount of imports (1)   2. (a) Cut the amount; (b) not change the amount; (c) demand less elastic for 'basics', so higher prices needed to cut imports (3)   3. Cut trade, cause slump and less efficient production (2)

**7.3** *Investment* 1. (a) +£2906 m (b) +£7309 (1)   2. Relatively lower interest rates in the UK, better opportunities overseas, end of exchange controls (2)
*Ford* 1. (a) Spending on new factory; (b) own company (1)   2. Low wage costs, exchange rate changes, etc (2)   3. More spending, growth, jobs, etc (2)   4. Use less iron, UK too expensive in Europe, specialist steel makers now cheaper (2)

**7.4** *Exchange* 1. 1977 to 1980 (1)   2. 13% (effective rate) (1)   3. Higher interest rates in USA, etc (1)
*Support* 1. (a) Markets where people buy and sell £s and other currencies; (b) deals for short-term capital gain. (2)   2. Poor trade would lead to payments deficit. (1)   3. Buying £s; letting others know it was doing so (2)   4. (a) less threat to inflation; (b) help industry to compete (2)

**7.5** *UK terms* 1. 1% rise (1)   2. (a) Better then worse off; (b) less then more competitive (2)   3. Changes in relative inflation, and the exchange rate (2)
*Tourists* 1. £s fall, so cut (1)   2. US better off, GB worse off abroad (2)   3. Consumers of foreign goods and services gain, producers in competition with foreigners lose out (2)

**7.6** *Payments* 1. (a) Oil, cars, pineapples; (b) profit, tourism, transfer; (c) bank deposits, buying factory (3)
*Factsheet* 1. (a) Services, income on property, transfers; (b) credits less debits for visibles and invisibles; (c) changes to the official reserves, etc (3)   2. Official financing = +0.60 +0.21 (£000m), so balance if met = −0.81 (£000m) (2)   3. Good surplus in services and fuels, slight surplus in manufactures, but deficit in food and materials (2)

**7.7** *Japanese* 1. Extra spending or tax cuts (1)   2. Higher incomes and spending in the UK means more imports (1)
*Figures* 1. June, August, Sept (1)   2. (a) −£1 billion; (b) +£730m (1)   3. + £74m (1)   4. (a) Weaker balance of payments may lead to lower exchange rate; (b) and so to extra inflation (2)   5. Deflation, tariffs, quotas, etc (3)

**7.8** *EEC* 1. European Economic Community of countries following common policies on trade, etc (1)   2. From tariffs, and a share of VAT money (2)   3. (a) Regional support, etc; (b) opportunities for trade in a common market (2)   4. Deficit leading to depreciation. (2)   5. Trade in large and open market, social and political ties, etc (3)

# Examination Questions

## Section A – short answers

1. Doctors, teachers and retailers are examples of .......... industry. (SREB)

2. The payment to that factor of production known as enterprise is ........................................... (SREB)

3. The ability of workers to change from one particular skill to another is known as the ............................. mobility of labour. (SREB)

4. A count of the population is called a ............ (LREB)

5. The Transport and General Workers' Union is an example of a ......................... trade union. (SREB)

6. The kind of economic activity which involves the production of raw materials is called ........................ production. (LREB)

7. What is meant by limited liability? (LREB)

8. That part of the economy which is owned and controlled by the government is known as the ............ sector. (SREB)

9. A firm which owns cocoa plantations as well as chocolate manufacturing factories is an example of ............. integration. (LREB)

10. The type of retail organisation owned by the members who shop there is called ............................. (LREB)

11. The responsiveness of demand to a change in price is known as ............................................. (SREB)

12. When one firm can control the supply of a commodity, it is called a ............................................ (LREB)

13. A .................. account with a bank enables its owner to draw cheques; the owner of a .................. account receives interest on the money held in it. (LREB)

14. Put the following in order of liquidity, by writing 1 for the most liquid, to 4 for the least liquid:
    (a) a table worth £50 ...........................................
    (b) a £10 note ....................................................
    (c) £20 in a deposit account in a bank .......................
    (d) £50 in National Savings Certificates ....................
    (LREB)

15. The banker to the government is called the ............... (LREB)

16. The following table shows the National Income and the Index of Retail Prices for a country.

| | 1970 | 1980 |
|---|---|---|
| National Income in £m | 500 | 750 |
| Index of Retail Prices | 100 | 125 |

Describe the trends shown in both National Income and in prices. (LREB)

17. Money National Income has increased by 50%, real National Income has increased by 20%. Explain this difference. (LREB)

18. The method of calculating the National Income in the U.K. which adds together the total earnings of all the factors of production in one year, is known as the ....... method. (SREB)

19. A large part of local government expenditure is provided by the central government in the form of a ......... (SREB)

20. A tax is said to be ........................... if the rate of tax rises as income rises. (SREB)

21. If a government spends more than it receives in revenue from taxation and other revenues, it is said to have a budget ......................................... (SREB)

22. A service earning foreign exchange for the U.K. is called an .................. export. (LREB)

23. A method of restricting trade by limiting the import of certain goods to a fixed number is called a ..... (SREB)

24. The balance of payments account of a country gives the following information for 1980.

| | £m |
|---|---|
| Visible exports | 1750 |
| Visible imports | 1250 |
| Invisible exports | 840 |
| Invisible imports | 630 |

Calculate the country's balance on current account. (LREB)

25. The relationship between the prices of a country's exports and the prices of its imports is called the ......... .................. (LREB)

## Section B – extended writing

1. For what reasons may the size of a country's population change? [20] (LREB)

2. (a) What is the difference between an "industrial" trade union and a "craft" trade union? [8]

(b) Describe the services which most trade unions provide for their members. [12]
(SREB)

3. What sort of decisions would the owner have to make about the factors of production if he intended to open a garage? [20]
(LREB)

4. "The ending of regional imbalance has been an objective of successive governments in the United Kingdom."
(a) Describe the problems associated with regional imbalance. [8]
(b) Briefly describe three measures which governments have taken to try to overcome the regional problem. [6]
(c) Discuss the effectiveness of the measures which governments have taken to overcome the regional problem. [6]
(JMB)

5. What is a monopoly? How might a firm obtain monopoly power? [5,15]
(OLE)

6. (a) What are the functions of money? [12]
(b) Why would each of the following be inadequate as a basis for our monetary system:
(i) cigarettes, [2]
(ii) gold, [2]
(iii) coal, [2]
(iv) cattle? [2]
(OLE)

7. (a) Distinguish between the types of securities which are available on the Stock Exchange. [10]
(b) How does the Stock Exchange operate as a market? [10]
(LSEC)

8. (a) What are the economic objectives of the Budget? [10]
(b) Illustrate your answer by reference to a recent Budget. [10]
(WJEC)

9. (a) Describe two of the methods used by countries to restrict their import of foreign goods. [4]
(b) Explain the reasons for these restrictions. [8]
(c) What is the economic case against restrictions? [8]
(LREB)

10. Describe the principal categories of the "invisible" trade of the United Kingdom, and show how they affect our balance of payments. [20]
(WJEC)

# Section C – response questions and projects

1. (a) Examine the graph and diagrams provided; use information from them to answer the following questions.
(i) What does the graph tell us about world population?

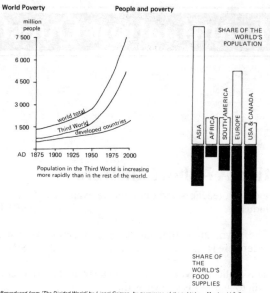

World Poverty    People and poverty

Population in the Third World is increasing more rapidly than in the rest of the world.

Reproduced from 'The Divided World' by Lionel Grigson, by permission of the publishers, Macdonald & Company (Publishers) Limited, copyright Macdonald Educational Limited, 1975.

(ii) In which area of the world is it increasing most rapidly? Which part of this area has the greatest population?
(iii) Name one region of the world that is likely to have a food shortage and one where there is a food surplus; give a reason for your choice in each case.
(iv) Give an example of a developed country and say what is meant by this term. [6]
(b) In a paragraph, explain what has caused the rapid growth of population during the twentieth century. [5]
(c) Explain what has resulted from the 'population explosion' and what can be done to solve the problems it has created. [9]
(WMEB)

2. Study the data below which shows the trends in employment between 1970 and 1980.

EMPLOYMENT TRENDS:– 1970 – 1980 (Great Britain)
(Source: Economics Progress Report H.M.S.O.)

(a) Define the term "unemployment" as accurately as possible. [2]
(b) What was the approximate level of registered unemployment at the beginning of 1977? [1]
(c) What is meant by the term "working population"? [2]

172

(d) Describe the main features of the trend in registered unemployed as shown by the chart. [4]
(e) Briefly outline THREE possible causes of high unemployment. [6]
(SREB)

3. The diagram below refers to the market for bread.

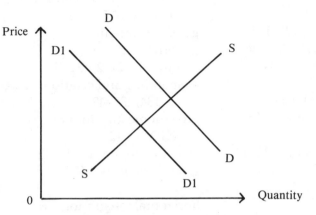

(a) Give *THREE* reasons why the demand curve might have changed from D to D1. [3]
(b) What is meant by the term "complementary good"? [2]
(c) Give *ONE* example of a good which is complementary to bread. [1]
By using the information on the diagram above, explain the likely effects on the price of flour. [9]
(SREB)

4. Study the data below which shows the rate of inflation (solid line) and the rate of increase in wholesale prices (dotted line) between 1970 and 1982.

(a) Define the term "inflation" as accurately as possible. [2]
(b) What was the rate of inflation at the beginning of 1977? [1]
(c) What is the difference between "wholesale prices" and "retail prices"? [2]

INFLATION – Percentage change on a year earlier
(Source: Economic Progress Report H.M.S.O.)

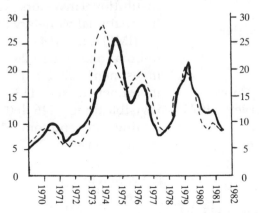

KEY:  ———— = retail prices (rate of inflation)

--------- = wholesale output prices

(d) Describe the main features of the trend in the rate of inflation as shown by the chart. [4]
(e) Briefly outline THREE possible causes of inflation. [6]
(SREB)

5. Study the following table of the Balance of Payments for a certain country in a recent year.

|  | £M |
| --- | --- |
| Exports | 20121 |
| Imports | 27157 |
| Government services (net) | −1684 |
| Private transfers (net) | +2777 |
| Interest, profits and dividends (net) | +1418 |
| Shipping (net) | + 12 |
| Investment and other capital flows (net) | − 2886 |
| Balancing item | + 410 |

(a) On the basis of the above information only calculate:
(i) the visible trade balance, [1]
(ii) the invisible trade balance, [2]
(iii) the balance of payments on current account, [2]
(iv) the balance for official financing. [3]
(b) Comment on the state of this particular country's balance of payments and suggest what policies the government might have adopted to deal with it. [12]
(OLE)

6. Study the structure of local industry in your area, describing the different types of work performed by local residents, and explaining the patterns you observe.

7. Study a topical economic issue involving trade unions and employers, such as a wage claim or a factory closure. Explain the economic issues involved.

8. Study a particular local firm, describe its work, customers and suppliers, and explain the economic forces governing its behaviour.

9. Describe a local market such as that for houses, or cars, or fruit and vegetables. Measure and explain the differences and changes in prices over a period of one or two months.

10. Describe the pattern of spending and sources of revenue of your local authority. Study the main changes in the authority's budget from one year to the next, and explain the effects of those changes on your community.

173

# Index